Palgrave Studies in Priso

Series editors
Ben Crewe
Institute of Criminology
University of Cambridge
Cambridge, UK

Yvonne Jewkes
School of Applied Social Science
University of Brighton
Brighton, UK

Thomas Ugelvik
Criminology and Sociology of Law
University of Oslo, Faculty of Law
Oslo, Norway

This is a unique and innovative series, the first of its kind dedicated entirely to prison scholarship. At a historical point in which the prison population has reached an all-time high, the series seeks to analyse the form, nature and consequences of incarceration and related forms of punishment. Palgrave Studies in Prisons and Penology provides an important forum for burgeoning prison research across the world. Series Advisory Board: Anna Eriksson (Monash University), Andrew M. Jefferson (DIGNITY - Danish Institute Against Torture), Shadd Maruna (Rutgers University), Jonathon Simon (Berkeley Law, University of California) and Michael Welch (Rutgers University).

More information about this series at
http://www.palgrave.com/gp/series/14596

Catarina Frois

Female Imprisonment

An Ethnography of Everyday Life in Confinement

Catarina Frois
Centre for Research in Anthropology
ISCTE – Instituto Universitário de Lisboa
Lisbon, Portugal

Palgrave Studies in Prisons and Penology
ISBN 978-3-319-87614-6   ISBN 978-3-319-63685-6   (eBook)
DOI 10.1007/978-3-319-63685-6

© The Editor(s) (if applicable) and The Author(s) 2017
Softcover re-print of the Hardcover 1st edition 2017
This work is subject to copyright. All rights are solely and exclusively licensed by the Publisher, whether the whole or part of the material is concerned, specifically the rights of translation, reprinting, reuse of illustrations, recitation, broadcasting, reproduction on microfilms or in any other physical way, and transmission or information storage and retrieval, electronic adaptation, computer software, or by similar or dissimilar methodology now known or hereafter developed.
The use of general descriptive names, registered names, trademarks, service marks, etc. in this publication does not imply, even in the absence of a specific statement, that such names are exempt from the relevant protective laws and regulations and therefore free for general use.
The publisher, the authors and the editors are safe to assume that the advice and information in this book are believed to be true and accurate at the date of publication. Neither the publisher nor the authors or the editors give a warranty, express or implied, with respect to the material contained herein or for any errors or omissions that may have been made. The publisher remains neutral with regard to jurisdictional claims in published maps and institutional affiliations.

Cover illustration: Catarina Frois

Printed on acid-free paper

This Palgrave Macmillan imprint is published by Springer Nature
The registered company is Springer International Publishing AG
The registered company address is: Gewerbestrasse 11, 6330 Cham, Switzerland

This book is dedicated to João Pina Cabral

Image 1 Odemira Prison Facility Façade

Acknowledgements

This work was made possible with the generous support from Foundation for Science and Technology Starting Grant Investigator FCT (IF/00699/2012), and Gerda Henkel Foundation (AZ 07/KF/15) within the Program Security, Society and the State.

I wish to acknowledge the Portuguese Directorate-General for Prison Services for having granted authorization for this study, namely Semedo Moreira, and Odemira Prison Warden, Paula Martins, as well as prison officers and staff who kindly received me at the institution. A particular thank you is due to the inmates and the guards that more than accepted my presence, and shared their days and experiences with me.

Throughout the years, several friends and colleagues—sometimes even without being conscious of it made a difference in my life and the way I pursue works like the one this book brings to light: Carmen Osuna, Mark Maguire, Gregory Feldman, Daniel Goldstein, Susana Viegas, Helena Machado, Susana Narotzky, and Miguel Vale de Almeida.

As always, Antónia Lima was one of the greatest supporters during the weeks and months of my comings and goings from Odemira; I hope somehow she recognizes her continuous presence in the pages that follow, and the same applies to João Pina Cabral, to whom this book is dedicated, with friendship and care.

My parents were invaluable in their efforts in keeping me focused on what was important besides work: spending time with my family, by the pool, or by the fireplace. Even though after all these years my daughters Francisca and Marta are already accustomed with endeavors like the one this book materializes, the encouragement they give me is the best reward I could ever hope to achieve.

Finally, a few words to my husband, Diogo: life is complete only with your love, generosity and companionship.

Contents

1 Introduction—"A Doll's House"   1

2 Portugal, a "Mild-Mannered" Country:
Penal and Penitentiary Overview   27

3 Entering Odemira Prison Facility   51

4 "Will You Be Back Again Tomorrow?"
Everyday Rhythms of Imprisonment   73

5 The Effects of Imprisonment   99

6 Tension, Authority, Rights   123

7 The Rule, the Letter, the Spirit of the Law   145

8 Institutionalizing Exclusion   167

Contents

9 "Getting in is Fast, Getting Out is Harder!" 191

10 Conclusion: Prison as a "Mirror" of Society 207

References 217

Index 229

List of Figures

Image 1	Odemira Prison Facility Façade	vi
Image 2	Prisoners' restricted area	71
Image 3	Interior of a cell	97
Image 4	Inmates working in the "boxes"	189

1

Introduction—"A Doll's House"

Odemira is a town on Portugal's southwestern region, known as Alentejo, situated in a lush valley with a river running through it. Its population of approximately 3000 inhabitants lives far from any major urban center, just outside the radius of one of the country's most popular touristic areas on the Atlantic coast. It is a typical Alentejo town, for the better and for the worse: the natural and urban beauty of its whitewashed houses spraying down the sides of an almost untouched valley; the peacefulness of rural life somehow offset by the demographic desertification that afflicts this part of the country, slowly destroying local commerce, services and communication. Odemira Regional Prison Facility,[1] a prison for women with a population of approximately 50 inmates, stands on one of these hillsides. Being the only female prison facility in the whole of Portugal's southern region, which occupies approximately 400 square kilometers, most of its population is comprised of women from that area, allocated there either on remand or as convicted felons.

I came across this prison almost by chance at the end of 2015, when working on a broader research project[2] started almost two years before in 10 prison facilities all over the country (out of the 49 currently operating). In the course of this work, I had visited the oldest and largest central prison for women (Tires prison facility, nearby Lisbon, the country's capital) and was thinking of including the other major female prison (Santa Cruz do Bispo Female Prison, in the Northern region of Oporto) which had opened in 2005 and was reputed for its "excellent material conditions". However, a colleague who worked in the prison services suggested that I visit Odemira instead. In his opinion, the fact that this was a modest-sized prison far away from major cities, would make authorizations and scheduling with its directing board an easier affair, thus enabling me to start work much faster.

It seemed like an interesting option for a number of reasons. Experience had already shown that even with an authorization from the Directorate-General of Prison Services, directing boards tended to limit internally the access of academics doing research on prison environments. Prisons closer to urban centers—and therefore closer to universities—were naturally more sought out by students and researchers, which meant a greater probability of being put on a "waiting list" for long periods of time. Odemira's geographic situation presented an obstacle for academics without the financial means and time to conduct research that involved long stays in a remote location (such as students completing their bachelor studies). In addition, it would also present a great opportunity to engage with the inmate population from a part of the country I largely ignored, and which remained generally rather unexplored by Portuguese prison studies literature.

Several months before my first visit to Odemira, one of my students, who worked for the Directorate-General of Prison Services, and who was acquainted with my broad research in prison settings, told me: "Compared with the places you have visited so far, you will find this more like a little doll's house. It's very small and it has almost as many guards as inmates!" This comment echoed enticingly. After so many months working in overcrowded, oversized and harsh environments, prisons with capability for up to 1200 inmates, the idea of finding a more proximate scenery pushed me to make the decision. On the other hand, and even if somehow strange, the image of a "doll's house", of an environment where everyone knew each other, made me think that perhaps this was the opportunity to try to overcome some of methodological and bureaucratic constraints I had almost invariably stumbled upon in the other prison facilities.

Throughout the years of research in prisons, I had found many frustrations in the process of establishing relationships with inmates, guards and other correctional treatment staff. The most relevant was related to the short staffing of prison officers, which invariably conducted to limited time and restraint access to certain prison areas. For example, on the initial applications for authorization one is requested to specify the exact number of inmates, guards and staff intended to be interviewed, with pre-defined criteria such as crime and conviction categories, nationalities and origin, etc. It was also need to define exactly the duration of fieldwork—one day, one week, one month?

While this information allowed prison services to schedule and manage the requests from academics, the idea of "hanging around", engaging in informal conversation, allowing chance and circumstance to dictate the direction of my investigation (a modus operandi which is so dear to the ethnographical method) were completely out of the question. And this was pronounced when it came to restricted areas, and namely those spaces—such as cellblocks or wings—where it would precisely be possible to practice such methods, following inmates and officers in their everyday life. Therefore, whereas administrative areas were easy to access and circulate without major restrictions—notwithstanding the awkwardness and suspicion aroused among staff members by having a stranger walking around apparently "doing nothing"—permanence in areas restricted to inmates was strongly conditioned, and strictly forbidden in the case of male prisons. In such places, access is restricted even to female staff working there on a daily basis as teachers, nurses, and lawyers, and including female prison officers. Thus, "for reasons of security", mostly connected with overcrowding and short-staffed prisons, it was impossible to guarantee the protection of outside visitors.

The hundreds of hours of conversations I maintained with inmates, guards and correctional treatment staff in such establishments were mostly held in the same rooms where inmates usually met with their attorneys, were presented to their sentencing judges, parole hearings, or received their weekly visits, under conditions which Drake, Earle and Sloan define as "interview-based research methodologies that tend to be episodic, short-lived and often take place outside of spaces the informant routinely occupies" (2015: 3). This is not to say that such methodology lacked validity—far from it. The conversations a researcher can hold in this kind of neutral space, isolated from the usual setting the inmate spends his/her day, can promote moments of an almost confessional nature, harder to obtain when the individuals find themselves in their everyday surroundings. Nevertheless, I was well aware that such confessional spaces isolated certain variables, which could only be properly relativized and contrasted with a follow-up in a more quotidian environment.

In other words, the *persona* emerging in a compact room, after the door was closed and a one-to-one interaction was engaged, was not the same as the one habitually interacting with guards and fellow prisoners outside of it. The atmosphere, rhythms and demands differ drastically in either space. Leaving, if only momentarily, the space of forced co-habitation, strict rules and limited autonomy they had come to know, also presented a source of tension and emotional conflict.[3]

In practice, besides a few guided tours around the cellblocks, refectories, classrooms, workshops, and courtyards, during those almost three years of prison research I had gained a very limited experience of inmates' living spaces. Even when working at Tires, where my presence (as a woman) would supposedly be less conspicuous or intrusive, the overcrowding and shortage of staff restricted my movements to a small unit separated from the main blocks where most inmates were held. From this limited experience in these environments, I was impressed especially by the noises, which provided a kind of prison soundtrack made up of constant chatter—and sometimes shouting—the jangling of guards' key chains, the clanking of bolts being turned and gates being closed, telephones ringing, metal detectors beeping, and the general humming noise produced by the hundreds of people sharing the same confined space.[4]

Odemira prison was a far cry from the scenario just described. Therefore, what started as a short visit programmed to last two weeks, ended up turning into an intensive and immersive experience lasting a whole year. The decision for this extension was not immediate and resulted from a number of converging factors. As explained in Chap. 3, after the first few days at Odemira (during which I followed my previous method of individual interviews in a tiny isolated room) I doubted I could ever return. In this case, this decision had not been provoked by the typical problems with limited access, but instead by the heavy and negative impact that the stories of inmates had on me. Nevertheless, this place offered a unique chance to do something which had been impossible so far: to talk with every single person there who was willing, whether they were inmates, prison officers, technicians, teachers or nurses.

For the first time, such a comprehensive knowledge of a whole prison population actually became a feasible goal. Odemira was indeed an institution modest in size, and a place I could at least (try to) know better. The warden was immediately forthcoming; something that cannot be totally unrelated to the fact that this was a female prison and I a female researcher. She presented no obstacles or unwarranted problems to the authorizations I had obtained for my academic project from the Directorate-General. The director herself, whose career had included working in male prison facilities, stated: "This is a different kind of prison". Likewise, the officers' attitude towards my presence there proved an essential contribution for the smooth progress of my research. Having previously visited "some of the worst facilities in the country", as they used to say, gained the director's authorization to carry out this investigation, and quickly blended in with the rest of the staff, joining them at meals, becoming involved in the daily chores and generally socializing with everyone without distinction, were some of the factors that gained me the trust and good will necessary to make my work there all the easier. Even though few of the officers granted me formal interviews, our conversations were continuous and everyone talked openly about their views on the prison system in general and Odemira in particular, about their work and their past professional experience. This prison became my "village"—a place where I gradually became familiar with the habits, the spaces and its inhabitants.

In the course of a year, I visited Odemira every month, for one-week periods, usually from 9 a.m. until 7 p.m. During this time, I could spend a day talking with a lot of people, or just hang around observing and getting the feeling for the place and its daily rhythms, perhaps not as someone who "belonged", but surely as someone who, despite still an outsider, ended up becoming a familiar presence. I was an observer, but I also became a subject of observation, and as will become clear, this issue of visibility and presence turned out to be very significant on more than one occasion. As the months went by, and my presence became habitual, the personal histories of inmates naturally revealed nuances and complexity otherwise difficult to acknowledge.

While it is true that one year in prison tends to resemble any other year (just like the days seem to be all alike), we must not ignore that just as anywhere else, very much may change in a person's life, both outwardly and inwardly, even in a short span of time. Some of the women who were on remand when I first began fieldwork, had since stood trial and become sentenced inmates while others had received the trial verdicts and been released on probation. Some had been admitted and others released (one had even been released and readmitted). Some had their court appeals decided and their sentences shortened, while others still faced new convictions added to their current sentences.

Again, if one day in prison resembles every other day, in one year there are birthdays and other celebrations, there are holy days, mother's days, Christmas. The routines, with their apparent monotony, were different throughout the seasons—the shorter winter days with less working activities and more school seemed more lethargic, while abundant work and training courses filling the longer summer days gave them a more frantic pace. On the other hand, and despite the routines dictated by prison rules and regulations, *time* has a different value in prison (Cohen and Taylor 1972). One day, one hour, one year, can either be just like the next or become crucial in determining how one copes with the experience of life within walls, or with the present moment. The anxiety of waiting for a decision regarding a request for parole or a furlough; how a conflict or misunderstanding with a fellow prisoner is handled; how a phone call or a letter bearing news from home may soothe or exacerbate the impotence of confinement.

Inside prison, time becomes the measure for what one can "cope" with, for testing the person's endurance to confinement—its environment and other occupants—before one finally surrenders and gives in to it; before one reaches a point of acceptance or definite rejection of the conviction/transformation that has been imposed. Just as "being inside" bears a certain meaning to an inmate, to a researcher "being let inside" makes it possible to distinguish its nuances and the impact of imprisonment on those who experience it. Prolonged and continuous fieldwork allows us to observe, to feel and to put into perspective the narratives and discourses of the agents, in this case those inhabiting a prison within a given time frame. In this respect, my own visibility and presence proved to be particularly important. Regular monthly visits brought me credibility amongst inmates, somehow assuring them of my genuine interest and commitment to know how they lived and who they were as women, as persons. In fact, they were the first to complain when they felt that it had been a "long time since the last visit", as if reproaching me for my absence over the past few weeks. On the other hand, the fact that I hung around with them in the courtyard, during meals or in the cell hall (the first time such an endeavor had been conducted in this prison) in their perspective made me a witness to their life experience. In some cases it also made me a confidant, someone who knew their story and could understand its developments and specific meanings.

Women's Prison, Women in Prison, and Women Imprisoned

We can assume that a prison facility is a place characterized by ambivalence, by permanently negotiated authority, by the accidents of everyday life. By focusing on a women's prison, we must be aware of two underlying and equally important dimensions. In a metaphorical sense we are dealing with *imprisoned women*—imprisonment here indicating much more than physical confinement—and in a very strict sense that we are considering *women in prison*, and thus in terms of their gender identity. The distinction between subjectivity and objectivity calls for an analytical exercise that poses an inevitable initial premise: a prison facility is a place for people who have committed actions punishable by law with the privation of freedom.

The Penal Code defines that inmates should be separated into different groups—according to crime categories, sentence lengths, age, levels of security, judicial status, gender, and so on—thus acknowledging that the prison population is not a homogenous group. As such, prison facilities, despite being under a common regulation, present distinctive features that reflect specificities intrinsic to their respective populations, but also other particularities that are taken into account: material conditions, the diversity and quantity of available services—working, educational, therapeutic—or the number of professionals working there, namely in terms of prison officers. Just as a youth prison differs from, say, a prison for adults, so too prisons for men differ substantially from prisons for women. Some of these discrepancies are immediately perceptible and are gender related: in Portugal the majority of officers in female prisons are also female, male guards being typically assigned to administrative tasks (and the reverse situation happens in male prisons). In terms of accommodation, cell conditions are also different, and may be equipped with a bidet and shower, or even have special units for mothers who have young children with them.

From what we can observe in the literature produced in other countries, female incarceration in Portugal, and indeed in Odemira, do not present substantial distinctiveness. The typical profile of the incarcerated woman seems to concur with international data (see, amongst others, Boutron and Constant 2014; Carlen 1983, 1985, 2002; Carlen and Worrall 2014; Covington and Bloom 2003; Bosworth 2016; Moore and Scranton 2014; Tabbush and Gentile 2013). However, more than simply corroborating a tendency we should be interested in observing and reflecting upon a problem that must be addressed politically, socially and culturally. Indeed, when we look into the histories and experiences of these women before they ever face imprisonment, we realize they had already been leading *imprisoned* lives long before. Imprisoned by poverty, social exclusion, and abuse often since childhood and then replicated throughout their adult life.

As I discuss over the next chapters, most inmates at Odemira lived in a situation of extreme precariousness, born into families of low socioeconomic status (usually accompanied by situations of violence and maltreatment), with a high rate of illiteracy or education levels far below the national average. At the time of their conviction, the vast majority were unemployed or working in unskilled and temporary jobs, relying on state welfare services or charity organizations to meet their basic daily needs. A large percentage were also single mothers or lived with partners who were not the father of their children, with teenage or young motherhood (before the age of 18, the Portuguese legal age) being the norm. In turn, this was also corresponded by a high number of children in the care of relatives other than their progenitors, or situations of repeated institutionalization—whether voluntary handed over by their mothers or retrieved by state agencies such as social security services or the Child and Youth Protection Services.

We must also bear in mind that these factors may not all converge simultaneously in every case. Acknowledging these women as somehow already leading an imprisoned life cannot in any way lead us to presume they were *fated* from the start. That would amount to obliterating their agency, ignoring their responsibility and ultimately denying their will. We find women—even if a minority—at Odemira and in many other prisons, who hardly fit into the pattern described above. Some inmates come from structured families, completed their secondary or even higher education, maintained steady jobs and livelihoods. Nevertheless, this book cannot avoid addressing this stereotype, contributing to reflect and problematize around it so as to infuse the density it demands. Why are these women confined? What were the defining moments, and how did certain factors converge so that one day they found themselves inside a prison cell? Ultimately, what is their story?

Finding an answer to these questions is where a qualitative analysis reveals all its suitability. Because each individual construes his/her own narrative, each person needs to recognize or relate to an identity—even if later, scientific distance works to establish distinctions, interpret information, compare and relativize data, and identify trends. For the women who participated in this study (and the same would apply to other imprisoned men and women) the circumstances, motivations, and causes behind their (illegal) actions form a combination which they look upon as a unique experience, and in fact some of the cases seem to follow what could be understood as an almost text-book example: the drug addict who prostitutes herself and does petty robberies to support her habit; the young woman who finds herself in financial problems and resort to drug trafficking; the woman who is an almost lifelong victim of domestic violence and one day kills her partner and abuser. All of them distinguish an element of inevitability in their trajectory, as if it were just a matter of time before they reached that point and even if, while verbalizing it, attribute the outcome either to personal causes such as "despair", "fear", or "bad luck"; or to external circumstances like "unemployment", "injustice", or "discrimination".

Furthermore, considering gender introduces an analytical and theoretical sphere that has found a significant bearing within the field of prison studies, and more specifically on the theme of "women in prison"—a dimension which to some extent questions the normative model of the societies/communities in which it arises. Much of the reflection on this particular topic revolves around the problem of challenging gender roles. In other words, of questioning what the role of women is expected *to be*? Any attempt to provide a valid answer will necessarily have to take cultural specificities of the context in question into account, and allow us to understand how they were judged in court, and how they judge themselves and their peers.

In a country such as Portugal—which is still predominantly Catholic and conservative, exhibiting features of a patriarchal domestic model—largely unbalanced in terms of gender equality (reflected not only in broad terms of working opportunities, but more specifically in questions of salary, parental responsibility, etc.), it is not surprising that the traditional gender roles are also the model which most of the women at Odemira identify with (Pina Cabral 2003; Lima 2003, 2016; Wall and Amâncio 2007; Wall 2012). This aspect is, if anything, further enhanced by the origin of most inmates.

Whereas in major urban areas there is a much more widespread and diversified education and work availability, independence from the family of origin or from spouses, for instance, is much easier than in the rural or semi-rural communities where the majority of Odemira's inmates come from. Here, women are inevitably more "confined" to the domestic sphere in which they were brought up and feel they belong. Therefore, during incarceration, on the one hand they reclaim (and even exacerbate) traditional gender identities, for example by evaluating each other on the basis of their domestic zeal, how well they tend to their chores, to their personal appearance, to their personal cleanliness, and so forth. On the other hand, they openly reproach and ostracize those who do not seem to correspond to this norm. Such an attitude, which seems to be directed outwards (to impress upon other inmates, guards, and even lawyers or other outside visitors), inevitably turns into self-censorship, since they somehow become chained to their own prejudice.

An Ethnography of Everyday Life in Confinement

> So-called participant observation has a way of drawing the ethnographer into spaces of human life where she or he might really prefer not to go at all and once there doesn't know how to go about getting out except through writing, which draws others there as well, making them party to the act of witnessing.
>
> Nancy Scheper-Hughes, *Death without weeping: the violence of everyday life in Brazil*

First and foremost, this is an ethnographic study of a small prison for women. As a qualitative methodology whose rationale relies on work carried out in situ, ethnography relies on continued observation extending through a period of time long enough to allow the researcher to engage with the context under analysis as much as possible.

Ideally, the purpose is not to confuse the subject of the study with the object being studied; that is, an ethnographer should not become part of the community he/she seeks to know, but must reach such a level of proximity and coexistence as to be able to share and experience the rhythms, habits, and forms of interaction that characterize the environment within which he/she has chosen to study. In summary, I would say that an ethnographer should gradually be able to recognize the unspoken. Anthropological literature on the ethnographic method is vast and varied, and has engaged a broad debate on whether its validity when applied to fieldwork done in remote locations can be equally transferred to investigations carried out "at home" (see Hastrup and Hervik 1994; Gupta and Ferguson 1997; Melhuus et al. 2010).

It is not my purpose to develop the discussion here; although it is widely shared amongst prison scholars that carrying out an ethnographic study inside a prison inherently implies in every situation a confrontation with the unfamiliar. We might almost say that, if even those who live or work there for months or years never come to feel that place as "home", how could a temporary visitor such as the ethnographer avoid experiencing a departure from the familiar, from the commonplace? Furthermore, ethnographic work in carceral settings implies an encounter with specific problems of subjectivity: empathy or repulsion towards our interlocutors—whether they are inmates, guards, or other correctional treatment staff—pity, compassion or outrage at what we are told or experience directly.

Similarly to ethnographies conducted in other organizational or institutional settings, access is also frequently an obstacle that does not depend on our will to surpass, or on the people we are following (Fassin et al. 2015; Frois 2009, 2013; Pina Cabral 2010; James and Toren 2010; Garsten and Nyqvist 2014). In the case of prison facilities, with the ethical and deontological issues that come into play, the researcher is met with additional challenges, including the difficulty of *being* in prison, of *returning* after a period of interruption, of *leaving* the terrain once and for all (see, for example, Crewe and Ievins 2015; Cunha 1994, 2002; Drake 2015; Jewkes 2012; Jewkes and Wright 2016). The relationships that can be established are tenuous, unstable, and managing underlying asymmetries implies tact and prudence, constantly shifting between trust and suspicion on several levels.

Once again, time was of the essence in this particular case. As already mentioned, I returned to Odemira regularly, and spent long periods of time with inmates and guards, inside and around the cellblock. The period of one year, from the first moment I entered Odemira until the day I decided to formally conclude my visits, brought me a familiarity that other shorter ventures (in other prisons) had made impossible, and which a longer incursion might have rendered redundant and even misleading. Such close and continued acquaintance with the institution's workings enabled me to identify different variables in its inhabitants' behavior, discourse and manner. The important point here is that one-to-one conversations do not always provide the same kind of information obtainable through interaction involving the presence of third parties, especially when we consider different group interactions—guards and inmates, directors and guards, technical staff and inmates, and so on.

The presentation of self, so insightfully described by Erving Goffman (1959, 1963, 1967) is in this context brought to bear, resulting in a permanent negotiation that does not—and this is perhaps the most important aspect—imply any contradiction or canceling out between the forms of interaction involved. In different situations, individuals expose, conceal, select or even manipulate specific features of their presentation to others: more submissive or compliant, more combative or critical, more reserved or thoughtful—according to what they believe that particular circumstance calls for.

The daily management of the multiple performances everyone is called upon to enact (and this is could be applied to any circumstance, that is, is not particular to prison environment) was one of the most revealing and frequently observed phenomena: the inmate who cried when she was alone with me as she confided the grief of imprisonment, and later in the courtyard was talking cheerfully among her fellow inmates, might have led me to doubt her earnestness and the meaning of her words; the officer who expressed sympathy and understanding of inmate's needs when she was walking around with me in the cell hall, and then described those same complaints as a mere whim as she reported them to her superiors, might make her pervious concerns sound hypocritical at the least; the correctional treatment staff member, claiming to abhor the prison officer body's corporatism, while at the same time declaring that in Odemira "everyone"—including inmates—was part of the same team, might be interpreted as cynical. All these discourses may be viewed as contradictory if we insist on viewing them all in the same light. Conversely, we can decide to acknowledge, as I try to do in this book, that the everyday life of any person is linked precisely by these kinds of contradictions, oscillations, misconstructions, and moods, depending on the person we are, or situations we find ourselves in.

I should stress yet another aspect I have sought to bring forth: the everyday life of a prison institution (see, amongst others, Crewe 2009, 2012; Schinkel 2014; Ugelvik 2014). At Odemira, the autumn and winter months are mainly occupied with educational activities, such as school, professional training courses, or recreational activities (music, poetry readings, etc.). As these are optional activities, inmates' participation is sporadic, and as a result their day-to-day become more monotonous and tedious, and this is true even for those women who do some kind of work "for" the prison, since usually these are unskilled part-time jobs such as cleaning or laundry duties.

Between April and October, this situation is totally inverted—these months coincide with wild berry harvest season and with it all the work of packing and storing, turning this prison into a virtual factory. Working the "boxes", as inmates call it, introduces an atmosphere that brings change not only to the physical spaces but also to the rhythms and routines. Nearly all the inmates want to take part in this activity, mainly for financial reasons: it's the most well-paid work that can be found at this prison, and it means having the money to buy some measure of independence, even if just for little things like tobacco, coffee, or to send a little money home. According to the guards and the warden, the pedagogical dimension of the activities available in prison (which some might term as their rehabilitating function) is a strategical tool to shape the behavior of a person in confinement.[5]

This brings us to a final introductory reflection on the theme of "ethnography of everyday life in confinement". The day-to-day in such a small community, living within a highly regulated and standardized environment, is not free from conflict, conniving, envy, and so on. Tensions rise, for instance, at times when there is any kind of "shortage"—money for cigarettes, coffee, hygiene products, or other commodities. The frustration that comes from privation enhances the limitations to autonomy and the sense of powerlessness and lack of choice inherent to most spheres of life in confinement: loneliness, the imposed cohabitation with others, the limits to contact with outside relationships (the number of phone calls or visits awarded), or items (letters or parcels).

On this point, Odemira presents characteristics that may be considered advantageous or doubly punishing for those confined. The first aspect is connected to the physical space. In terms of its architecture, Odemira belongs to a category that became known in Portugal as "county jails". It is a two-floor building comprised of an administrative area and front office, the director's office, the prison guards' quarters with two shower rooms, the staff cafeteria and dining room, the visitors area and a few other general-purpose rooms. In the same building, a heavy metal door with a bolt leads directly into the cell hall and the prisoners' restricted area: on the ground floor, a hall of roughly 30 by 4 meters is surrounded on both sides by two rows of cells. The walls are covered in pink tiles and the ceiling is opened up by a skylight. On the first floor, a balcony leads to further cells, making a total of 24 cells on both floors including double cells and cells for four, most of them for smokers. The distribution of inmates' is managed by the head of guards. All the cells were equipped with a cupboard for each inmate, as well as a bunk bed or single beds, and a toilet. Most cells also had television sets or stereos brought in by their occupants.

The upper floor also has a larger collective cell or dormitory, where most of the gypsy population was housed. As I was told, there were different motives for this division: the law recommends that people from the same family incarcerated (whether imprisoned at the same time or not) should be kept together. That was the case at Odemira, where I found several generations of the same family confined there. These women actually claimed to prefer such an arrangement themselves, not only because the dormitory was a larger space, but also because it had two toilets (separated with doors, rather than the curtain usually found in other cells) and it was smoke-free. No one ignored that ethnicity was a factor, but neither the prison direction nor the inmates regarded it as the primary concern.

Besides the cells, the ground floor also included a laundry room, a kitchen area that gave direct access to the refectory (which also served as a common room between meals), two exterior courtyards which were not much bigger than the cell hall, a shower room, a separate bathroom and a general-purpose room (normally used during the fruit packaging season). On the upper floor, besides a second shower room and toilet, a library occupied the entrance to a larger space used as a classroom.

Of the two outside courtyards, only one was available to inmates during their free time. The other one, accessed through the laundry room, was used to handwash clothes and hang them out to dry (neither of the courtyards had any kind of covering), and had a tiny annex where, years before, the nursery had been located, back when inmates with young children were admitted here. In short, this meant that for most of the day, inmates only had two large spaces where they could spend their free time—outside in the yard and inside in the cell hall, which was virtually just the doorstep to their cell.

While deprivation of freedom is intrinsic to imprisonment, we may say that in Odemira the physical constraint seems to be enhanced by the compactness of the place. Physical movement itself is cramped, and in turn inertia sets in, leading to an apathy that comes from lack of change in scenery and activity. During the winter months, when the weather conditions are harsher due to the cold and rain, inmates feel even more cloistered up inside, with the 50 women mostly confined to the inside precinct. Physical proximity is obviously one of the first consequences.

One may ask whether this proximity could lead to a greater sense of intimacy, or strengthen the bonds among peers. As will become obvious, most inmates at Odemira find that it is quite the opposite. Scrutiny, criticism and a continual sense of being under evaluation—not so much by the guards as by their peers—promotes conformism and passivity, and leads to strategies of isolation and self-protection. The absence of trusting relationships and the superficiality of "friendships" among inmates makes the feeling of emotional loneliness even more acute. This kind of proximate solitude—coupled with the atmosphere of inactivity felt during certain periods of the year—lead to self-reflectivity and inwardness, while outwardly seeming to promote greater compliance with the rules and norms of prison life.

This book seeks to unveil how much of this change is willed, imposed or even considered necessary by inmates and prison officers. At this moment it suffices to make a note of the idea, pointed out by several women during my stay, that "time runs slower in a small prison", regardless of the advantages they may find in the prison's reduced dimension compared to experiences in larger prison facilities, which they also describe as "confusing spaces, riddled with problems between guards and inmates", where a person is "never left in peace". In any case, the narrow space and the relatively low numbers of inmate occupancy—the other two female prisons in Portugal have an average population between 400 and 500 inmates—combined with the physical proximity between guards and inmates, gives Odemira all the advantages and drawbacks of an almost familiar environment.

There are four to five prison guards on permanent duty amongst the almost 50 inmates (who may be assigned to different occupations), besides the daily regular visits and rounds made by chief officers. The power asymmetry underlying the distinction between guard and inmates, though not totally eliminated, are considerably softened due to the constant interaction and familiarity produced by months and years of close coexistence (Fassin 2015; Genders and Player 1995; Liebling 2008; Liebling et al. 2012).

As will become clear, what inmates in other studies have described as severe experiences of oppression (see, for instance, the work of Moore and Scranton 2014), namely the negative perception of guards' constant presence and monitoring of their behavior and interaction, both officers and inmates describe as exactly the opposite. Guards are the first to admit that "this prison does not serve as an example" to portray the Portuguese prison system, while inmates themselves describe their keepers as "exceptional persons", highly committed and available. As a case study, Odemira seems to resemble a practice that has mostly characterized experiences in North European countries (Baldursson 2000; Johnsen et al. 2011; Pratt and Eriksson 2013; Ugelvik and Dullum 2012), where prisons are usually more restricted in size, focused on greater proximity with inmates in their everyday life, promoting an interaction that may not necessarily eliminate the distress caused by confinement, but can make it a less harmful experience.

We must not forget, however, that this prison is an exception rather than a typical example within the Portuguese context, which in the last decades has been characterized by prison overcrowding, and general shortage of material and human resources. In other words, Odemira seems to escape the kinds of problems that afflict the majority of Portuguese prison facilities—decayed infrastructures, conflicts among inmate populations and overburdening of professionals, all of which render prison guards and technical bodies unable to respond adequately to all situations.

Some authors object to finding positive features in any part of imprisonment, as if this somehow betrays the experience of those who have to suffer its privations, or as if this might somehow serve to legitimize what undoubtedly is the clearest example of a total institution in contemporary society. On this point, this work avoids extreme stances either way. Prison is a place of suffering on many levels, and in this regard Odemira is not peculiar. Yet, no two prisons are alike, and this is easily forgotten when dealing with institutions that are at the same time so prone to stereotyping and so widely concealed from public perceptions (Jewkes 2012, 2015).

Within their diversity, it is so important to observe and point out the harmful effects of imprisonment, as it is to understand and distinguish among its different forms and degrees. The best way to gain insight into its ambiguities and gradations, is to lend voice to those who experience it, without digging ourselves into absolute dichotomies as we discuss questions of power, legitimacy, submission, confrontation, and so on—but rather engaging in a reflection on these issues as they emerge and are reflected in the discourse of those who live and experience them through imprisonment.

* * *

Carrying out a study on a prison facility, its actors, its everyday life, its particularities and events, there is one important feature that can gain greater or lesser analytical relevance—the criminal act (Comaroff and Comaroff 2016; Comaroff 2010; Parnell 2003; Parnell and Kane 2003). Sometimes this element may seem to be undervalued or neglected, by inmates and guards alike. Prison officers, for instance, even though they may have a formed opinion about the crimes committed by a particular inmate, often embrace an idea that can be translated into an expression like "the judge has already convicted them for the crime that bought them here, so it's no longer relevant for my work". They consider the trial that preceded imprisonment must not serve as a reference for a second judgement and condemnation on their part. Actually, it is also possible to observe this attitude among inmates, who avoid speaking openly with each other about their crimes, finding that this topic enters a private sphere that should not be under their peers' scrutiny.

Within the bounds set by inmates' willingness to discuss the topic, crime is assumed as a constant presence throughout this book, as an essential factor for our understanding of their life trajectories. In other words, if it is incontestable that a person's identity before and after imprisonment is defined by their previous experience, then the way they conceive, verbalize and put their past into context, namely the criminal acts which condemned them, is crucial to a better understanding and insight of their present condition (Crewe and Bennett 2012).

In practice, it is extremely hard to gauge this dimension through everyday life observation. Even supposing that inmates may be more disposed to speak openly about their crimes in private conversation, it is normally a theme they will not discuss in the presence of other inmates, being usually even considered a taboo topic, as I came to realize. The physical proximity mentioned earlier, and whatever degree of intimacy might arise from sharing a common living space, does not necessarily translate into sharing this kind of information—quite the contrary.

From what could be observed during fieldwork, one of the unspoken rules at Odemira when it comes to the topic of crime is a kind of "don't ask/don't tell" policy. Nevertheless, these women are sentenced for periods that vary between a few months and several years (the longest sentence belonged to an inmate serving 16 years), and consciously or not, the criminal act is probably the factor that most decisively defines and characterizes a person in this situation—before him/herself, before his/her peers and before the judicial and penitentiary system.

These observations can be corroborated by different means and in different situations. Throughout this research, I was able to verify that the "attitude towards crime" and the "attitude towards the victim"—two items that are usually found in any formal assessment performed on inmates during imprisonment—suffer the inflexions that characterize processes of gradual rationalization and distance from the facts, the evolution and transformations in the judicial processes, as well as a greater or lesser acceptance of the condemnation, and the validity of justice and impartiality on the part of those who delivered it.

Every time inmates recount their personal history, every time they describe their crimes—as well as the justifications and explanations they offer—new elements emerge and add further reasoning, deeper context and even new interpretations of the facts. This does not merely result from a process of self-reflection alluded to earlier, but is also due to prolonged contact with other life histories, whose similarity or contrast influence the repositioning of their own identity. Comparison with other inmates and with fragments of their stories—leading them either to discriminate or to empathize with others, to minimize or condemn their actions—influence how they come to see themselves and their own actions, especially their crime. In view of this, I believe that the present work cannot afford to dismiss crime *as an action*, not just because it is part of these women's experience at the time when I speak and interact with them, but also because it inevitably shapes how they present themselves to others—cellmates, guards, director, sentencing judge, visiting relatives, and so on.

Every prisoner knows, whether they are aware of it or not, that their present actions are being gauged to determine changes in their behavior; they will be brought to bear in the assessment of their conduct on a daily basis; they will determine their future. This constant evaluation inevitably has the past as its main reference—and more particularly that turning point in their lives which has been textually inscribed in the reading of their sentence. Whenever an inmate files for an appeal to reduce her sentence, is evaluated for furlough or applies for probation, she will be once again confronted with the facts. More than that: she will have to deal with being appraised by others.

Book Contents

Dividing into chapters an investigation that deals with a confined space such as a prison, which concentrates dozens of people with particular characteristics, proved to be more difficult than I initially expected. Combining the empirical work of everyday life observation with analytical interpretation required finding both an appropriate structure and a narrative thread that must go beyond a succession of episodes, but at the same time does not digress into a theoretical abstraction. The way I found to successfully communicate the complexity of daily life inside a prison facility, was to divide my work into chapters that somehow followed the timeline of my one-year of fieldwork at Odemira. Chapter 2 outlines a brief overview of the main changes that have occurred in recent Portuguese penitentiary history since the most important prison reform of 1936 until nowadays while describing some of the most important changes in penal legislation, and their implications on the Portuguese prison system.

Paradoxically, we observe that the doubling of the inmate population over this period has been met with the increasing number of prisons being closed down, having for some decades now brought the carceral system to a situation of chronic overcrowding, shortage of material and human resources, degradation of infrastructures and near collapse of prison services. Odemira prison facility stands out from this general panorama, presenting specific features that are discussed in Chap. 3, which outlines a brief historical overview of this small facility, focusing especially on the period of continued operation as a female prison since 1995. Entering Odemira, the reader is presented with some methodological notes taken on the first days of fieldwork, and the initial contact not only with the institution but also its population, and some of the complexities that encouraged me to turn this work into more than just another study based solely of short interviews, but instead on a longer and continued permanence.

Thus, and since for the first time I was allowed to actually "enter a prison"—that is, to go beyond the doors of administrative area and into the prisoners' restricted areas—Chaps. 4, 5 and 6 are dedicated to describing the everyday life inside this prison: inmates' routines, conversations, conflicts, complaints, problems, difficulties, and so forth. These chapters also focus on some specific themes, such as work, family, motherhood, crime, following up in greater depth some of these women's life histories as a means to address issues such as discrimination, exclusion, violence, and poverty. In summary, we will see how the concepts of "inside" and "outside" are as decisive as they sometimes become so tenuous that they cease to be physically felt; almost become purely psychological categories; that "feeling the prison", to use inmates' own words, implies the experience of punishment and learning through error, but also an opportunity to interrupt a cycle and a trajectory that seemed to have spun out of control. But to what degree were such trajectories and experiences inevitable, or reactive, so to speak?

These issues are discussed in Chaps. 7 and 8. The first of these looks into the judicial rulings that condemned Odemira's prisoners, and debates whether their female gender identity had bearing on those decisions—whether it can be seen as an attenuating factor or conversely as an aggravating circumstance; if discrimination, censorship, or condescendence weigh into those decisions. While the question of gender is unquestionably paramount in the context of relations between individuals and institutions, the practice of justice and the application of the law are also discussed as subjective and moral procedures. In turn, Chap. 8 follows up on the relation between inmates and institutions, but this time bringing the debate out of prison, and looking at institutions such as Social Security, state institutions like the Child and Youth Protection Services or the Victim Support Organization, and local entities as town councils and other local organizations.

As we follow inmates' past interaction with these entities, we dissipate whatever doubts one might still have that crime never is a person' first option, and in many cases it was actually their very last resort. Chapter 9 brings us back inside prison to find uncertainty as the main feature of imprisonment, observing how the past is constantly being revisited by prisoners and ultimately shapes their everyday actions. The waiting for court decisions and authorizations, for pending sentences or reduced sentences; moments such as hearings with supervisory judges periodically remind inmates of the reason they were first brought of prison, constantly updating their status as criminals, but more than that, they are moments for appraising, judging and decreeing their transformation/rehabilitation.

In the Conclusion, I reflect upon three interrelated dimensions: methodological dilemmas, ethical commitments and the inherent political implications of a prison ethnography work. While it is certain that prison intends to remove human misery and suffering of the convicted from the public view, as Michel Foucault stated, we might also ask ourselves to what extent anyone might be interested today in getting to know—given that knowledge implies responsibility—who lives in prison and what that experience is like?

Notes

1. From now on I will refer to Odemira prison only as "Odemira".
2. This project was financed by Gerda Henkel Foundation and developed between 2015 and 2017, entitled "Human Security in Prison. Perspectives, Subjectivities and Experiences. A Contribution to the Anthropology of Security".
3. I thank Miguel Vale de Almeida for the suggestion of trying to understand what benefits this limitation could bring to debates about prison methodology.

4. Although I also conducted interviews allocated to the main pavilions—one for remand inmates, the other for convicted—in this small unit I was able to engage with the prisoners without space or time restraints since there was only 15 women there, due to their age, mental issues, or mobility difficulties.
5. The editorial found in the prison's newsletter, *Entre Margens* (Between Margins) of May/June 2016, written by the director herself, reflects upon this issue: "The school year is over. It was an intense year, and an arduous task for most of the inmates who attended, since they had to conciliate study with work. The values and knowledge gained will become essential tools for their life in freedom. Portugal, like the rest of Europe today, is going through a serious crisis, making it even harder to enter the work market. [...] As a priority, we have been concentrating our efforts to make this activity a permanent feature of Odemira Prison. It is also the best way to gain working habits, which will be so essential when the time comes to face the world beyond these bars. [...] Education is no less important. As a conclusion, we should stress that the stages inmates gradually conquer contribute to empower and improve inmates, enabling at the same time to expand their awareness and thus avoid future mistakes. Good luck, we are all here, working together to help you in this crucial phase of your life."

References

Baldursson, Erlendur. 2000. Prisoners, Prisons and Punishment in Small Societies. *Journal of Scandinavian Studies in Criminology and Crime Prevention* 1 (1): 6–15.

Bosworth, Mary. 2016a. *Engendering Resistance: Agency and Power in Women's Prisons*. New York: Routledge.

Boutron, Camille, and Chloé Constant. 2014. *Être mère en Pérou: droit ou double peine?* Champ Pénal/Penal Field. XI.

Carlen, Pat. 1983. *Women's Imprisonment. A Study in Social Control*. London: Routledge & Kegan Paul.

Carlen, Pat, ed. 1985. *Criminal Women. Autobiographical Accounts*. Cambridge: Polity Press.

———, ed. 2002. *Women and Punishment. The Struggle for Justice*. Devon: Willan Publishing.

Carlen, Pat, and Anne Worrall. 2014. *Analysing Women's Imprisonment*. Devon: Willan Publishing.
Cohen, Stanley, and Laurie Taylor. 1972. *Psychological Survival. The Experience of Long-Term Imprisonment*. London: Penguin.
Comaroff, Jean. 2010. Anthropology and Crime: An Interview with Jean Comaroff. *PoLar: Political and Legal Anthropological Review* 33 (1): 133–139.
Comaroff, Jean, and John Comaroff. 2016. *The Truth about Crime. Sovereignty, Knowledge, Social Order*. Chicago: Chicago University Press.
Covington, Stephanie, and Barbara Bloom. 2003. Gendered Justice. Women in the Criminal Justice System. In *Gendered Justice. Adressing Female Offenders*, ed. Barbara Bloom, 1–20. Durham: Carolina Academic Press.
Crewe, Ben. 2009. *The Prisoner Society: Power, Adaptation, and Social Life in an English Prison*. Oxford: Oxford University Press.
———. 2012. Prison Culture and the Prisoner Society. In *The Prisoner*, ed. Ben Crewe and Jamie Bennett, 27–39. New York: Routledge.
Crewe, Ben, and Jamie Bennett, eds. 2012. *The Prisoner*. New York: Routledge.
Crewe, Ben, and Alice Ievins. 2015. Closeness, Distance and Honesty in Prison Ethnography. In *The Palgrave Handbook of Prison Ethnography*, ed. Deborah Drake, Rod Earle, and Jennifer Sloan, 124–142. London and New York: Palgrave Macmillan.
Cunha, Manuela. 1994. *Malhas que a Reclusão Tece. Questões de Identidade numa Prisão Feminina*. Lisbon: Centro de Estudos Judiciários.
———. 2002. *Entre o Bairro e a Prisão. Tráficos e Trajectos*. Lisbon: Afrontamento.
Drake, Deborah. 2015. Finding Secrets and Secret Findings: Confronting the Limits of the Ethnographer's Gaze. In *The Palgrave Handbook of Prison Ethnography*, ed. Deborah Drake, Rod Earle, and Jennifer Sloan, 252–270. New York: Palgrave Macmillan.
Drake, Deborah, Rod Earle, and Jennifer Sloan, eds. 2015. *The Palgrave Handbook of Prison Ethnography*. New York: Palgrave Macmillan.
Fassin, Didier. 2015. *L'Ombre du Monde. Une Anthropologie de la Condition Carcérale*. Paris: Seuil.
Fassin, Didier, et al. 2015. *At the Heart of the State. The Moral World of Institutions*. London: Pluto Press.
Frois, Catarina. 2009. *The Anonymous Society. Identity, Stigma and Anonymity in 12-Step Associations*. Newcastle upon Tyne: Cambridge Scholars Publishing.
———. 2013. *Peripheral Vision. Politics, Technology and Surveillance*. Oxford and New York: Berghahn.
Garsten, Christina, and Anette Nyqvist, eds. 2014. *Organisational Anthropology. Doing Ethnography in and Among Complex Organisations*. London: Pluto Press.

References

Genders, Elaine, and Elaine Player. 1995. *Grendon. A Study of a Therapeutic Prison*. Oxford: Clarendon Press.

Goffman, Erving. 1959. *The Presentation of Self in Everyday Life*. New York: Anchor Books.

———. 1963. *Stigma. Notes on the Management of the Spoiled Identity*. New York: Simon and Schuster.

———. 1967. *Interaction Ritual: Essays on Face-to-Face Interaction*. New York: Anchor Books.

Gupta, Akhil, and James Ferguson, eds. 1997. *Anthropological Locations. Boundaries and Grounds of a Field Science*. Chicago and London: University of Chicago Press.

Hastrup, Kirsten, and Peter Hervik, eds. 1994. *Social Experience and Anthropological Knowledge*. New York: Routledge.

James, Deborah, and Christina Toren. 2010. Introduction. Culture, Context and Anthropologists' Accounts. In *Culture Wars: Context, Models and Anthropologists' Accounts*, ed. Deborah James, Evelyn Plaice, and Christina Toren, 1–18. Oxford and New York: Berghahn.

Jewkes, Yvonne. 2012. Autoethnography and Emotion as Intellectual Resources: Doing Prison Research Differently. *Qualitative Enquiry* 18 (1): 63–75.

———. 2015. Foreword. In *The Palgrave Handbook of Prison Ethnography*, ed. Deborah Drake, Rod Earle, and Jennifer Sloan, ix–xiii. London and New York: Palgrave Macmillan.

Jewkes, Yvonne, and Serena Wright. 2016. Researching the Prison. In *Handbook on Prisons*, ed. Yvonne Jewkes, Jamie Bennett, and Ben Crewe, 2nd ed., 659–676. London and New York: Routledge.

Johnsen, Berit, Per Kristian Granheim, and Janne Helgesen. 2011. Exceptional Prison Conditions and the Quality of Prison Life: Prison Size and Prison Culture in Norwegian Closed Prisons. *European Journal of Criminology* 8 (6): 515–529.

Liebling, Alison. 2008. 'Titan' Prisons: Do Size, Efficiency and Legitimacy Matter? In *Tackling Prison Overcrowding. Build More Prisons? Sentence Fewer Offenders?* ed. Mike Hough, Rob Allen, and Enver Solomon, 63–80. Bristol: Policy Press.

Liebling, Alison, David Price, and Guy Shefer. 2012. *The Prison Officer*. 2nd ed. London and New York: Routledge.

Lima, Antónia. 2003. *Grandes Famílias, Grandes Empresas. Ensaio Antropológico sobre uma Elite de Lisboa*. Lisboa: Dom Quixote.

Lima, Antónia Pedroso. 2016. Care as a Factor for Sustainability in Situations of Crisis: Portugal between the Welfare State and Interpersonal Relationships. *Cadernos Pagu* 46: 79–105.

Melhuus, Marit, Jon P. Mitchell, and Helena Wulff, eds. 2010. *Ethnographic Practice in the Present*. Oxford and New York: Berghahn.

Moore, Linda, and Phil Scranton. 2014. *The Incarceration of Women. Punishing Bodies, Breaking Spirits*. London and New York: Palgrave Macmillan.

Parnell, Philip. 2003. Introduction. Crime's Power: Crime, Law, and the State. In *Crime's Power. Anthropologists and the Ethnography of Crime*, 1–32. New York: Palgrave.

Parnell, Philip, and Stephanie Kane, eds. 2003. *Crime's Power. Anthropologists and the Ethnography of Crime*. New York: Palgrave.

Piacentini, Laura. 2007. Researching on Russian Prisons. A Consideration of New and Established Methodologies in Prison Research. In *Handbook on Prisons*, ed. Yvonne Jewkes, 152–173. Devon: Willan.

Pina Cabral, João. 2003. *O Homem na Família: Cinco Ensaios de Antropologia*. Lisbon: Imprensa de Ciências Sociais.

———. 2010. The Door in the Middle: Six Conditions for Anthropology. In *Culture Wars: Context, Models and Anthropologists' Accounts*, ed. Deborah James, Evelyn Plaice, and Christina Toren, 152–169. Oxford and New York: Berghahn.

Pratt, John, and Anna Eriksson. 2013. *Contrasts in Punishment. An Explanation of Anglophone Excess and Nordic Exceptionalism*. London and New York: Routledge.

Tabbush, Constanza, and María Florencia Gentile. 2013. Emotions behind Bars: The Regulation of Mothering in Argentine Jails. *Signs: Journal of Women in Culture and Society* 39 (1): 131–149.

Schinkel, Marguerite. 2014. *Being Imprisoned. Punishment, Adaptation and Desistance*. London and New York: Palgrave Macmillan.

Ugelvik, Thomas, and Jane Dullum, eds. 2012. *Penal Exceptionalism? Nordic Prison Policy and Practice*. London and New York: Routledge.

Ugelvik, Thomas. 2014. *Power and Resistance in Prison: Doing Time, Doing Freedom*. London and New York: Palgrave.

Wall, Karin, ed. 2012. *Famílias em Portugal*. 2nd ed. Lisbon: Imprensa de Ciências Sociais.

Wall, Karin, and Lígia Amâncio, eds. 2007. *Família e Género em Portugal e na Europa*. Lisbon: Imprensa de Ciências Sociais.

2

Portugal, a "Mild-Mannered" Country: Penal and Penitentiary Overview

The expression "Portugal is a mild-mannered country" is a coined phrase in Portuguese popular culture to define the country and its docile, submissive, quiet and orderly population. Three episodes set in very different moments of Portuguese history may be evoked to illustrate this idea: it was the second European country to abolish the death penalty, in 1867, which would somehow reveal a humanitarian view in punishment; the military-led revolution that in 1974 put an end to a 48-year-long dictatorial regime was renowned for its peaceful unfolding, symbolized by the carnations handed out by the population, with which the revolutionary forces decorated their rifles and tanks as they marched into the capital Lisbon. Lastly, whereas other countries did not escape episodes of turmoil and violent protests in the wake of the sovereign debt crisis that affected several southern European countries, in Portugal the most significant manifestations of popular discontentment during the period of external financial intervention (2011–2015), were the massive silent marches that took over the streets of most major cities in Portugal, and the revival of an old

---

I wish to thank Afonso Bento and Ana David for their valuable contribution in the writing of this Chapter.

revolutionary song ("Grândola Vila Morena") as the anthem sung in many public demonstrations (Accornero and Pinto 2015).[1]

It may come as a surprise to discover that, in contrast with this reputation for mild manners, since 1980s Portugal has consistently been one of the European countries with a highest incarceration rate per capita (varying from 135 to 147 per 100,000 inhabitants). The irony somehow folds back on itself when we consider that the Annual Internal Security Reports and Eurostat Statistics have revealed a decreasing trend in the registered crime rates in a country that is usually described as one of "the safest in Europe" (on this point, see Frois 2013, 2011). This discrepancy between low crime rates and high incarceration rates is not an exclusively Portuguese phenomenon when considering the European panorama. The most notorious example of this is actually the United Kingdom,[2] usually pointed out as an example of the paradigm that prison sentencing has prevailed as the main form of punishment in certain societies.

From the ample debate held in specialized literature (not only in the juridical, but also criminological and sociological fields), we could assume that condemning an offender with deprivation of liberty is a necessary condition to satisfy the popular notions that "justice is being done", or that "the justice system works", an idea accurately summed up by Austin Sarat when he states, referring to the United States of America very specific case in this subject, that "The way a society punishes demonstrates its commitment to standards of judgment and justice, its distinctive views of blame and responsibility, its understandings of mercy and forgiveness, and its particular ways of responding to evil." (2014a: 1).[3]

Portuguese prison statistics (namely from the last three decades) show that the use of preventive detention is one of the most favored measures—20%–30% of the cases—applied by magistrates to defendants/suspects awaiting trial. In purely objective terms, this decision suffers from a particular shortcoming. The Portuguese Penal Code specifically assumes that remand prison should be of last resort, bearing in mind that it is "the gravest coercive measure that can be applied to a person suspected of committing a crime, and thus only applicable when all other coercion measures prove inadequate or insufficient". Depending on the type and seriousness of the crime, after conviction, so too the commitment to a prison facility should be pondered as exceptional, rather than the only inevitable destination for someone who has committed a crime.

Judging by the existing numbers, however, this is far from being the interpretation made by the overwhelming majority of first instance magistrates and judges. The last two decades clearly reveal that, despite the existence of an array of alternative punitive procedures that equally fulfill the function of holding offenders accountable for their criminal acts—such as monetary fines, community service, electronic bracelets, house arrest, and so on—these tend to be considered by judges as overly lenient when weighed against the "social alarm" caused by the crimes in question (and later we shall see what these are).

This has been a recurring discussion within the political, judicial and penitentiary circles; the representatives of the Ministry of Justice and the Directorate-General of Prison Services themselves have long since been the first ones to oppose what seems to have been the excessively punitive action of Portuguese magistrates. However, when we analyze the context in which these manifestations of clamor and criticism are proffered, we acknowledge that they are motivated by factors that are extraneous to the problem itself. In other words, there is no thorough and broad reflection upon the purpose, use and efficiency of the imprisonment, or even—from a different perspective—of the effects of incarceration on those convicted for the practice of criminal acts. The discussion usually revolves around much more practical aspects: the Portuguese prison system is beset by structural problems connected with issues of overcrowding, infrastructure conditions and shortage of human resources.

Two opposing phenomena have stood out over the last three decades: the decreasing number of prison facilities versus the increasing number of inmate populations. In a strictly financial rationale of resource management, several prison facilities (of different sizes and in various locations) have been closed down one after another. At the beginning of the 1970s there were 112 prison facilities operating in Portugal for a total population of 6000 inmates. In 2016, for the 14,200 existing inmates there were under half that number of facilities, a total of 49.

Prison overcrowding, however, is actually but one of the problems the system is facing, leading responsible entities to admit that there is a serious risk of "system breakdown", as the General-Director of Prison Services stated during a parliamentary committee hearing in March of 2016, if measures are not taken urgently. In fact, the director's bluntness during that hearing made quite an impression on MPs. After thanking them for the opportunity he was being given to present what he called the "bleak picture" that emerged from a glance at the country's prisons, he proceeded to go over the available data.

This representative of the prison services had come prepared with several documents: graphic charts revealing the overcrowding in several facilities (where single cells had to be adjusted to accommodate up to four inmates); photographs documenting decayed buildings in danger of imminent collapse; tables showing the shortage of prison guards and correctional treatment staff in relation to the prison population, and so forth. He also described other extreme situations, such as prisons where inmates had to sleep in the hallways due to lack of available (or inhabitable) cell space, or food shortages that made it impossible for certain prisons to ensure meals for its whole population. The director repeatedly admonished (as the Minister of Justice had done also) that such situations should be dealt with urgently, given that "the state has the right to deprive offenders of their freedom, but could not deprive citizens of their dignity." (Frois 2017).

This analysis was not limited simply to the shortage of resources he had to deal with on a daily basis. He directly held magistrates accountable for prison overcrowding, considering that they relied far too much on preventive detention measures and tended excessively towards maximum prison sentences. Regarding the execution of prison sentences, he further observed that the vast majority of inmates in Portugal are made to serve the totality of the sentences, rarely benefiting from any kind of sentence reduction. In other words, even though the law stipulates scheduled dates for reviewing the sentence, at which point it may be substituted by an alternative measure, the judges seem extremely reluctant to take this path. In short, in Portugal there is far too much prison sentencing, the sentences are far too long, and as a rule they are much too often served to their legal limit.

To have a full grasp of the problems raised in this debate—none of which are new—we must go back a few decades to trace the evolution of the law regarding penal matters. In this attempt, at the same we will be underlining its cultural specificities, inasmuch as political and legal histories also reflect a county's customs and practices. In order to do so, the starting point will be to observe how the Portuguese penitentiary system was originally structured, and then try to describe how it "grew" from there, more specifically since the beginning of the democratic period, in the mid-1970s.

The Portuguese Penitentiary System: Concepts and Practices

Although 1867 is the year when the operation and regulation of "modern" prisons and punishments—such as they were defined at the time—were first considered as a whole, it was only with the 1936 Prison Organization Reform that a law was written reflecting and systematizing the period's penitentiary spirit. Conceived following a study on the experiences that were being carried out in other European countries, this reform had two main goals: to set up a new organization and management of prison facilities on the one hand, and to implement a humanist worldview of prison sentencing on the other. Based on the assumption that there were different categories of offenders and crimes, the new system conceives a prison system that can accommodate such diversity, and thus it starts by acknowledging that:

> The construction, conditions, and localization of existing buildings are terrible, and their number insufficient for the existing inmate population, wherefore the excesses of capacity have become a hindrance to their disciplinary and educational action, since inmates are made to live in an inadmissible promiscuity—preventive inmates side by side with convicted felons, the insane mixed in with the sane, the occasional delinquent co-existing with the hardened career criminal. (1936 Prison Reform, Article 1)

Throughout the 1940s and 1950s, a large number of prisons were built following models that respond to the different typologies and identified specificities, such as sentence length or population number: the small county jails for sentences under three months; the central or regional prisons for sentences longer than three months and less than two years—with a strong emphasis on the "regeneration of delinquents" through work; security prisons for the more serious crimes, or those that caused "deeper social alarm". Besides the separation according to gender, this reform gave special attention to other distinctions that had been basically ignored so far: the creation of a prison school for youths between 16–21 years of age, asylum prisons, security prisons for "difficult correction criminals", and overseas penal colonies for "incorrigible criminals".

The nature of the dictatorial regime that had recently risen to power in Portugal introduced yet another category of crime whose agents presented a very specific profile—the political prisoners—for whom the regime built a new facility in mainland Portugal (which added to the some of the already existing facilities adapted for this purpose), and several penal colonies overseas.

This reform was not characterized only in terms of the penitentiary thought behind it. By acknowledging the existence of differences amongst the types of "delinquency", and the consequent need for differentiated institutions to accommodate them, it also assumed that prison should aim to and rehabilitate and re-socialize the individual, and not just serve as a place of containment and punishment.

> The prison regime should not provide inmates with an atmosphere that will harm their moral betterment, and even less should it lower the moral standards they had upon their entrance. It is the least that can be demanded of a prison facility, although obviously, beyond these negative effects, the prison should further seek to act in the sense of the inmates' moral elevation. (1936 Prison Reform, Article 29).

The main emphasis was on the correctional or educational element, achieved through the labor and moral education of the inmates, more specifically through the individualization of the sentence, thus presupposing its regular review and appraisal at any time of its enforcement, namely in long-term sentences. This means that the duration of a prison sentence, seen as a measure of censurability and seriousness of the crime, and also as defining the regime of its execution, influences as well how the prison services should conduct their action. Short-term sentences (from three to six months) should mostly serve an intimidating purpose, while longer term sentences must contemplate a gradual system of inmate's re-education and readjustment, for which the contribution of the different prison professionals is summoned—from the director to the medical doctors, from the religious counselors to the teachers, workshop supervisors, guards, and so on:

> All of this must be accomplished—and herein lies the condition and the secret of success—with the full commitment and increasing participation of the chief interested party [the inmate]. In order to achieve this goal, we must address head on the prisoner's moral and material misery, taking part in his concerns and problems, taking an interest in the fate of his close ones, and finally preparing his convalescence, which upon release needs to continue being followed up, in strict cooperation with the work of his patrons; faithful and certain that this time and effort will never be a total waste, even when occasionally disappointment is the only result of all the hard work and hope (1936 Prison Reform, Article 53).

The period mediating between the reform of 1936 and the one that followed, witnessed several relevant changes in penitentiary terms, namely the creation of the Sentencing Court in 1944. Up until then, sentence supervision was left up to the penitentiary administration, and the court was only responsible for convicting and sentencing. When the Sentencing Court was created, those competencies were carried out with the assistance of the judge who appraised and decided on the offender's dangerousness, and the enforcement of security measures, as well as on any decision regarding requests for early leave during the sentence. As a result of the distinction between inmates and the focus on work and education as essential features of an inmate's rehabilitation, during this reform's lifetime—which lasted almost the entire duration of the *Estado Novo* dictatorial regime—the number of prisons operating in Portugal rose almost to 200 facilities, including all the above-mentioned categories and models (Adriano 2010).

The changes introduced in the period immediately after the end of the dictatorship, in 1974, must be understood more as the result of that period's particular circumstances than as a new structured project. A clear example of this was the shutting down of all political prisons (the prisoners had since been freed) operating in Portugal and its overseas colonies. The new penitentiary reform of 1979 was, from its outset, intent on defining the purposes of all freedom deprivation measures, stressing amongst them the rehabilitation and reintegration of inmates. Thus, above intimidation, repression or punishment, the aim of prison sentences is to operate a transformation on those it targets: "Art. 2.1: The execution of measures involving deprivation of liberty should be guided towards reintegrating inmates in society, ensuring their future chances to lead socially responsible lives free of crime; Art. 2.2: The execution of measures involving deprivation of liberty also serve as a protection for society, preventing and deterring other criminal acts." Two factors stand out, once again upholding that deprivation of liberty should be "attenuated" in its execution. Firstly it should, as much as possible, approximate reclusion to "the conditions of life in freedom, thus avoiding the negative effects of freedom deprivation" (Art. 3.2). Secondly, it should seek to individualize sentencing: "Sentence enforcement should, as much as possible, stimulate the participation of the inmate in his social reintegration, especially in drafting their individual sentence plan and summoning the cooperation of society towards achieving those ends." (Art. 3.4).

The 1979 reform reflects international guidelines, namely from the UN and the Council of Europe, and Portugal's full commitment to the main international conventions on the matter at the time, implying the recognition of inmates' juridical status, provided with social rights and acknowledged as a party in the juridical relationship with the state and not merely as the passive subject in a relationship of power with the penitentiary administration. As far as the prison facilities were concerned, in addition to the shutdown of a large number of prisons all around the country, allocation of inmates was now done according to different levels of security—maximum, medium and minimum—and the distinction between different prison establishments consistent with their characteristics (gender, age, juridical status, place of residence, etc.).

Within the framework of the Portuguese juridical and legal system, the prison sentence is solely concerned with "general" and "special" prevention. By "general" it means discouraging criminal actions, reinforcing the confidence of the community on the validity and enforcement of its juridical-penal dispositions. "Special" prevention is focused specifically on the offenders, with the goal of preventing them from committing new crimes. The current law—Law n° 115/2009, of October 12, 2009 from the Code of Enforcement Prison Sentences and Imprisonment Measures—serves the public imperatives of ensuring citizens' security, promoting the system's humanization and bolstering the efficiency of the means for social reinsertion. In other words, if prison is not to contribute towards the inmate's "anti-socialization", it means that the prison's concrete setting should not reinforce the stigmatizing social weight already carried by the judgement and the sentence; the limitation of rights cannot permit, except insofar as they are imposed for compelling reasons, urgent and adjusted to the inmate (and not to the facility's operating requirements); the inmate's general living conditions should resemble those of life in liberty; and the relations between the inmate and the outside world should be promoted. (Code of Enforcement Prison Sentences and Imprisonment Measures, Articles 2 to 6)

Legal Changes and Prison Population in Portugal after 1974

The Portuguese political revolution of 1974 gave way to dramatic changes in the country's legal outlook. During the years following the democratic revolution, the balance between shifting social circumstances and applicable legal codes was not always easy to achieve. As several scholars have remarked in different ways, one of the pervasive traces in Portuguese society after the revolution was a fundamental discrepancy between the demands and practices of its social and political agents, and the formal changes introduced in the state apparatus and its different legal norms (Sousa Santos 1990; Ferreira 1999; Barreto 2000; Bravo 2000; Costa 2003).

This was particularly evident in the area of criminal justice. With the Penal Code in 1982, a gap emerged between a set of laws widely renowned as progressive and advanced—which emphasized and prioritized the resocialization of offenders—and a pattern of growing prison population and prison overcrowding. In fact, at the same time that a wide variety of alternatives to short prison sentences was promoted—such as fines, community work, and suspended sentencing or probation regimes—these legal provisions proved to be ineffective to overturn the general growth tendency registered in the prison population (Costa 2003).

Even though the fact that prison rates have doubled may be explained by a phenomenon of social liberalization during this period in Portugal—alongside a transitional phase of economic instability and an increase in criminality—neither the magistrates seemed predisposed to fulfill the spirit in which the Penal Code was originally intended (in that they failed to explore its possibilities for alternative sentencing), nor was the code itself able to deal with the new types of criminality that began to emerge at this time; namely drug-related crimes. In any case, during the last decades of the twentieth century the fact was that prison population continued to grow and, by 1995, Portugal had one of the highest rates in the European Union. As a consequence, during the 1980s, prison overcrowding started to affect the penitentiary system, becoming such a notorious problem that the Portuguese government resorted to successive amnesties and presidential pardons (in 1981, 1982, 1986, 1991, 1994, 1999).

Which factors weighed in this persistent growth of the prison population throughout the 80s and 90s? The answer is twofold, and must be sought not just in the letter of existing criminal law, but also in its praxis by justice officials. It is consensually recognized that the general dispositions pertaining to criminals and criminality changed during the 80s. All over Europe and the United States, insecurity and fear caused by a rise in criminality (or sometimes only its perception) fueled a "law and order" kind of approach, emphasizing punishment and retribution over leniency and rehabilitation (Cunha and Durão 2011; Wacquant 2009).

Portugal was not immune to these tendencies. As in other places, one of the short-term results of the so-called "war on drugs" was a sharp and sudden growth in prison population numbers. It was not only a matter of the number of detentions generated by the enforcement of these laws,[4] or the length of the sentences imposed, but also of how the principles underlying these specific laws had a "contamination effect" over the rest of Portuguese criminal justice. As Eduardo Maia Costa, a former district attorney of the city of Lisbon, remarked:

> The drug laws fostered a criminal policy that uses penal law as the main instrument for social control (or even for socialization), and focuses on criminalization, extending sentences and even aggravating the deterioration of prison conditions… The 'war on drugs' has worked as the strategic 'spearhead' for the new criminal policy, which has influenced the penal code itself, as the clearly more punitive nature of the 1995 and 1998 revisions demonstrate. (2003: 95)

It should not be surprising that factors such as overreliance on prison sentences (as opposed to possible alternative penalties), increment in medium and long-term sentences (between two and five years, and five or more years, respectively), intense use of pre-trial detention, and increase in average time of detention (as the result of widespread reluctance in granting probation), played a fundamental role towards the situation of penal overcrowding occurring from the mid-80s until the turn of the century. Despite maintaining rehabilitation as one of their main objectives, the Penal Code revisions of 1995 and 1998 were instilled with this renewed punitive spirit. While continuing to contemplate the use of alternative measures, such as community work or the payment of fines, they also extended the sentence limits for "crimes against people" (from 20 to 25 years) and introduced general prevention as an accepted goal of imprisonment.

These modifications heightened the widespread pattern of "bifurcated" criminal policy (Cunha 2002, 2015), in which "petty" criminals have greater chances of avoiding prison, while the sentences for more serious offenders are extended, and they spend longer periods of time in prison:

> This produces a *stocking* effect, or in other words, a cumulative process in the numbers of inmate populations, in which renewal is slower because they remain longer periods in prison, which in its turn continues to receive increasing numbers of long-term convicts. On the other hand, this enhanced severity is also reflected on the work of judicial agents—supervisory courts included—in part because they act as the executioners of a diffuse public perception of insecurity, often interpreted as an appeal for repression they feel they must respond to. (Cunha 2008: 15)

During the first decade of the twenty-first century, the number of imprisonments registered a consistent decrease (from 13,918 in 2002 to 10,807 in 2007). Although difficult to pinpoint the specific factors that might be directly responsible for these fluctuations, some possible clues for this occurrence can be advanced.[5] In terms of the decrease in the prison population between 2001 and 2008, it may be related to the 1999 Amnesty, which seems to have had lasting effects. Considering the low Portuguese birth rate at the turn of the century, some authors would argue that demography played a significant role in this decrease (Semedo 2004, 2005, 2006). However, 2008 witnessed a sudden inversion of the past six-year consecutive fall, going from 102 inmates per 100,000 inhabitants, to approximately 138 in 2015.[6] From 2009 onwards the prison population resumed its growing trend and the majority of inmates only exit jail when their sentences are complete, which means there is a great reluctance in granting conditional releases.

Furthermore, between the end of the 90s and the first decade of the twenty-first century, a series of episodes publicized by the media prompted the production of specific legislation in the area of criminal justice. As an example, one could consider the 2007 Penal Code that become known as the "Casa Pia reform" in reference to a major sex scandal that transpired during the early 2000s involving a large number of people (including celebrities, politicians and even a minister), who were accused of molesting minors from a well-known children's home called "Casa Pia". Domestic violence, which was defined as a public crime in 2000, is another crime against the person that has gained increasing attention from the Portuguese judicial system, having been extended to include many different categories: violence against women, elderly people, child abuse, violence against parents, and (in 2013) domestic violence perpetrated by women against men. In 2008, for the first time since 1991, the number of inmates convicted for "crimes against people" (which includes crimes such as murder or aggression, but also sex crimes) exceeded the number of inmates convicted for "drug-related crimes". The global problems and legal "wars" currently being waged all over the world—such as the already mentioned "war on drugs", whose impact on the Portuguese prison population at the beginning of the 80s was especially notorious—do not invalidate the need to address internal problems, which have marked legislative production in penal matters, related mainly with domestic violence crimes, economical crimes, sexual crimes, road crimes, and so forth.

Prison Studies in Portugal: An Overview

There is abundant and relevant literature in the field of prison studies in Europe. The wide variety of themes and approaches combining empirical and quantitative analyses have enabled the production of comparative research, as well as the identification of national and international trends.

As a multidisciplinary field, the production of qualitative monographies and methodological theorization has allowed prison studies not only to understand prisons and their populations, but also their interaction with other relevant phenomena, such as political ideologies, cultural habits and customs, and socioeconomic circumstances.

Acknowledging that prisons are not impervious to the outside world, however, does not make our delving on its specific features any less essential, or continuing to question particular phenomena, such as comparing existing models, for instance, between places where prisons provide inmates with the comforts and conditions available to any common citizen (Ugelvik and Dullum 2012), vs. situations of overcrowding, violence and repression found elsewhere (Buondi 2016); or the role of the state as mediator or guarantor of welfare policies in the face of the wide array of public systems and subsystems responsible for providing support for its citizens (national or foreign). Furthermore, the literature in this field is enriched by its wide thematic variety: studies focusing on gender issues (e.g. Bosworth 2016 [1999]; Crewe 2009; Zedner; Carlen 2002; Moore and Scranton 2014; Carlen and Worral 2014); on punishment, power, resistance, or identity (Fassin 2015; Fassin et al. 2013; Ugelvik 2014; Drake 2012; Schinkel 2014; Simon and Sparks 2013); on the different agents involved—prison officers, prison management, and so forth: (Bennet 2016; Liebling et al. 2012); on borders, stigma, racism and discrimination (Bosworth and Flavin 2007; Aas and Bosworth 2013); on kinship and family relations inside and outside of prison (Comfort 2008; Scharft Smith 2014), and others.

This extensive bibliography helps us, as social scientists and as citizens, to identify and reflect upon both the positive and negative practices that characterize different ideologies, models, praxes, and even different prison facilities, on a variety of scales, from the international perspective to the regional and even national scale (e.g., Pratt 2007; Pratt and Eriksson 2014; Ruggiero and Ryan 2013).

In Portugal, the field of prison studies has shown a significant growth over recent years, although its focus has mostly been restricted to the period since 2000, addressing related topics such as deviance, juvenile delinquency, crime and security, surveillance, or identification technologies (Durão 2008; Fatela 1989; Frois 2008, 2013; Cunha 2015; Machado 2015; Duarte 2012; Carvalho 2003). In the early 90s, a group of scholars from the Centre for Juridical Studies (a Ministry of Justice entity) identified the necessity to make judges understand the "profound motivations which lead certain individuals down criminal paths...and the real implications of depriving an individual of his liberty" (Medeiros in Semedo 1994: 6). This concern led to the funding of pioneer work carried out by three anthropologists—Semedo (1994), Cunha (1994) and Pereira Bastos (1997)—whose work involved qualitative and in-depth case studies in male and female prisons as well in asylums, respectively. These references derive their relevance especially from their role as reminders not only of the long period of political and police repression, but also of the possibility to investigate and penetrate settings that had thus far remained completely inaccessible to the public eye.

The work by José Semedo (1994) reads as a detailed account of both the formal apparatus of the male prison institution of Linhó, and the more informal and spontaneous perceptions, relationships and dilemmas of inmates, officers and other workers. Beyond providing the historical, legal and sociological background of the institution, this ethnography is concerned with the mechanics of social relationships inside that prison, the first of the kind to be conducted in Portugal. Semedo's most important finding was the realization that there was no solidarity between inmates, but rather a set of fluid and opportunistic associations, which occasionally convene to accomplish certain goals. This came as a surprise to the author, whose working hypothesis was that relationships inside prison would be formed according to the same patterns and criteria as those formed outside of it: "Even in joint ventures, it is the pursuit of individualist goals that presides and leads [inmates] to associate with their colleagues. Therefore, the factors forming the basis for inmates' association are much more linked with short-term interests, than with criminal or sub-cultural affinities" (1994: 204). So far this continues to be the only in-depth ethnography in a male prison setting, conducted throughout three years of research.

Manuela Cunha led two investigations separated by a 10-year gap, in the country's oldest female prison. Operating since 1954 on the outskirts of Lisbon, Tires prison facility was for 50 years the only female prison in Portugal. When Manuela Cunha started her work in the 1980s, her portrayal revealed a prison with all the characteristics of a Goffmanian "total institution", seeking to strip subjects of their individual identity, namely through its isolation from the outside world. The heterogeneity of its population (in terms of crime types), bound solely by the burden of a deep social stigma, was instilled with the normalizing idea of womanhood and motherhood, as discussed in the works of authors such as Pat Carlen or Mary Bosworth.

The activities female inmates were employed in at the time were typically "feminine"—embroidery or seamstress work, for instance—and had been organized precisely to "serve" several other male prisons that had meanwhile been opened in the vicinity. Even the inclusion of a unit for women with children sought to preserve and encourage the duties of inmates as mothers and housewives. Having marked the period in terms of its insight into prison facilities in general, and female incarceration in particular, Cunha's next work, involving a "return to Tires" (as she put it) one decade later, once again revealed its crucial importance for Portuguese research, though this time not so much on incarceration—the author herself stated that this was not "a study on a prison"—but rather on the changes introduced in the penal system during this period and their reflection on the female inmate population.

Convicted in their majority for drug-related crimes—resulting from alterations to the drug law mentioned earlier—many of these women were arrested and convicted along with other family members from the same boroughs. Thus, when the author talks of "relatives, friends and neighbors", she is actually alluding to the small social and kinship constellations coexisting at the same time in penitentiary settings—the women held in Tires and the men scattered throughout other neighboring facilities. Thus, *Entre o Bairro e a Prisão* (2004) [From the ghetto to prison] also seeks to show how the borders between the inside and outside are gradually dissolved through the circuits and trajectories that increasingly become part of these women's everyday existence; a population that in this case is not bound by specific ethnical or racial, but rather by territorial or geographical, areas commonly described as "problematic".

In a different vein, António Pedro Dores (2003, 2010, 2013) has been one of the most prolific Portuguese researchers on the field. Among other works, the author has produced a number of politically oriented books—Dores is known for his activism and fierce criticism of prison—including "Prisons in Europe: Starting a Debate" (2003), in which he collected the presentations made by several experts (national and foreign) in the "1st European Conference on Prisons" held in Lisbon. The networks that grew out of that meeting were at the root of the international project known as "European Observatory for Prison Research".[7] The aim of the project, which Dores took part in, was to analyze prison conditions in different European countries, and to compare them against the standards set by international law.

The sociologist Anália Torres contributed to the advancement of our understanding of the Portuguese penitentiary landscape through her analysis of the circulation and use of drugs in prison settings. By using an extensive and quantitative methodology—based on surveys answered by inmates, medical services and wardens of all 49 Portuguese prison establishments—the author delivers a portrait of the *Prison–Drug* connection in two different periods. The overall conclusion drawn by Torres is that drugs—whether as a business or as a substance for consumption—ruled the daily life in Portuguese prisons. The numbers presented in the first book (Torres and Gomes 2002), are persuasive: 52.8 % of the Portuguese prison population were not only convicted for drug-related crimes, but also shows patterns of drug abuse.

Torres et al. (2009) analyze a second period—between 2001 and 2008—by repeating the methods of the previous study. This time around, the author found that the number of inmates who committed drug crimes and engaged in their consumption had decreased to 30.7 %. On the other hand, the study also revealed that the group more exclusively involved in the business side of drugs had increased to 35 %. This shift was doubtless linked to the Portuguese drug laws passed in the year 2000, decriminalizing drug consumption.

Two other authors stand out in the field of prison studies in Portugal—Rafaela Granja and Silvia Gomes—through their two distinct approaches to female and male prison facilities (with a focus on the country's northern region, taking advantage of the opening, in 2005, of the first women's prison is part of the country). Rafaela Granja turned her attention to the experience of family relationships inside and outside prison, considering both female and male inmates, as well as the relatives who visited the prison facilities she worked on. Exploring the relationships, overlapping and ambiguities contained in the equation "family, crime and exclusion", the author identifies what she calls "vulnerable resistance"; that is, "a process of creative negotiation by which imprisoned men and women seek to expand the possibilities to play their family roles from within prison, and continue to define themselves as active involved members of their family group" (Granja 2015: 141, see also Granja et al. 2014).

Granja's work explores relevant aspects in our understanding of how men and women experience family life in reclusion, but also how gender roles are embodied by both those in confinement and the relatives who manage the everyday life of the "family" left behind on the outside.

Silvia Gomes, also extending her attention to male and female inmates alike, focused specifically on foreign citizens and members of minority ethnic groups (namely gypsies), and their relation with the phenomenon of criminality, thus bringing forth the debate around the subjective, though often reified notion, which tends to attribute greater dangerousness and propensity for crime to members of these groups by contrast to national citizens. Considering the characteristics of immigration in Portugal over the last decades (and not necessarily just the origin of foreign citizens actually imprisoned), the author focuses on three main groups: people from the PALOP community (Portuguese Speaking African Countries: Angola, Mozambique, Guinea-Bissau, Cape-Verde, São Tomé and Principe), from Eastern Europe countries and from the gypsy ethnic group. Combining the data from prison statistics with inmates' narratives, Gomes not only offers a broad view on these individuals' trajectories, but also corroborates data that are common to other countries; namely, regarding the over-representation of these communities within the penitentiary environment.

Within the field of Portuguese prison studies, there is yet one relevant feature deserving special mention, and it has to do with the issue of gender, regarding both the authors and the focus of their works. Indeed, the majority of researchers working on prison and reclusion are women— the most illustrative example of this is the volume *Mulheres e crime. Perspectivas sobre intervenção, violência e reclusão* [Women and Crime: Perspectives on Intervention, violence and reclusion] written entirely by women and on women—with an exclusive focus on female incarceration, its effects and consequences, both on the inmate population and their families. There is probably a very practical explanation for this fact that doesn't inevitably reflect a personal choice or preference on the part of researchers (connected, for instance, with issues of feminism, as Bosworth points out as a personal choice, 2016).

All female authors have underlined—as I have done myself—the importance of access in the development of this type of research. Although we have no means of gauging the level of access a male researcher can obtain inside a male prison, one thing is clear, and that is the difference in access that female researchers are allowed, depending on whether they are conducting their work in a female or male prison. While inside a male prison, interaction with inmates is restricted to the facility's administrative area, inside closed rooms and away from the inmates' restricted area in a formal interview atmosphere; inside a female prison—obviously depending on the facility's specific conditions and authorizations obtained from the directing board and officer's body—access to all prison areas may be virtually unrestricted, thus permitting informal contacts with the population, and a much more flexible management of research time and observation of prison life.

The Gap Between Theory and Practice

So far I have identified some of the key moments in Portuguese penal thinking, from its formal inception and implementation up to the present day. We saw that the underlying theoretical models regarding the function and purpose of prison—implying sentence humanization and individualization, acknowledgment of the prisoners' juridical status, indispensable correctional treatment activities and opportunities, as well as its resocialization function—were surpassed by the actual social and juridical reality. This problem may be summarized in a few lines: the progressive shutdown of prison facilities since the end of the 1970s until the beginning of 2000 had the severe consequence of increasing prison overcrowding, accompanied by the progressive degradation of those prisons that remained in operation.

Initially justified as an efficient measure of human and material resource management, from the moment small prisons were closed and their inmates relocated, the result was precisely the opposite of the initial intention to rehabilitate offenders or even promote the approximation of prison conditions to a free environment. Despite the visible structural transformations in the country after the democratic revolution in 1974, and especially since Portugal joined the Economic European Union (nowadays European Union)—in terms of citizenship rights, for example—these changes were not reflected in the penitentiary environment, which seemed to remain stuck in time. Prison overcrowding, for instance, has the adverse effect of making it impossible to guarantee the goal of having an individual cell per inmate, and double bunk beds were soon transformed into triple bunk beds. In case of necessity, any cell, dormitory or even corridor could easily be used to double or even triple a prison's capacity, with the corresponding prejudicial impact on the prisoners' living conditions.

Left without the proper means to renovate the existing facilities and conduct much needed improvements, only in the end of 2000s would the bucket latrine be finally eradicated in Portugal. Before that, it was common to witness such anecdotic situations as having cells in which inmates had their own television sets and audio systems, but did not have basic sanitary facilities.

The separation of prisoners (by crime categories for instance) contemplated in penal law, or the sentence individualization and penitentiary treatment, have all become part of the great oxymoron that characterizes today's penitentiary system: overcrowding makes it impossible to separate remand from convicted prisoners, and the same applies to the separation of especially vulnerable prisoners (e.g., the elderly, addicts, sexual offenders) from the general population. Shortage of social workers and correctional treatment staff renders any prospect of therapy or skills improvement inoperative, and in most cases it is the guards they seek assistance from when they have a problem that would usually be provided by the correctional treatment staff. Even though labor is not mandatory by law, the sheer non-existence of work offered in the majority of prison facilities (if we discount the tasks needed for its operation, such as cleaning, laundry or kitchen duties) not only renders inmates sedentary, but consequently leaves most of them without any source of income besides the support provided by the family.

Regarding the duties and performance of prison officers, several problems can be pointed out throughout the last decades. One major change has to do with the type of professional training they received before being admitted into service. It was only since the 2000s that this education began to provide more than just the knowledge of regulations and legislation, and techniques of self-defense—and started to include conflict resolution skills, psychology, and sociology. While there are still guards who claim with perplexity that nowadays "the imprisonment regime is too soft and the inmates do as they please", and that "prisoners nowadays have more [civic] rights than obligations"; other officers who do not share this point of view instead complain that they lack the proper conditions to perform their tasks.

Whilst the Portuguese prison population doubled its figures, the number of prison officers remained stationary, and unevenly distributed by the existing facilities. Therefore, in major prisons with capacity for more than 500 inmates—and especially those housing both remand and convicted inmates—there is a generalized situation of understaffing. The examples are diverse: two guards assigned to guard a courtyard with more than 150 inmates at the same time; four guards responsible for a prison wing holding 200 inmates; or the sheer impossibility of attending to anything more than the prisoners' most basic needs. Over the last decade, and especially when the country was under a severe economic and financial crisis, prison officers unions frequently came forward in protest against their working conditions (especially regarding safety and security, both their own as the staff and the inmates under their supervision).

What we may observe from an analysis of parliamentary debates on the penitentiary situation is that this is not a new issue—far from it—and that the problems have already been abundantly and clearly identified. However, that is not the same as saying that these have resulted in any change, or that new measures have been taken to fight the progressive degradation and prevent a situation of imminent collapse of the whole penitentiary system (in the words of the Director-General). Though Odemira is obviously also affected by this general lack of resources, the next chapters evidence that due its particular characteristics in terms of scale, number of officers allocated, close relationship between its main actors—warden, prison officers, correctional treatment staff, prisoners and even the community—have preserved this prison facility as an exception rather than making it just one more case to add to the norm.

Notes

1. The work of Diego Palacios Cerezales on "popular protest and public order" in Portugal from mid-nineteenth to the late twentieth century, presents an extensive debate on the contradictions underlying what should hypothetically constitute the people's response to "the use of force by the state" (2011: 14).
2. The literature on the topic is extensive and well documented; consider particularly the volumes collecting a wide variety of essays on these themes, in Jewkes (2007) and Jewkes, Crewe and Bennett (2016).

3. The volume edited by Austin Sarat (2014a, b) entitled *Punitive Imagination* equates the rhetoric of "law, justice and Responsibility" with the North American case and offers an original contribution for our reflection upon different conceptions, representations and purposes of punishment in the country with the world's highest incarceration rates. In the same line, consider particularly the works of Loïc Wacquant for their thorough reflection on this topic (Wacquant 2000a, b, 2002, 2009). For a comparative study on the incarceration policies of three different US states, see the works of Vanessa Barker (2009) and Lorna Rhodes (2004) covering research in seven prisons.
4. Attention must be paid to the number of offenders convicted for drug related crimes, which increased from 1028 in 1989 to 3902 in 1998 (Ferreira 1999). At the same time we should also acknowledge that the predominant type of crime in Portugal, which is "Crimes against Property", has in most cases a relation to drugs or drug consumption.
5. In 2015, the majority of inmates (2120) were released because their sentences were over, which surpasses the number of inmates released because they were offered conditional liberty (1718). In 1998, a higher number of inmates were released because they were offered conditional liberty (1637), than of inmates released because their sentence was complete (1593). However, as Ferreira (1999) clarify, a more detailed and accurate analysis would require data that could point out, on the one hand, the number of inmates that required probation in a given year and, on the other, the number of request which were approved.
6. Information sourced from the World Prison Brief: http://www.prisonstudies.org/country/portugal
7. http://www.prisonobservatory.org

References

Aas, Katja Franko, and Mary Bosworth, eds. 2013. *The Borders of Punishment: Migration, Citizenship, and Social Exclusion*. Oxford: Oxford University Press.

Accornero, Guya, and Pedro Ramos Pinto. 2015. 'Mild Mannered'? Protest and Mobilisation in Portugal under Austerity, 2010–2013. *West European Politics* 38 (3): 491–515.

Adriano, Paulo Jorge. 2010. *Penitenciária Central de Lisboa. A Casa do Silêncio e o Despertar da Arquitectura Penitenciária em Portugal*. Unpublished Master thesis, Lisbon.

Barker, Vanessa. 2009. *The Politics of Imprisonment. How the Democratic Process Shapes the Way America Punishes Offenders.* Oxford: Oxford University Press.

Barreto, António. 2000. Crises da Justiça. em *Justiça em Crise? Crises da Justiça,* org. António Barreto, 13–28. Lisbon: Dom Quixote.

Bennet, J. 2016. *The Working Lives of Prison Managers. Global Change, Local Culture and Individual Agency in the Late Modern Prison.* London and New York: Palgrave Macmillan.

Bosworth, Mary, and J. Flavin, eds. 2007. *Gender, Race and Punishment: From Colonialism to the War on Terror.* New Brunswick: Rutgers University Press.

Bosworth, Mary. 2016b. *Engendering Resistance: Agency and Power in Women's Prison.* London and New York: Routledge.

Bravo, José. 2000. Justiça Penal em Portugal: Crise para além do Ruído. In *Justiça em Crise? Crises da Justiça,* ed. António Barreto, 263–275. Lisbon: Dom Quixote.

Buondi, Karina. 2016. *Sharing this Walk. An Ethnography of Prison Life and the PCC in Brazil.* Chapel Hill: University of North Carolina Press.

Carlen, Pat, ed. 2002. *Women and Punishment. The Struggle for Justice.* Devon: Willan Publishing.

Carlen, Pat, and Anne Worrall. 2014. *Analysing Women's Imprisonment.* Devon: Willan Publishing.

Carvalho, Maria João. 2003. *Entre as Malhas do Desvio.* Lisbon: Celta.

Comfort, Megan. 2008. *Doing Time Together: Forging Love and Family in the Shadow of the Prison.* Chicago: Chicago University Press.

Costa, Eduardo. 2003. A Lei Escrita e a Lei na Prática em Portugal. In *Prisões na Europa: Um Debate que Apenas Começa,* ed. António Pedro Dores, 93–102. Oeiras: Celta.

Crewe, Ben. 2009. *The Prisoner Society: Power, Adaptation, and Social Life in an English Prison.* Oxford: Oxford University Press.

Cunha, Manuela. 1994. *Malhas que a Reclusão Tece. Questões de Identidade numa Prisão Feminina.* Lisbon: Centro de Estudos Judiciários.

———. 2002. *Entre o Bairro e a Prisão. Tráficos e Trajectos.* Lisbon: Afrontamento.

———., ed. 2015. *Do Crime e do Castigo. Temas e Debates Contemporâneos.* Lisbon: Mundos Sociais.

Cunha, Manuela, and Susana Durão. 2011. Os Sentidos da Segurança: Ambiguidades e Reduções. *Etnográfica* 15 (1): 53–66.

Dores, António Pedro, ed. 2003. *European Prison: Starting a Debate.* Oeiras: Celta.

Drake, Deborah. 2012. *Prisons, Punishment and the Pursuit of Security.* New York: Palgrave.

Durão, Susana. 2008. *Patrulha e Proximidade. Uma Etnografia da Polícia de Lisboa.* Coimbra: Almedina.

References

Duarte, Vera. 2012. *Discursos e Percursos na Delinquência Juvenil Feminina*. Vila Nova de Famalicão: Húmus.
Fassin, Didier. 2015. *L'Ombre du Monde. Une Anthropologie de la Condition Carcérale*. Paris: Seuil.
Fassin, Didier, et al. 2013. *Juger, Réprimer, Accompagner. Essai sur la Morale de L'État*. Paris: Seuil.
Fatela, João. 1989. *O Sangue e a Rua. Elementos para uma Antropologia da Violência em Portugal (1926–1946)*. Lisbon: Dom Quixote.
Ferreira, Vitor Peña. 1999. Sobrepopulação Prisional e Sobrepopulação em Portugal: Evolução Recente, Situação Atual e Alguns Factores que a Explicam. *Temas Penitenciários* 2 (3): 7–38.
Frois, Catarina, ed. 2008. *A Sociedade Vigilante. Ensaios sobre Identificação, Vigilância e Privacidade*. Lisbon: Imprensa de Ciências Sociais.
———. 2011. Video-Surveillance in Portugal: Analysis of a Transitional Process. *Social Analysis* 55 (3): 35–53.
———. 2013. *Peripheral Vision. Politics, Technology and Surveillance*. Oxford and New York: Berghahn.
———. 2017. Privação de Liberdade, privação de dignidade. Violência em Contexto Prisional. *Etnográfica*.
Granja, Rafaela. 2015. *Para cá e para lá dos muros: Relações familiares na interface entre o interior e o exterior da prisão*. Unpublished PhD thesis, Minho University.
Jewkes, Yvonne, Jamie Bennett, and Ben Crewe, eds. 2016. *Handbook on Prisons*. 2nd ed. London and New York: Routledge.
Liebling, Alison, David Price, and Guy Shefer. 2012. *The Prison Officer*. 2nd ed. London and New York: Routledge.
Machado, Helena. 2015. Genética e Suspeição Criminal: Reconfigurações Actuais de Co-produção entre Ciência, Ordem Social e Controlo. In *Ciência, Identificação e Governo*, ed. Cláudia Fonseca and Helena Machado, 38–55. Porto Alegre: Coleções Editoriais do Cegov.
Moore, Linda, and Phil Scranton. 2014. *The Incarceration of Women. Punishing Bodies, Breaking Spirits*. London and New York: Palgrave Macmillan.
Palacios Cerezales, Diego. 2011. *Portugal à Coronhada. Protesto Popular e Ordem Pública nos Séculos XIX e XX*. Lisbon: Tinta-da-China.
Pereira Bastos, Susana. 1997. *O Estado Novo e os seus Vadios. Contribuição para o Estudo das Identidades Marginais e sua Repressão*. Lisbon: Dom Quixote.
Rhodes, Lorna A. 2004. *Total Confinement: Madness and Reason in the Maximum Security Prison*. Berkeley: University California Press.
Ruggiero, Vincent, and Mick Ryan, eds. 2013. *Punishment in Europe. A Critical Anatomy of Penal Systems*. London and New York: Palgrave Macmillan.

Sarat, Austin, ed. 2014a. *The Punitive Imagination. Law, Justice and Responsibility*. Alabama: The University of Alabama Press.

———, ed. 2014b. Examining Assumptions. An Introduction to Punishment, Imagination, and Possibility. In *The Punitive Imagination. Law, Justice and Responsibility*, ed. Austin Sarat, 1–18. Alabama: The University of Alabama Press.

Scharft Smith, Peter. 2014. *When the Innocent are Punished. The Children of Imprisoned Parents*. London and New York: Palgrave Macmillan.

Schinkel, Marguerite. 2014. *Being Imprisoned. Punishment, Adaptation and Desistance*. London and New York: Palgrave Macmillan.

Semedo, José. 1994. *Vidas Encarceradas. Estudo Sociológico de uma Prisão Masculina*. Lisbon: Centro de Estudos Judiciários.

———. *Relatório Estatístico 2004*. Lisbon: Direção Geral dos Serviços Prisionais, Serviços de Organização, Planeamento e Relações Externas.

———. 2005. *Relatório Estatístico 2005*. Lisbon: Direção Geral dos Serviços Prisionais, Serviços de Organização, Planeamento e Relações Externas.

Simon, Jonathan, and Richard Sparks, eds. 2013. *The SAGE Handbook of Punishment and Society*. London: Sage.

Sousa Santos, Boaventura. 1990. *O Estado e a Sociedade em Portugal: 1974–1988*. Porto: Edições Afrontamento.

Torres, Anália, and Maria do Carmo Gomes. 2002. *Drogas e Prisões em Portugal*. Lisbon: CIES/ISCTE.

Torres, Anália, et al. 2009. *Drogas e Prisões: Portugal 2001–2007*. Lisbon: CIES/ISCTE.

Ugelvik, Thomas. 2014. *Power and Resistance in Prison: Doing Time, Doing Freedom*. London and New York: Palgrave.

Ugelvik, Thomas, and Jane Dullum. 2012. *Penal Exceptionalism? Nordic Prison Policy and Practice*. New York: Routledge.

Wacquant, Löic. 2000a. *Prisons of Poverty*. Minneapolis and London: University of Minnesota Press.

Wacquant, Loïc. 2000b. The New 'Peculiar Institution': On the Prison as Surrogate Ghetto. *Theoretical Criminology* 4: 377–389.

Wacquant, Löic. 2002. The Curious Eclipse of Prison Ethnography in the Age of Mass Incarceration. *Ethnography* 3 (4): 371–397.

———. 2009. *Punishing the Poor. The Neoliberal Government of Social Insecurity*. Durham and London: Duke University Press.

3

Entering Odemira Prison Facility

Before going into detail on the daily life inside Odemira prison, such as it was experienced during the one year of fieldwork between October 2015–2016, it is important to present the history of an institution that has undergone some transformations—considering both its original purposes and the cumulative practice—that distinguishes this facility within the general scope of the Portuguese prison system. Tracing such a genealogy is not an easy task, since the official data and documents available at the archive of the Prison Services Directorate-General contain significant gaps. The first records indicate that before the mid-twentieth century, Odemira County did not yet have a proper "jail", but only a small holding area inside the premises of the court building situated in the town center, as was the custom then. The basement and ground floors served as cells, where men and women were held without the basic sanitary, medical or living conditions.

The 1936 Prison Reform Act described in the previous chapter decreed the construction of county jails in small towns such as Odemira (which was built in the 1950s). These were small buildings designed to accommodate convicted felons serving short sentences (three to six months), the management of which was entrusted to a jailer living on the premises with his family. Odemira's regional prison facility, with a capacity for 28 men and 13 women, was inaugurated in the follow-up of this reform. From the scant information available regarding this period, we discover that during its first 20 years, the prison held an annual average of 5 to 10 inmates (male only), and given the brevity of their stay and the low number of inmates, there was no activity program in place, except for occasional wicker basket making.

When in 1977 the government issued an order to close down these premises—an order that extended to most county jails throughout the country—both the jailer and the inmate population protested. Such a decision would imply the transference of its population to more distant locations, and since most inmates were locals, it would effectively mean their separation from family and friends. Nevertheless, by the mid-1980s Odemira clearly presented serious infrastructural and managerial problems.

Research into the archives clarified this situation, revealing a document written by a social worker reporting on her monthly visits to inmates. The document is a letter sent to the Directorate-General of Prison Services describing the main problems found there: inmates spent most of their days without any occupation or activity, they were virtually isolated and disregarded by the community, and their living conditions were poor, with risks for their safety and well-being. There was no heating or hot water, and inmates had neither bed sheets nor bath towels. The cells were in a general state of degradation, and inmates slept in the same clothes they wore during the day to keep warm at night. The shortage of financial resources reflected on the lack of qualified staff, and whenever the jailer was absent, his wife would be left in charge to manage the facility and monitor inmates. Odemira prison was actually closed down during the mid-80s, not only due to its small occupation rate, but also because the post of prison jailer was extinguished and substituted by a professional body of prison officers. Over the following 10 years, several solutions were proposed for this building, including the transference of the local fire department or its conversion into a police station.

With the aid of state funds and considerable local investment, Odemira prison reopened in 1995, after extensive renovation work on its infrastructure. Given that at the time there was only one female-only prison facility in operation (Tires prison), Odemira was turned into a prison for women from the country's southern region, originally with the capacity to accommodate inmates with small children in their care. The area that was previously the jailer's premises was turned into an administrative area, including two dormitories for guards, a kitchen, and a dining room equipped with a small cafeteria.

The reports for the first years of this new operation allow us to observe the important transformations operated in penitentiary administration on a national scale, insofar as the changes occurred in Odemira can be seen to reflect the extensive reorganization of the prison system following the closing down of county jails and the significant increase of the inmate population in Portugal during this period. These documents also reveal relevant information regarding the inmate population; namely, the increasing number of convictions for drug-related crimes, and more specifically the high proportion of inmates with drug addiction problems, both of which are in line with national trends.

With a capacity to house 56 inmates, the allocation of 117 women upon its inauguration set the initial occupation rate at 200%. The population was in its majority comprised of Portuguese citizens or immigrants from Portuguese-speaking countries (particularly from Cape Verde, Guinea Bissau and Brazil); 75 % of inmates were convicted for drug-related crimes, and approximately half of them had a history of drug abuse. The oldest inmate was 70 years old and the youngest 16 (very similar to the present age-range), and there were fifteen children (under three years) living with them.

The warden's report for the first year emphasizes the problems with the prison's management, starting with his own inexperience at the job, as well as most of the female officers who were only now starting their professional careers. The report also mentions other unforeseen insufficiencies, particularly the lack of skilled personnel to supervise inmates, with consequences for their own imprisonment and release, such as, for example, "[considering] the lack of information, outside supervision and follow-up, inmates face serious problems when they are unexpectedly released without the necessary means to return home." Added to this, during the first years the prison functioned without an internal regulation code, and the only services that were officially ensured were security—by prison officers—and meals. In other words, Odemira was not prepared with education services, professional occupation offers, or continued medical assistance—specifically for drug addiction or diseases such as hepatitis or HIV.

The annual reports sent to the Directorate-General of Prison Services show that serious efforts were made by the warden to establish protocols and partnerships to change this situation. Between the years of 1997 and 1998 basic education was implemented, and activities such as traditional rug making, floriculture, beach cleaning, and wild berry picking were implemented. The prison population reaches almost 150 inmates during this period, maintaining the preponderance of drug-related crime offences. Since Odemira did not possess a separate unit for inmates with children, despite being equipped with a small nursery (where the laundry room is presently found), the mothers were moved with their children to the cells on the ground floor:

> The children living with their mothers inside the prison facility were given special attention, and thus the ground floor was prepared to accommodate them (a more suitable space without any stairways and more adequate living quarters). There are 10 cells for the inmate mothers, who share a double cell equipped with single beds for each child. Enrolment in the local preschool is encouraged for children over two years old, and only the nursery remains open in the prison. This arrangement would allow our children to enjoy the same social interaction and conditions as children not in reclusion, thus providing more adequate means to foster their psychological and emotional development. (Odemira Regional Prison Facility, Annual Report 1998)

As far as family was concerned, the policy (which has remained unaltered to the present day) was that whenever relatives were incarcerated at the same time, they would preferably share the same cell or put into dormitories "so as to respect and strengthen bonds of kinship, friendship and affection". As the prison gradually improves the inmates' possibilities and resources, a change is seen to occur in its internal disciplinary procedures; that is, in the way the prison guards perform their task. On this point, the report from the year 2000 (five years after reopening) underlines the following feature, under the heading "Discipline":

We [the warden and the social worker] have detected an institutional culture that favors frequent disciplinary measures over a more pedagogic intervention after the facts. In light of this, an effort has been made to instruct the technical staff on this point. The number of filed complaints has diminished considerably [from 139 to 46]. We attribute the significant decrease in infractions and punishments to stricter measures for more serious infractions and a more lenient and pedagogic approach to other less serious cases. We therefore conclude that overall, the effect of this line of action on the institution's everyday life is positive.

In other words, Odemira warden introduced a discipline policy that promoted dialogue and immediate action as a means to prevent potential problems rather than the usual practice of formal complaints involving bureaucratic proceedings that needed judicial mediation to apply different punishment measures. In parallel, the more serious situations, such as cases of physical assault, drug use or contraband, were sanctioned with greater severity. In the 15 years since these data were released, we find that this approach has gradually gained increasing advantage.

As the next chapters will strive to make clear, the prison environment and the different relationships established within it are defined by a sense of cooperation, and on the rare occasions where situations of conflict arise, the guards are the first to be called upon by the inmates to mediate the situation. The close relationship between officers and inmates, the latter often voluntarily seeking the former to solve everyday problems (whether to seek advice, ask for help or just to "talk"), prevents this authority from being challenged, and instead serves to legitimize, acknowledge and even invoke it.

In the absence of any activity reports for the period between 2001 and 2010, and given the significant gap in the available information, the direct testimony of officers who are still working in the prison, as well as of inmates imprisoned there from 2001 to 2015, became the main source in the reconstitution of the institution's history during this period.

According to the officers, in the first 10 years since reopening (that is, between 1995 and 2005), the inmate population varied within the range of 120–150, clearly indicating a situation of permanent overcrowding which demanded maximizing all the available space for accommodation, including setting up bunk beds in corridors. In addition, several women had their children with them (there were up to 20 children in the prison at one time). Inmates performed a wide variety of tasks, including seasonal work such as beach-cleaning crews or teams of wild berry pickers, and other more permanent activities, such as rug making, schooling or other training courses.

In 2005 there took place an event that had a profound impact on prison life in Odemira, and whose repercussions are visible even today: the plan to transfer all its inmates to Tires prison. Originally, the idea was to shut down this prison, and to adapt an existing male facility in the southern city of Olhão that was inoperative at the time—even though other neighboring prison facilities had reached a situation of near breaking point. Local authorities promoted a public petition to stop this process, and it turned out to have a wide popular support. The motives invoked by the council's representatives were mostly concerned with the positive economic impact of the prison on local commerce; namely, attracting the business brought by people visiting their inmate relatives, but also as an important asset in the fight against the demographic desertification in which the region found itself, especially considering that families of prison workers had also come to settle there.

The town council also alleged that shutting down Odemira prison would defraud the significant financial investment made to renovate the facility 10 years ago. In spite of these efforts, in the space of two weeks, 50 inmates were transferred to Tires in several convoys, taking everyone by surprise—not only the local authorities, but also the inmates and the officers themselves. This, however, was not an isolated case. The Minister of Justice at the time had set out to close down almost half of the 56 existing prison facilities, in a plan to reduce costs in the name of "management efficiency". Regarding this episode, one officer gave the following account:

> Thirty inmates (mothers and children included) were transferred to Tires in one week. The deputy director [of Prison Services] came personally here to inform us that the prison was being closed down and that we were all going to be transferred to the Olhão prison facility. At the time the news was received as a negative thing, both by those of us who lived here [a few

and by others who didn't live close by because Olhão was even further away. It's true that the prison had some problems in its infrastructure, in terms of plumbing, electricity, etc., and that it was urgently in need of repair.

The girls [referring to the inmates] were caught by surprise, and I don't remember anyone who didn't reject this new idea. But later, more or less at the same time, the directorate-general changed [its directing board] and the orders were now "not to close the premises". We weren't officially informed, the whole thing was just left at that. The government turned around, everything was reverted and as a result everything remained as it was.

When this guard claims that "everything remained as it was", she is referring strictly to the prison being kept open (or at least that's what we can infer retrospectively) since in fact a lot was changed. The women who had already been transferred to Tires were never returned, and gradually occupation stabilized at 80 % to 90 %, that is, 45 to 50 inmates. With the transference of inmates with children, the idea of accommodating mothers and infants in Odemira was definitely abandoned, and nowadays the facilities with this capability are Tires Prison and Santa Cruz do Bispo Female (which started operating in 2005).

Although currently this prison does not accept women with children in their care, we do find cases of recidivist inmates now doing time who had previously been imprisoned here with their children (who were now grown up). Some of them referred to that period as a "beautiful time, with all those little children running around". Conversely, for the officers that memory was precisely the opposite, and they had no desire to go back to it. One of the guards confided: "Catarina, you are a mother. Now imagine what it's like locking down the cells at night, with little children clinging to you pleading 'It's not dark, please don't close the door yet …' it was heartbreaking. Children should not be imprisoned. The noise of key chains jangling and locks being bolted probably still haunt them today!"

We are thus faced with these two very contrasting views: to the prison guards, the inexistence of a separate unit for mothers and children due to the limited available space would be a traumatizing experience that would negatively mark these children's lives (even if children were to spend most of the day "outside" the prison) and should thus be avoided. According to the female guards, as women (and some of them also as mothers), this daily contact, the closeness and bonding with the children, ultimately put an additional emotional burden on their work. Nevertheless, as we shall see, for many inmates who were now imprisoned, separation from their children was a major source of suffering and thus, they have an entirely different perspective about this issue.

"Working" with Women

Although the present overview deals with two very different periods (1995–2005; 2005–2015) in the history of this institution, they both share one common element: the officers who work there. In its overwhelming majority comprised of women (including administrative officers), the prison officer staff has remained stable. Some have worked there since inauguration day, even if career promotion has led some of them to move up to senior positions within the institution. Therefore, while in other prison facilities constant officers' rotation is a common practice, especially in the major urban centers where the highest number of prisons is concentrated, Odemira presents an exception. Its remote geographical location and lack of easy access make it an undesirable destination for potential outside candidates and most of those working at Odemira live in its vicinity (although few officers actually lived in the town itself).

The prolonged habituation of prison staff is commonly considered as potentially negative, since, as Moore and Scranton (2014) have aptly illustrated, overfamiliarity with procedures and routines may generate conformism, indulgence, and in some cases may lead to abuses of power or situations of despotism. At Odemira, however, this circumstance has not produced the same effect. The officers' involvement with the working of the institution, constantly being stimulated by the warden through the signing of partnerships and protocols with outside entities such as local businesses, training centers or the City Council itself, helps these professionals to make inmates the main focus of their concerns.

The close coexistence between those who ensure the prison's operation and its "inhabitants", gives origin to a relationship that could be considered unusual (although a feature often underlined by those who have conducted research in small prisons like this one). Unlike larger prison facilities where different bodies are allocated to separate pavilions—inmates blocks, prison officers quarters, administrative services, medical ward, and so on—Odemira's exiguous space in itself works to avert this physical separation. As already mentioned, the same part of the building was shared by administrative offices—including the warden—officers' dormitories, as well as a common kitchen and cafeteria. Meals were habitually taken together, especially at lunchtime, both the director and deputy director were assiduous presences rather than the exception, avoiding superfluous distinctions from other staff members.

A habit was made to take a daily stroll after lunch down to the town center, to which all were invited, regardless of their station or occupation. Therefore, the kind of conflicts or contrasting views that are traditionally inscribed into the relations between prison officers and administrative technical staff were not frequent. In other prisons I have worked on, a prison officer's rhetoric is often frequently permeated by complaints about "civilian personnel" (social workers, for example) not understanding the problems of security that are implied in the working of a prison. Social workers, in their turn, tended to claim their invaluableness to the penitentiary system by opposition to officers' securitarian perspective and the protection of their own corporation. In other words, in Odemira the close coexistence of guards, administrative staff, teachers and nurses, whether out of necessity due to lack of space, or because somehow a way was found to overcome traditional discord, resulted in their combined action.

This does not imply the disregard of hierarchy, or that situations of tension never occurred. However, at Odemira it was unanimously understood that above all else, it was crucial for directing bodies and head officers to share the same line of action in terms of dealing with inmates and the prison management systems. More important than having an exhaustive and detailed set of rules to follow, both the chief officers and the warden seem to agree that if a good relationship and a common perspective were not achieved, the different bodies could easily obstruct each other's work. In such cases, the rules, regulations, authorizations, and so on are easily transfigured from useful tools into obstacles and a source of permanent contradiction, whether the problem arises in the sphere of internal procedures or the more general management operations.

Further stressing our perception of Odemira's distinctive character is the fact that its officers consider this prison not to be a suitable facility for new prison officer trainees. For someone who wishes to "learn" how to become a prison guard—dealing with tension, danger, conflict, complications—Odemira is "a place to avoid" they say. Perhaps the best illustration of this was given to me by two chief officers who worked there. One of them was only a few years away from retirement and most of his professional career had been spent working in large male prison facilities. At one point he had asked to be transferred to Odemira precisely because he wanted "to end [his career] on a high note" as he put it. In other words, he found that he no longer possessed the physical and emotional stamina needed to perform his duty in an environment where the degree of demand surpassed the threshold of what he thought he could bear as a human being. The other case was a prison officer who had asked for transference after 20 years in a prison for male inmates convicted for serious and very serious offences, with sentences ranging from 7–15 years. Odemira was very far away from his place of residence, and perhaps worried that one could think he had been somehow demoted, or had "changed for the worse", he made a point of explaining the motives for his move:

> One day I got home after a 12-hour shift in that "madhouse". I found my youngest son playing around like children do, fidgeting with everything and never standing still. I remember telling him a couple of times to quiet down, but he kept on going, until there was a moment when I simply "lost it" and I got up and smacked him. The following day I went in to work and the first thing I did was file for transference. I could not stand that atmosphere any longer; it was getting to me psychologically. I have to travel farther to get here, but it's worth it, it's just a whole different ball game.

The prison where this officer had worked before was different from Odemira in every respect. It was a male prison with a population that at the time rounded 600 inmates, and where staff were confronted daily with multiple occurrences: all kinds of fights and conflicts (gang-related, debt-related, etc.), drug trafficking, of contraband, and general disregard for prison rules (illegal use of cell phones, alcohol brewing inside the cells, etc.). The weekly raids carried out to the cells invariably produced an array of illegal substances and objects (artisanal weapons, drugs, etc.).

Prison officers also had to deal with the high number of visits the prison allowed which were particularly delicate moments, in which tension levels could rise abruptly, triggering fights amongst inmates or confrontations with the guards. Overall, the daily work in this prison was characterized as stressful and testing. As my interlocutor was describing the moment when he smacked his son at home, he claimed to feel a kind of exasperation rise within him, which he didn't recognize as his own "normal self". He admitted that sooner or later he would have succumbed to the pressure, as he had witnessed with many other colleagues in his profession. After some years in Odemira, he claimed that this was a special prison, where "everything was different", going on to give some examples:

> I feel rejuvenated here. But mind you, I continue to do my job exactly as I always did. The difference, for example, is that since I've been here I never again did raids where I came up with knives, drugs, cell phones; I never again had to report on inmates and initiate disciplinary procedures; or go to trial because an inmate filed a complaint against me alleging abuse; or fear for my own physical integrity when I start work every day.

This officer also underlined the difference in behavior between incarcerated men and women—a distinction I repeatedly heard voiced in roughly the same terms by several other officers and that we can find replicated in several studies—and which was summed up in the following expression: "When a man goes to prison, he goes in by himself, but a woman takes all her problems with her."

In the opinion of both officers and correctional treatment staff, imprisoned men are solely concerned with their day-to-day inside walls. Women, on the other hand, typically claim to suffer mostly with the situations left outside, which they still try to manage and control: their children, their companion, their parents, their household, the monthly bills, and so on. For prison officers, feminine reclusion is emotionally a more demanding job due to the constant personal requests for help and counsel. With male inmates, they say, it's the opposite. The officer is considered an "enemy", and they will do everything to avoid staff's interference, as one officer put it: "They resolve things amongst themselves, very rarely asking for anything from us".

If working with women is generally acknowledged to differ from working with men, in this prison the distinction is somehow further enhanced by the facility's small dimension. All the officers know every single inmate individually; they know their name, their cell, their personal history (at least since they were imprisoned there). In this respect, Odemira is unlike the majority of prisons, whether because usually inmates are distributed throughout different blocks or wings assigned to different officers work shifts, or because in large prisons with greater rotation of inmates, they are usually identified by number rather than by name. Thus, the idea that a trainee officer would chose Odemira—where there is such a close proximity between administrative staff, officers and inmates, where they would not face some of the kind of problems "usually" characteristic of prison facilities—as the place to do his/her internship is considered to be as counterproductive. Regardless of how long this hypothetical internship lasted, the candidate would never become truly prepared to deal with much more hostile and stressful environments.

In terms of the prison officers' work volume, Odemira is also unique when compared with larger facilities. Granting that guards are responsible to take inmates out routinely to court hearings or medical appointments (implying long travels to other country districts, considering once again the prison geographical location) it bears no comparison with the average of 5, 10 or 15 daily runs that characterize the officers' routine. Furthermore, unlike the general Portuguese prison panorama, Odemira presents what is considered as the "ideal" number of officers on duty to perform all shifts without a shortage of human resources, and this may be a determining factor for its smooth operation. For an average population of 50 inmates, there are approximately 35 officers who take on 24 hours shifts followed by 48 hours of rest.

Entering Odemira: The First Days

Odemira's population remained stable throughout the months of my fieldwork, despite a few "arrivals" and "departures" (and even a read-mission). Specific cases will be described in greater detail over the following chapters, but for now it is important to focus on a general view. Perhaps the best way to start attempting to identify and understand these women's everyday life in confinement is by describing how this research started, in what was supposed to be "one more" prison to visit in the course of a wider research project.

The work plan was similar to the one I already used in other prisons, concerned, for instance, with covering the widest variety of experiences of imprisonment: first-time offenders, recidivist inmates, convicts transferred from other prisons; and parameters: identifying different age ranges, crime categories and sentence lengths, and so forth. Aiming to interview an average of 15 women, the initial selection of those who were to be contacted was drafted with the warden's help, applying these criteria among inmates that she considered were willing to participate. There was only one inmate straightaway described as possibly "complicated", due to what the warden characterized as a "psychological instability", but in general she was confident that most inmates would be cooperative.

During this procedure I found some criminal offences that I had not foreseen, and which could be added to my sample; namely, fraud, domestic violence, and child maltreatment—here was a possibility to find out more. On that first day I learned that the youngest inmate was 19 years old—serving a 52-day prison sentence for failing to pay a fine of €400—and the oldest was 74 and on remand awaiting trial for drug trafficking.

The first week was spent interviewing inmates in a small room located outside the cellblock in the prison's administrative area, normally used either to hold meetings with attorneys or as an office for the nurse. From those first contacts I distinctly remember the perception that the general discourse of these interviewees was somewhat different from what I had become used to within the prison system, which typically included a list of complaints about the prison's poor conditions, the staff, and the mistreatments or indignities inmates were subjected to. I did hear complaints as well—the women referred to the cold and dampness of the cells; the water heating not powerful enough, so that the last to take showers usually had to take them cold; and the lack of activity during certain months—but the general tone was, if not resignation, one of acquiescence with their prison sentences. Furthermore, their discourse revealed a high degree of self-reflection and a concern with self-change: expressions such as "prison has given me time to think, to understand" were recurrent. Perhaps most noteworthy was a feeling, which at the time I could not fully grasp, of being faced with poverty, deprivation, lives characterized by a crudeness and latent violence—towards themselves, towards others and from others. This does not at all imply these women could be pigeonholed into a homogenous economic, social and cultural category, a fact that has been abundantly noted by the vast literature on prisons, underlining the heterogeneity of inmate populations (Jewkes et al. 2016). Nevertheless, some stories, explanations and regrets repeated themselves: drug abuse, husbands who beat them, unemployment, "bad luck" or misfortune of "being with the wrong people in the wrong place at the wrong time", being homesick and longing for their children.

After this first week I left Odemira, exhausted and unable to listen or see anymore (Crewe and Ievins 2015; Jewkes 2012). Somehow I wasn't prepared for life conjunctures that many authors succinctly describe, when referring to female imprisonment as having "a far bigger range of problems to do with social exclusion—unemployment, low educational attainment, mental and physical health problems, victimization and addiction. Because of their role as primary carers, the impact of prison produces a greater strain on women, on their families and on the rest of society." (Medlicott 2007: 245) In other words, the social exclusion and poverty were mirrored in the life, expression and narratives of women who beat on their children, who were beaten by their companions; histories of drug addiction involving theft, robberies, drug dealing; a life of conflict with justice, welfare services, difficulties with social workers and child protection services; institutionalization; deceit, manipulation, shame, guilt, regret, despair.

Over the next chapters I present some of these women and their stories. Gina, a Mozambican convicted for drug trafficking, facing a 7-year sentence and an additional deportation penalty, even though she had been living in Portugal for over 15 years with her family; Teresa, who was in her early twenties, and had been arrested in the airport smuggling drugs on a flight from São Paulo, Brazil; Mariana, who had killed her husband after years of suffering abuse; and Rita, an accountant convicted for fraud in a crime she had committed 10 years earlier and had been unable to reimburse. Virginia, who not only had to deal with a past of drug abuse and crime, but also having one of her children die while she was serving her third prison sentence; Francisca, charged with mistreatment of her four small children, who expressed outrage for her conviction, blaming her oldest daughter for having plotted with Social Security services to incriminate her; Carla, a long-time drug addict who sought at all cost to remain close to her family, claiming to "follow her daughter's footsteps" by filing for transference requests to prisons that were closer to wherever her daughter moved.

Although these weren't at all unique or unprecedented cases, after several years of coming across similar stories with inmates in other prisons, on this occasion several facts converged to provoke a different impact on me. Firstly, as a woman, as a wife, as a mother. To some extent, the empathy with some of the life experiences was greater than the things that distinguished us. For the first time I felt something that had never happened before while working in male prisons: a sense of closeness.

In some cases I could immediately understand—and in other cases I was at a loss to understand—these women's grief, the motives behind their own choices, the apparent inevitability of some experiences and decisions. Moreover, I somehow seemed to recognize the relevance—and the inmates seemed to assume as much—of such trivial things as having shampoo and conditioner to wash hair, or the time to wax legs or eyebrows. I could understand how menstruation might "indispose" one to talk or be sociable, but also how important it was on other occasions to have someone to talk openly about such things as marriage. Expressions like "You know what men are like" or "You have children so you can understand how hard it is to be separated from them" were recurrent in our conversations, and these personal traits became a key to establishing the kind of rapport during fieldwork that to some degree I did not realize was missing. On this point Laura Piacentini's reflections about her work in Russian prisons are highly revealing:

The bulk of the discussion on doing prison research focuses on how penetrating the unique physical barrier of the prison educes burdensome non-physical barriers in terms of gathering information (building social rapport while suspending moral judgements); coping with an intricate ethnography (establishing position and purpose in an unfamiliar 'deep place'); and navigating the complex relationships between captives and custodians (the myriad power relations that operate within this unique environment). (2007: 155)

Inside that interview room, I played the roles of "professor", "doctor", "woman", "wife", and "mother". With no immediate gender distinction, it was assumed that I could instantly perceive intimate details of other women. This does not mean that some distinctions between us were forgotten, namely that they were indicted or convicted persons and I was not in the same situation; or that they were forced to be there, whereas I had come of my own accord and could leave when I wished.

Throughout the fieldwork, to some degree both the inmates and the officers seemed to consider that since I was away from home I was capable of understanding what it meant to be separated from the children,[1] not being there for them in their everyday chores, the anxiety deriving from five-minute phone calls in which one must decide how to distribute that short time between the people one want to talk to—speak a little with all of them or longer with each one on different days? And in making this kind of decision, to leave someone out, who should that be—husband, parents, sister?

Building this kind of empathic relationship with the inmates at Odemira—which admittedly had not occurred in male prisons in the same way—might raise some epistemological difficulties, but these are not solely linked with the issue of gender. There are many other reasons that might contribute to explain the strong initial impact of my contact with this specific prison facility, and that includes all the persons functioning within it, not just inmates, but also officers, administrative staff, and the warden. To put it bluntly, it was the first time I found inmates describing positive aspects of prison confinement. A significant part of these women alleged that incarceration allowed them "to think", "to change", to reflect upon their past and envisage their future. They managed to do so not because they talked about their crimes to each other or with specialized social workers—psychologists, therapists or social assistants—since in fact there was no kind of therapy being offered here, but on their own, while they were working, just passing the time in the courtyard, or in idle conversation with the officers on duty. They could do it, according to their own reasoning, because they had time, the kind of time they didn't seem to have at their disposal when they were on the outside.

Additionally, it was the first time that persons in confinement verbalized comments like "the officers in here are amazing", or demonstrated pride about the prison warden, who had helped them, for example, to buy new dresses for the Christmas party. Perhaps paradoxically, some women claimed that imprisonment had brought them autonomy: while at Odemira they could make decisions about their own lives without someone—usually referred as the husband or the partner—criticizing and thwarting their choices, deciding for them, or making them abdicate their own will (cf. Bosworth 2016; Carlen 1985; Comfort 2008; Granja 2015). This is related, as will be abundantly noted in the following chapters, to their own personal trajectories before incarceration; namely, within family, marriage, work relations, and so forth.

In sum, as Moore and Scraton reflect upon in their review of the literature on "Gender, violence and unsafety": "When people enter prison they bring with them the specific context relating to the events for which they have been prosecuted…while carrying the resilience and/or burdens of personal history" (2014: 50). At Odemira, described by the inmates as a "quiet", "easygoing" and "peaceful" place, these details made a difference in everyday life. This was especially true for those inmates who had already been imprisoned in larger prisons, where they had found "chaos" and "confusion".

Obviously, this scenario might seem only too idyllic. After all, we are thinking about a prison, which by definition is a place that limits freedom, where people are removed from their environment of choice and prevented from pursuing their life and from evolving. Being imprisoned implies an interruption, a repression, a separation—from family, friends and work (Solinger et al. 2010). Nevertheless, the manner in which inmates at Odemira talked about crime, their families, themselves, about imprisonment even, once again was different from the usual accounts I was familiar with. There was rage, revolt, and anger, but its targets were not necessarily the same: the prison officers were not considered the enemy; the director or the staff were not strangers. While prison was not a place they had chosen to be, they still claimed there were positive aspects deriving from this experience. This realization became an intellectual challenge for me, since on the one hand it apparently contradicted the general trend of the "state of the art" presented by the literature on this subject (and my own findings in other prison settings; see Frois 2016, 2017) while, on the other hand, it called for a deeper understanding of the experience of imprisonment and of their subjects' life histories.

Therefore, considering that the daily lives of these inmates become necessarily intertwined in their shared experience from the moment they enter prison, it follows that it is difficult to understand any single one of these persons without accounting for everything and everyone who has become a part of their life during the days, months and years of confinement. Notwithstanding their individuality, their personal history and narrative, we have to assume that prison, as a physical space, literally limits their worldview. Analogously, their identity—even when recalling a past that inevitably refers to the outside world—is informed and determined by their experience of confinement and relations with other inmates, prison staff and justice system. If a person's identity is always construed by relation to a context, when inmates seek to convey a narrative about their past and the events leading up to their imprisonment, we discover that it is their present condition, and the place where they now find themselves which becomes most decisive in constructing their discourse.

Notes

1. The topic of family relationships and imprisoned parents is widely covered in the prison literature. A very good example of the problems that arise when parents are imprisoned is Smith (2014), focusing specifically on the children.

References

Bosworth, Mary. 2016c. *Engendering Resistance: Agency and Power in Women's Prison*. London and New York: Routledge.

Carlen, Pat, ed. 1985. *Criminal Women. Autobiographical Accounts*. Cambridge: Polity Press.

Comfort, Megan. 2008. *Doing Time Together: Forging Love and Family in the Shadow of the Prison*. Chicago: Chicago University Press.

Frois, Catarina. 2016. Close Insecurity. Shifting Conceptions of Security in Prison Confinement. *Social Anthropology* 24 (3): 309–323.

———. 2017. Privação de Liberdade, privação de dignidade. Violência em Contexto Prisional. *Etnográfica*.

Granja, Rafaela. 2015. Para cá e para lá dos muros: Relações familiares na interface entre o interior e o exterior da prisão. Unpublished PhD thesis, Minho University.

Jewkes, Yvonne. 2012. Autoethnography and Emotion as Intellectual Resources. *Qualitative Inquiry* 18 (1): 63–75.

Jewkes, Yvonne, Jamie Bennett, and Ben Crewe, eds. 2016. *Handbook on Prisons*. 2nd ed. London and New York: Routledge.

Medlicott, Diana. 2007. Women in Prison. In *Handbook on Prisons*, ed. Yvonne Jewkes, 245–267. Devon: Willan.

Moore, Linda, and Phil Scranton. 2014. *The Incarceration of Women. Punishing Bodies, Breaking Spirits*. London and New York: Palgrave Macmillan.

Smith, Peter Scharff. 2014. *When the Innocent are Punished. The Children of Imprisoned Parents*. London and New York: Palgrave Macmillan.

Solinger, Rickie, Paula C. Johnson, Martha L. Raimon, Tina Reynolds, and Ruby C. Tapia, eds. 2010. *Interrupted Life. Experiences of Incarcerated Women in the United States*. Berkeley: University of California Press.

Image 2 Prisoners' restricted area

4

"Will You Be Back Again Tomorrow?" Everyday Rhythms of Imprisonment

On the first occasions inside the inmates' restricted area, I was able to observe rhythms that I had so far been unaware of, and the meaning of which I did not immediately understand. Upon crossing into the inmates' area from the administrative offices, most inmates were out in the courtyard, where I joined them. It was a small patio, approximately the same size as the prison hall, bare except for two garden benches that were patently insufficient to accommodate all the women who had gone out to bask in the sunlight. The yard was enclosed on all sides by walls that were almost as high as the patio was wide, giving one the sensation of being stuck at the bottom of a tank. Not even the mural paintings that covered one of the walls depicting a huge colored tree inscribed with motivational messages—"Family is the joy of life", or "Life is easy when you have a positive attitude"—managed to make the place more amiable. Some of the women were sitting down with their backs against the walls, either gathered around in small groups chatting, or on their own. It was mid-morning in October, and it seemed that there wasn't much to do.

At a given moment, and without any warning, the women started to get up, one after the other, and headed back towards the cell hallway. All the cell doors were closed, but I watched as a line started to form at the far end wall, in front of a door that was also locked. The officers were going about their work: one was out in the yard, another one sat behind a desk; they hadn't issued any kind of order and didn't seem to pay notice to the movements. More women joined the line, and a considerable crowd formed an organized queue of pairs or groups of three.

Some women carried on reading the books they were reading, still standing up, while others continued their conversations. The last to join the line were the oldest—two gypsy women in their 70s—who got up from the only chairs inside the premises, and cut to the front of the line, placing themselves before the closed door. I asked one of the inmates what was going on, why had they left the patio to form that line? It was lunchtime.

The arrival of two more officers in the inmates' area seemed to trigger unlocking the door, and three by three the women started to enter the refectory, each one picking up a tray and taking a place at the empty tables inside. Only when a table had been fully occupied would another group advance to sit at the next table. The first to enter the room were the older women, obeying what seemed to be an unspoken agreement amongst the inmates, who would jokingly cry out "Let the elderly through!" before following them into the refectory. This behavior on the part of inmates towards the elder members was not a gesture borne out of mere courtesy or deference: there were at least two other inmates who, though not as old, seemed to have fragile health. However, these women's physical suffering was especially noticeable, particularly in one of them who could not walk without the aid of a cane and was rarely seen standing up.

Clad in black from head to toe, they were the characteristic image of the gypsy widow: tall, bulky women in deep mourning dress. Always accompanied by relatives, they were the object of special attention from other inmates and prison officers alike. Both of these women were serving their third term in Odemira, always on drug trafficking charges. At the same time that the officers warned me not to be fooled by their gentle appearance—saying, "those two have done some nasty things"—more than once they told me that prison wasn't the right place for these women, that they should instead be placed in a home for the elderly, where they would be better taken care of. On some occasions during the winter months, when the cold and dampness affected their movements, the prison warden (as an exception to the procedures) allowed them to remain in their cells during the afternoon period.

Lunch was monitored by the prison officers, overseen by one of the chief officers, who remained in the refectory for the duration of the meal. On entering or leaving the area, some inmates would use the short periods before and after a meal to "have a word" with the chief or with one of the officers with whom they were on closer terms. They needed something or had a difficulty that needed help solving from the correctional treatment staff or the warden herself. Their requests were varied: knowing if a package they were expecting had been delivered; if a relative had deposited money in their accounts for personal expenses; if they could make a phone call outside the prescribed hours; or asking for permission to talk to the doctor or the nurse without a previous appointment due to a sudden headache or toothache, and so on.

Usually, after everyone has been served, the chief officer asks if anyone wants seconds (which often occurs, since inmates unanimously agree that "the food is very good"), after which those who have finished their meal ask for permission to leave the table and put their trays back. As would be expected, the first to be served are the first to leave. No more than 20–25 minutes elapsed from the moment the door was opened until lunch is over. Being only around 50 women, they all eat at the same time, and as soon as the last one is attended, the inmates on kitchen duty move into a different area of the refectory where they start collecting the trays and doing the washing. In less than an hour the space is ready to be used again, this time as a common room with the television on.

There was nothing to do, just chatting, just hanging around. The women returned to the yard, some of them to smoke, others to resume their reading, others to wait for the bar to open for coffee. This cafeteria was a small space embedded in the refectory, opening up to the cell hall by a narrow window. Inmates make their orders at the counter, and take their coffee or drinks out to the courtyard. In terms of its size, the space was, therefore, not so much a cafeteria as a kind of takeaway stand. Once a week (on Fridays), there were pastries on sale, and the bar also served as the prison "shop" where every fortnight inmates could buy personal items, such as hygiene products, groceries, and so forth.

No more than half an hour later, I once again noticed a new line, this time comprised of a smaller group, being formed in front of another closed door: these inmates were waiting for the nurse who hands out the medication. By now, some of the women didn't go back outside; they just lingered on, backwards and forwards. I quickly understood why: it was time to return to the cells they had left at 8:30 a.m. A long line was formed before the stairway leading to the cells on the upper landing. On the ground floor, it was interesting to notice small groups of inmates gathered at the door to their cells talking, as they would on their house doorstep with neighbors. The officers started the process of opening the cells, their actions once again falling into a cadence: the older women going up first, followed by the rest. One of the officers opens the ground floor cells and another one is in charge of the upper floor. They open the cells one by one, doing a number check of the inmates for each cell. The next hour and a half is spent in the cell watching television, resting, or just whiling the time away with their cellmates.

On this first day I peeked into one of the cells, to get a glimpse of what they were like. I was met by its occupants, who seemed eager to show me their living quarters, an enthusiasm I later realized derived from a sense of personal pride.

I was welcomed into an exiguous rectangular compartment of no more than six square meters. Along one of the walls, a bunk bed occupied almost half of the space available, and the rest was taken up by two small cupboards. At one corner, a small curtain hid a toilet seat. A barred window at the far end wall completed the setting. The motive for the inmates pride' seemed to be as evident as the room's sparseness. The beds were neatly made, everything was spotless and nothing seemed out of place. My hosts explained that orderliness was one of the rules that they took more seriously: "It's not because we are in prison that we're going to stop doing our beds, right? The 'bathroom' is cleaned every day, and the floor scrubbed with disinfectant!" I asked hypothetically what would happen if they had to share the cell with someone who did not follow this rule so strictly, if this was a common practice in all the cells. The officer who was accompanying me nodded in approval as the woman explained: "All inmates agree on this subject, and when someone new is admitted and is not familiar with this habit, the rest of us take it upon ourselves to explain how to keep their things and their tidiness. If someone refuses, we take it up with one of the officers, who will then deal with it." This attitude towards orderliness seemed to go beyond the mere acceptance of a rule, and as I came to realize, it also extended to other aspects connected with personal presentation. As the doors were locked down, the officers set off with a "see you later".

* * *

I was invited to lunch amongst the officers and the warden, an atmosphere I was to become used to. Some of them brought home-cooked meals; others heated pre-cooked dishes in the microwave. A television set was turned on, and the conversation revolved around the news being announced on that day's lunchtime update. An hour later it was time to open up the cells again, and I was keen to know how the afternoon was spent. On leaving their cells, the inmates once again dispersed throughout their landing area, and the refectory was converted into a common room where they watched television, played cards or napped with their arms on the table. The smokers mostly hung around the courtyard despite the chilly autumn weather. During the school year, those who "have" school go to the library, where there is a classroom, while those who work attend to their chores—cleaning, laundry, and kitchen duties. During this time of year there were no other activities, except for occasional music and poetry workshops. In other words, during the school year most women had nothing to occupy themselves.

I was allowed to attend a class, so in this first day "inside prison" I made my way to the library. Prison statistics clearly reveal that the average education level amongst the imprisoned population is very low; the majority of inmates drop out somewhere between primary and basic education, rarely completing compulsory education, which in Portugal is set at the twelfth grade. Most of the women at Odemira fall into this pattern: out of the 47 inmates there, 12 were illiterate, 14 had only attended primary school (the majority of which had not completed the fourth grade), 7 reached as far as the sixth grade, and the remainder had finished secondary education. Only two women had attended university.

The classroom was just an area in the library demarcated by a row of desks set out in a U shape, with a stool in the middle where the teacher sat. I put away immediately the diary and pen that I brought with me when taking a seat at an empty place next to one of the students: this was an adult literacy class. Looking around I noticed that all 10 inmates present were gypsy women and that they spanned a very broad age range. There were women as young as 30 and as old as 70. None of them could read or write, and the exercise that day was learning to write their own name—something that was still beyond most—the more advanced students were completing a table with the numbers 1 to 100. They had to fill the gaps with the missing numbers and it was a difficult task, one that very few were managing to complete on their own, and so they were constantly calling out to the teacher for help. The studies that have attempted to make a sociodemographic description of this ethnic minority in Portugal are from the outset hampered in their representative character by a restriction that derives from the fact that Portuguese law forbids any reference to ethnicity in surveys or statistics. As Gomes and Granja notes:

> The available data only consider the pair foreign/national, leaving out from possible analyses categories such as ethnic group, immigrant, foreign resident/non-resident. Statistics likewise cannot differentiate between resident and non-resident foreigner. Moreover, we have to consider the case of people who are born in Portugal but keep their parents' nationality, thus falling into the erroneous category of "second generation immigrants". Given that we have no data on ethnic groups, we are also faced with the problem of people who are statistically considered nationals, but who due to their phenotype, for practical effects have an everyday experience of being treated as foreign or immigrant, as in the cases of the so-called "repatriates"[1] or gypsy communities. (2015a, b: 42) (My translation.)

Due to the fact that they are not always registered, or only registered in their teens, the real total number of gypsies living in Portugal is not known exactly. Estimates vary between 40,000 and 90,000 scattered throughout the country, with strong concentrations in the north and central regions. In the south and Alentejo region, where Odemira is situated, is estimated to hold 20 percent of the total gypsy population. In terms of the imprisoned gypsy population, the only existing study was carried out by Moreira in 1999, and was based on internal data collected by the Directorate-General of Prison Services.[2]

According to its author, around 80 percent of gypsy inmates have never attended school, and 50 percent cannot write their own name. Commenting on these data, Gomes and Granja conclude, "the rate of formal and informal illiteracy amongst women reaches almost 90 percent" (2015a, b: 40).

The gypsy women at Odemira told me that their community had only started to allow young girls to attend school in the last decade. The reason for their reluctance had to do both with their fear of contact with non-gypsy boys, and on the other to the fact that the ideal marriage age was between 13 and 15. This meant that the girls would have to leave school either to start working in the fairs with their family, or stay home taking care of the house and the children, very rarely engaging in professional work outside the family sphere (Gomes 2013; Magano 2014; Casa-Nova 2009; Acedo 2015).

Drug trafficking, the crime for which 9 out of the 14 gypsy women held in Odemira were charged with or had been convicted for, was an activity that within this community involved almost all members of a family, the eldest typically heading the organization, while the rest of the family—sons, daughters, in-laws, and so on—did the actual distribution and selling around the neighborhood. With ages ranging from 23 to 70, only three of them were first-time offenders. The remaining were recidivist offenders, serving 7-year sentences on average.

The teacher had put a table up on the wall with the complete numbers for those who had finished writing their name. The 34-year-old woman sitting beside me still struggled with her first name: Sónia. After several failed attempts, she finally seemed satisfied with the result and moved on to the numbers. She became stuck when she reached number five, and I could see the frustration she felt with her hand's disobedience, so I tried to help her, giving her tips on the different ways she could make the shape, or suggested images that could serve as a pictogram—"a snake with a hat". We spent the next two hours tackling the curves and lines that made up this number, until she finally sat back and exclaimed: "I'm too old for this!" Other women were doing random scribbles, and only one of them was managing to follow the teacher, who kept going over the numbers pointing them out on the board. Most could count to 10, but none of them were able to follow from there, or even recognize the numbers that were being pointed out on the board. On my next visit to Odemira, Sónia was in a hurry to tell me that she had finally managed to "do number 5". I asked her to show me, and I sat and watched as she drew the snake. Though she had forgotten do put the "hat" on the curvy line, making her 5 indistinguishable from her S, she seemed very pleased with this accomplishment.

When the class was over, I went downstairs to see what was happening on the ground floor. A new procedure seemed to be underway: around 5:30 p.m. it was time for the afternoon shower period, and the cells had been opened again. All those who hadn't done so in the morning or before lunch, could now use the shower room on their floor. I saw women leaving their cells in their bathrobes and slippers, carrying their towels and a small plastic bucket containing soap, shampoo, hair comb, and so on. Some of them asked the officers for tweezers to do their eyebrows, or razors to shave their legs. I stood watching this movement from the cells to the showers and back again.

Throughout this activity, the officer's task was mostly ensuring certain routine procedures—opening and closing the door to the administrative area, attending to a request, and generally being ready for any event—usually chatting with their colleagues and with inmates as they went about these duties. During one of these periods, an inmate approached the officer, and made the following comment to one of them: "Ma'am, are you trying to make us all envious, showing off those nails all nicely made up?" This teasing comment prompted a lighthearted conversation about varnish colors, and soon they were exchanging tips on makeup and hairstyling techniques—the best way to shade the eyes, or straighten the hair, and so on. One of them was telling the others how she was going to do her hair next time, telling them how to do so without staining their towels with the dye. The officer also offered advice on this: "Use the green towels to wrap around your hair, they're older, and the dye always stains a lot, even after rinsing your hair thoroughly." I stood listening to this exchange of beauty tips, until one of the officers looked my way and gave me an explanatory smile: "The women get awfully vain in here. They gain a newfound pride in their own appearance. Some of them enter this place absolutely ravaged, and after a few weeks it's as if they have a body again, the color returns to their faces. It's the drugs that really eat them up. Of course they're not all in here for drugs, but many are."

This officer recalled what she considered to be an extreme case of a woman in her thirties who had been brought in for failure to pay a court fine set as an alternative to a prison sentence on petty theft charges. The woman was a drug addict and was in very poor physical condition when she arrived, weighing just over 40 kg to her 1.65 m. During the standard stripping on admission, the officers had been very disturbed by her thinness, by the disfiguration of a body that had been taken to the limit. It made such an impression that months later the officer still found it difficult to make sense of what she had seen:

> She comes from a well-off family. Her father came here to talk with us, and said that it was the family's own decision not to pay his daughter's court fine. She had been in and out of several rehabilitation clinics, and she always ended up running away. Now it was almost a relief for them knowing she was safely guarded, and he believed it would be good for her too. She would eat and sleep regularly, and have a real chance to get away from the drugs, to get clean.

While reflecting on this alleged newfound self-respect and even "female vanity" that these women—officers and inmates—claimed to be gained while in prison, I observed that as the women finish their showers, they started coming out to the yard with new clothes and had done up their hair differently. For a moment it seemed as if they had been prepping up for a dinner date, they were so smartly dressed. This care appeared to be generalized, and it strongly contrasted with the sweat suits and trainers that most male inmates habitually wear in other prison facilities I had visited.

While most of the time the women in Odemira put on a more casual wear as they go about their daily chores, after their afternoon shower, there was a marked and conscious enhancement in presentation. And in fact, women repeatedly emphasized their contempt for signs of "sloppiness", to the point where they even reproach certain past behaviors of their own from the time before being admitted into Odemira. Thus, though officially not compulsory, taking daily showers is for all purposes a requirement—"and if someone refuses, we tell the officer straight away". Likewise, one of the inmates explained the importance of disinfecting the cell: "This is different from our home, you see? We have to be more thorough because of the germs, since we have to share the space with so many people. It's true that we are always more or less the same group of people, but still, you can never be too careful." She described the disgust she felt when she saw someone asking her for her cigarette butt: "When I first arrived, I also used to do that and it didn't bother me, but now I feel disgusted just to think of it. If I run out of cigarettes, I prefer not to smoke than to ask someone for their butt. That's something I'll never do again!"

There were basically two ways to interpret this concern with hygiene, with asepticism, with personal presentation and cell upkeep. In the first place, it was a demonstration of the inmate's awareness and rejection of so-called "deviant" behavior, which they somehow associated with their criminal past. Secondly, it seemed to reflect a sense of identity closely related with gender, insofar as it valued features identified with an ideal of femininity (of what a woman *should* or *should not* be).

Viewed from this perspective, the cell could be made to represent the home, or household, as an orderly, well-kept space. Similarly, the attire, hair, nails, and general presentation in public seeks to project the image of the self-respecting woman, and conversely, of someone whose self-awareness seeks to command respect from others (Bosworth 2016: 103–114).

It was obvious that the officers reinforced such an attitude, and the chief officer even commented that whenever they had to take an inmate to a public event, such as a court hearing, where inmates from other institutions were also present, they felt a certain pride in "their own": "We are proud of our inmates; well-dressed, tidy, personable. Some of the men we find in these places look like bums—unkempt, dirty, even stinking." Nevertheless, and despite the fact that the officers indeed often assume the task of overseeing this aspect of the inmate's lives, calling out those who skip a shower, or do not make their bed properly, they insisted that it was the inmates themselves who monitored each other, and that they took these matters very seriously: "No woman likes to be cautioned, right? It's humiliating having someone telling you in front of others that your cell is a mess, or that you smell bad!"

Gypsies, Drug Dealers and "Recidists"

The afternoon went by seeing the women, like sunflowers, shift their place around the courtyard in order to catch as much sunlight as possible, since its high walls prevented the rays of sun from filling the whole yard at any given moment. After the afternoon shower and a pause for a cigarette, a new line started to build up inside the cell hall. It was 6:30 p.m. Dinnertime. The procedure was identical to lunch, only this time the women brought small thermos flasks, which they left by the refectory entrance and the inmates on kitchen duty would fill these up with hot water for the others to take up to their cells to make coffee or tea. Dinner was again monitored by three or four officers, supervised by a chief officer.

The same movements and actions start all over. This time I noticed that the women have brought their cutlery inside a plastic bag, taking them out before the meal and retrieving them at the end. It is plasticware, and each inmate has her own set. I also noticed that there were no cups or glasses. The dinner trays include a bowl of soup, a plate with the main course, and a piece of fruit. Besides these, there was also an empty bowl and a bagged sandwich with an extra piece of fruit and yoghurt. It is their "night snack", which they can take with them to the cell. The empty bowl is for drinking water, and it is identical to the ones used to drink milk from at breakfast.

The rest of the evening very much mimics the after-lunch routine, even though during the winter, with the days getting shorter, sunlight is replaced by electric light. Due to the cold, or to the rain, and given that the yard is completely unsheltered, only a few of them go back out after dinner for a quick smoke. The rest remain in the cell hall, which after sundown seems smaller and more cramped; a closed-off rectangle where there are only two chairs reserved for the oldest women. It is roughly 90 minutes between dinner and lockdown in which there is absolutely nothing to do. Huddled around small groups, the largest of which is the gypsies, most of the women chat away this waiting period. Some of them read, others sing to themselves, and others just pace the room back and forth.

As the day progressed, I began to find that without a watch I was losing track of time. But even more unsettling, I realized that I was also gradually losing other references, to the point where even the purpose and meaning of the place began to be lost on me, in a similar vein to that which Laura Piacentini claims by saying that "prisons do not represent 'normal life'…The prison is where one simply cannot avoid effect on vision, mobility and hearing" (2015: 87). It was as if the memory of life outside those walls was somehow losing its consistency. The uneasiness that I began to feel made me think of those inmates who spent the day strolling aimlessly around the precinct, as if bound only to the movement of the body through a meaningless environment. In this surrounding, a group of women were having a heated debate around some controversial topic. As I approached, one of them called out to me:

> It's good that you're here, mam; maybe you can help us with something. Article 21 is applied to large-scale drug trafficking, right? I'm asking because I was condemned on Article 21, but she [one of her mates] got Article 17. What is that for? It means she gets five years, right? It's aggravated trafficking, right?

All attentions were suddenly on me. After all, I was a "professor", so in their minds I should be able to clarify these finer legal points. But my legal knowledge was limited to general categories like possession, possession with intent to distribute, or small- or large-sale drug trafficking. When I openly told them that I could not help, I saw the suspicion in some of the women's eyes, as if thinking, "What kind of professor is she, who doesn't know these kinds of things?" One of them came to my rescue by saying, "She's not that kind of professor, she's here to write a book about us". The others seemed to be satisfied with this explanation, and went on to explain to me the dispute they were trying to settle without success.

One of the inmates, who was on remand, had been charged under one of these articles in the Penal Code. The others, already convicted, were trying to explain to her the type of offence that the article usually applied to, the corresponding sentencing range, and thus the amount of years in prison that she could be facing.

This was clearly a phenomenon that I had already seen in other prison facilities. Here too, inmates made a point of incorporating legal jargon into their vocabulary. When asked about the crime they had committed, they usually refer to the legal definition: "aggravated manslaughter" rather than "I killed my husband (or wife)"; "theft" or "burglary" rather than "I robbed people on the street" or "I broke into people's houses"; "battery" rather than "I beat my children". However, the familiarity with legal terms did not mean that these women had any legal literacy. In fact, most of them seemed largely ignorant about the whole legal system and its workings.

On my visits to Odemira, many expressed their bafflement regarding their own case, specifically in terms of how the judges had ruled, or the counsel their lawyers had given them. In some cases, this difficulty derived from things as simple as not understanding the questions directed at them during trial by the judges. On the other hand, their experience led them to construct certain notions. For instance, it was generally accepted that drug trafficking offences, especially in the case of recidivists, would usually result in mandatory imprisonment sentences. Regarding the lawyers, who were often described as "charlatans who take our money and leave us here", the inmates referred to specific situations, such as being advised not to make any statements during trial hearings. Among the group of women that had approached me, for example, some claimed that this had resulted in being accused of crimes they had not committed: "I admit what I did. It's true that I stole, but some of the other things they accused me of were not my doing, and the lawyer told me to keep quiet!"

Most of the conversations with gypsy inmates at Odemira turned into group talks. The curiosity raised by the presence of an outsider, together with their tendency to remain together most of the time, transformed these meetings almost into focus group sessions, in which their life experiences seemed to complement and complete each other, as each one added a piece of information to the other's account. In fact, in the course of a year's fieldwork, new members of this community arrived, some of which had family ties with other inmates already there, making kinship gain an ascendancy over other identity bonds, such as residential proximity, ethnic belonging or crime category. Their family bonds did not imply that they belonged to the same "drug ring"—trafficking being the most common crime among this group—or that this community formed what is legally known as a "criminal organization", where all members operate under one leadership. In most cases at Odemira, this activity seemed circumscribed to a single household, albeit sometimes within the same neighborhood or settlement.

In the case of Irina and Isaura—mother and daughter—it was the latter's house that was used as the selling point for the drugs. On the day they were arrested, there was a police raid in the neighborhood, which resulted in several arrests (including two other family members who were in the house at that time). The witnesses produced by the district attorney were drug users who had been detained in the raid and made a formal positive identification of the two women as the neighborhood drug dealers. At the time of her detention, Irina was 56 years old. Long separated from her husband, who "was good-for-nothing except for beating me up", Irina had borne 10 children, two of whom had died at an early age, and three others had ended up in prison for robbery, theft and drug trafficking. Her daughter Isaura was 33 and had three children, all minors, entrusted to one of her sisters who, as Isaura explained, "had never gotten herself involved in any of this business. It was just my mother and me."

This wasn't the first stay in prison, for either mother or daughter. Actually it was Irina's third prison sentence (always at Odemira), and Isaura's second—the first of which she served in a central prison where she could keep her baby boy with her—but it was the first time they were in the same prison together. Following a directive of Portuguese enforcement measures legislation, according to which inmate relatives are preferentially accommodated together, mother and daughter shared a common cell with other gypsy women who were also related to them. Irina described her life as "a life of suffering"—abused by an alcoholic and possessive husband; finding temporary work in street markets or in the fields; raising her children by herself with a lot of "sacrifice and poverty".

Unable either to read or write, nevertheless she had sought work around the factories in the Alentejo region—where she had lived her whole adult life—to no avail. She attributed this to the prejudice against the gypsy community, but also to the fact that her husband did not approve of her having a job. To this list she added other reasons to explain why she had finally resorted to drug trafficking:

> I have always worked very hard, doing any kind of work I could find, I've never shied away from work. But then came the Chinese competition, and then the ASAE (Portuguese Authority for Economic and Food Safety), so the street markets were no longer profitable. So you can imagine what it was like for me, on my own, with my children to provide for, my little grandchildren to feed. The social integration income is next to nothing. So what would you do if you saw your kids crying for food?

What she was trying to explain was that selling drugs was not her first choice as a source of income. Judging by her account, drugs presented a means to buy food, medicine, clothing—all the basic needs for her family in a situation of hardship and lack of work. The daughter, Isaura, concurred with this description, adding that in her own case she also had to deal with a problem of epilepsy. She was a "nervous person" and needed expensive medicines to treat her convulsions, but also for what she called her "pression" (by which she meant depression).

Both mother and daughter were outraged with their incarceration. It was not that they disagreed with the illegality of their acts, or did not outright admit that "drugs only bring disgrace to others", but because they claimed that in their case, drug trafficking had really been the only way out of a desperate situation—a question of survival. In other words, their lack of education and specialized skills, the restrictions on street vending that had traditionally been their main activity, combined with the discrimination and prejudice met by the gypsy community when they sought other kinds of work, had ultimately sealed their fate:

> They say gypsies are dirty, that we're all thieves, so nobody will employ us. How are we to sustain a household? I have never stolen a thing from anyone. We are clean. So why doesn't anyone give us work? Surely you can see that the social income is a trifling, right? It's just too much poverty!

Similarly, they felt that the prejudice found in their everyday struggle to find work repeated itself in the courtrooms, namely through the bias of judges. Even though the sentences applied to them were identical to all other inmates (gypsy and non-gypsy) charged and convicted for similar crimes of drug trafficking, they claimed as soon as a gypsy is presented in court, the judge has already formed an opinion his/her guilt. On the other hand, minimizing the gravity of their offence—"Come on, I was only carrying a couple of bags, and I got such a heavy sentence!"—was also used to support their argument of bigotry. For them, a "small" quantity did not justify 5- to 7-year sentences. They believed that their ethnicity had secured these convictions, not just their crime, despite admitting that there was also another aspect worth considering: their recidivism could explain the judge's readiness to convict them. Both Irina and Isaura argued that the solution for gypsies was not putting them in prisons, but giving them work and fighting prejudice.

While I was listening to their complaints, one of the gypsy matriarchs who had been attending the afternoon class earlier that day came over, and as she began to tell me about her case, the other gypsy women gathered around, nodding their assent to the older woman's accusations of discrimination against members of the gypsy community. I could not make out everything that was being said, since many of the terms were misstated—"recidist" instead of "recidivist" for example—which was understandable, since Antónia, as I had already witnessed, could not read or write. When I asked about her age, she became unsure, but one of her daughters there tried to help by saying "my older brother is 50 or so".

Antónia told me she had 11 children, "two of them not quite good in the head, poor things", and that she had worked her whole life: "We did the fairs, selling wicker baskets, bunches of asparagus, you name it. And I did it all on my own. My husband was a wicked man, very bad to us." The daughter kept nodding, as if to confirm the truth of what was being said, while the rest added pieces of their own stories: "My father was also very mean to my mother. Once he even put rat poison in our soup to kill us all. I remember seeing that the soup was blue, and telling my mother not to eat it, cause dad wanted to kill us."

Antónia went on telling her story, and none of the others interrupted what seemed like an endless yarn: "Yes, I remember we tied small bunches of asparagus, and many other things. But then one day we are put away here for just a couple of bags, and that's on account of us being "recidist" and gypsy! As soon as the judge sees a gypsy, he doesn't even blink, they must be a thief or a dealer; we don't stand a chance." The group echoes the woman's indignation: "They think gypsies are unclean, that we are all thieves, we are not given an opportunity!" says another voice in the group.

This time it was a gypsy woman in her 50s who joined the conversation. She had also been convicted along with her daughter. According to her, "The young woman had enrolled as a trainee in a beauty academy, but when it came to hiring her, they said she wasn't good enough. They didn't say it was because she was a gypsy, but we know how it is, right?" I turned once again to Antónia, wanting to know a little more about her criminal history, and when I asked her if this had been the first time in prison, she answered that it was the third or fourth time, and that she had other children in prison as well: "… and I have two little daft ones, they are bedridden, poor things…So you see, I've been here for six years already and nobody knows when I'll be getting out. They don't tell me. I can't see an end to this. The lady warden has even told me that we have to find someone to look into my case, because no one knows what to do with me."

The conversation was cut short as another line, this time as long as the lines for meals, began to form in front of the medicine dispensary. A different nurse from the one I had seen earlier was now standing at the door. There are very few women who do not take some kind of medication before going to bed, so I decide to join the line to continue talking with the inmates. Most of them were very comfortable telling me that they took "sleeping pills" or antidepressants. The small group of women who didn't take anything boasted of not depending on medicine to cope with prison, even though I found that almost invariably those who took some kind of antidepressant in prison already did so beforehand. It was a little past 7 p.m. when the cells were reopened to let inmates in for the night. Some of them asked me: "Are you coming back again tomorrow? We can talk some more!" After a little while, the cell hall became deserted. The officers told me that inmates were allowed to watch TV in their cells until 11 p.m., and lights were turned out manually by a guard at 1 a.m., except on weekends, when they were given more latitude.

Order, Security, Well-Being

The officers seemed almost surprised that I had "made it" through the day, and I sensed a little skepticism when they asked me if I was coming back the next day. While for me this might have been a unique opportunity to have unrestricted access inside a prison, to follow inmates' routines and movements, from the officer's standpoint theirs was an extremely demanding and emotionally exhausting profession. Especially those who were on regular eight-hour shifts, the daily experience of prison seemed to be as burdensome as it was for inmates themselves. Even without the main problems that typically afflicted larger prison facilities, their work required not just a constant readiness to solve daily problems, but also an emotional availability to deal with inmates' dilemmas. To ensure the harmonious cohabitation of almost 50 inmates it was crucial not to leave any conflict unresolved, to foresee any potential source of discomfort, and to detect signs of stress or suffering amongst the population before they built up to a major incident.

With schedules and rules strictly defined for almost all situations, the routines at Odemira were similar to any other Portuguese prison facility. Nevertheless, there were specificities to this prison, particularly in aspects that weren't so precisely regulated, as, for example, regarding the amount of time spent out of the cells. The law dictates that inmates must have "at least" one hour a day out of doors, but each warden is left to decide how this period is allotted. The rules regarding this open air time had changed over the last two years, as a measure intended to limit its inmates' autonomy and freedom of movement. On the warden's orders, all inmates were forbidden from remaining in the cell during the day, and were only allowed one hour in the cell during the officer's lunch break, and then after lockdown for the night (with the exception of weekends, during which the cells were kept open). Before this new rule, those inmates who didn't have work or any other occupation could remain in their cells after lunch, and were only obliged to participate in the chores assigned to them or that they were voluntarily engaged in, such as school, gym or music classes. One of the inmates who had lived through this transition complained: "It was a much better system, and now we're all made to pay for the errors of a few."

The new rules had been enforced as a result of two suicide attempts that had occurred in the previous years during this "free" time in the cells. Despite being in the company of her cellmates at the time, one of the women had managed to drink from the bottle of cleaning disinfectant. Another inmate tried to slash her wrists with a shaving razor. From then on, personal hygiene products were kept by the chief officer, and all inmates had to stay out of their cells during the daytime. This new requirement was extremely taxing for them, and even more so for the more elderly women whose fragile health prevented them from performing any physical task and were thus left to spend all of their time in the refectory hall, where they were permanently disturbed by the bustle of other inmates—watching television, playing cards, chattering and laughing—and the cold and humidity of the winter months or the heat of the summer months made their stay there physically much more uncomfortable than their cell beds. The warden explained the need to make such a rule: "There can't be any exceptions. This is the only way to keep an eye on all of them, and to prevent any other events like the ones that happened two years ago. Perhaps those occurrences were just warnings, but sometimes these warnings can go wrong, and we can't risk them hurting themselves or destabilizing the prison environment."

In both of the cases behind this change of regulation, the inmates in question had been described as "mentally unstable" persons, women who in the opinion of the warden, the officers and the correctional treatment staff should never even have been placed in a common prison to serve their sentence. One of them was very young, 24 years of age, and had a diagnosed history of depression, co dependent behavior and suicidal tendencies, particularly when under the influence of drugs.

Patricia, whom I had had the chance to meet, had been sent to Odemira for a string of petty theft crimes committed with her boyfriend. According to the prison officers, after the first weeks in custody spent getting clean from drugs, she turned out to be a cheerful and cooperative person. She started a romantic relationship with another inmate there who was further into her sentence and already benefitted from home leaves. Coming back from one of those leaves, Patricia's new partner managed to smuggle in some hashish. Out of the six inmates that the drug was offered to, only Patricia accepted.

The officers were alerted to this situation by her own behavior, which became erratic and psychotic, and finally she confessed to the drug use and told the officers how she had obtained it. The other inmate was immediately transferred to another facility, and shortly afterwards Patricia made her suicide attempt with the cleaning product.

After receiving treatment at the local hospital and a temporary stay in a hospital prison, where she had been admitted on the grounds that she was mentally dysfunctional, she was sent back to Odemira. The officers recalled that she had "returned a different person" and had "never been herself again". Medicated with antidepressants and anxiolytics, the officers did not understand why she had been returned to Odemira when she was so clearly debilitated: "She was practically a zombie, she badly needed looking after. What was a woman in that condition doing in a prison?" Even the rest of the inmate population found it hard to witness the state of this young woman, while the officers were permanently confronted with her inability to perform the most basic tasks due to the strong medication she was under. The warden considered that this case needed to be urgently addressed. It was clear to all that Patricia should be hospitalized and given psychiatric support, instead of being stuck in a prison facility with the rest of the common population (Liebling and Ludlow 2016; Moore and Scraton 2014; Liebling 1992; Rhodes 2004; Mills and Kendall 2016).

The other case that contributed to the change of rules had different contours and a distinct effect on the prison's day-to-day life. Generally avoided by most inmates due to her conflicting character and eccentric behavior, the prison's directing board and staff viewed this inmate as a constant challenge. Having been released from prison on completion of her sentence, three days after my first stay at Odemira, I remember that her name still figured on a board that hung on a wall in the chief's office room, which served to keep the registry of inmates' allocation. In her specific case, in front of the name—Madalena—was the indication that she was interned in the hospital prison at Caxias.

Her story was unique, insofar as in the 20 years of this facility's history as a female prison, this had been the only case of an inmate convicted for child sexual abuse. Sentenced to five and a half years for the sexual abuse of a minor friend of the family, she had been diagnosed with bipolar disorder, and her character described as manipulative, detached from reality and displaying traits of "promiscuous behavior". In the years spent behind bars, she never showed the ability or willingness to comply with basic rules of personal hygiene or orderliness, causing trouble with her cellmates, who often complained to the officers that she wet the bed, smoked rolled-up book pages, and was generally aggressive to others. Madalena had regular psychiatric visits, and took medication to keep her functional. However, both officers and correctional treatment staff were clear on her inability to have an independent life outside of prison, especially if she stopped taking her medication, either because she decided she didn't need it, or reached a point where she could not afford it.

As her sentenced reached its end and she was granted home leaves, Madalena started confiding to other inmates that she didn't want to be set free, which was understandable in light of the fact that, as the warden and vice-warden who followed her case told me, after the events with the minor leading to her imprisonment, the family had cut all ties with her. A few days before her release, Madalena made her suicide attempt, and was thus transferred to the hospital prison.

A month later, I was told that Madalena had come directly from the hospital to gather her things and get ready for release. Her time was up, and the staff were shocked that in the five years she spent in prison, no official solution had been reached to ensure that she continued her psychiatric treatment, to secure a place for her to live or a minimum wage to sustain her on the outside. All attempts to have her committed to a psychiatric facility had failed despite the efforts of Odemira's directing board. On the one hand, Madalena had not been legally declared unaccountable or incapacitated. On the other hand, she also refused a hypothetical commitment to a mental institution after her release from prison; all she wished for was to stay in this facility, which was not possible.

Even though in larger prison facilities cases such as these two might seem trivial, Odemira's warden pointed out that in such a small environment their impact on the inmate population had been severe. In some of them it inspired depressive traits, in others it made suicide seem a viable solution to their problems, so it was urgent to fight any copycat effect. The warden and the officers were unanimous in their opinion that a well-balanced environment depended as much on the cooperation between staff and inmate population, as on a sense of solidarity and responsibility amongst inmates, who would have to be the first to detect and report any disruptive or negative behavior in their ranks.

Although drug rehab programs are widely available within the Portuguese prisons, namely with substitution therapy (methadone), the system has many flaws not uncommon to the National Health System in general that are also evident in Odemira, particularly in terms of continued mental health treatment and supervision. The officers' daily monitoring is largely organized to cover for the obvious deficiency in the lack of individual and group therapy to treat specific problems of this female population.

Despite the provision of medication for cases of acute stress or anxiety disorders, and the regular presence of nurses trained to detect cases that need the intervention of a specialized physician, this is clearly an inadequate and insufficient arrangement. Most inmates are under prescribed medication, and they either started treatment after imprisonment or are continuing previous treatments. However, as the next chapters will make clear, the problems that afflict many of these women are not limited to medical pathologies that can be so easily diagnosed—anxiety, depression, insomnia, and so forth. Their life histories reveal a host of disturbances derived from their past experience and background—in many cases coupled with physical or psychological abuse—whose profound effects largely surpass any specific event or symptom.

De facto, the fragments of conversations with gypsy women recounted in this chapter allowed us to glimpse issues that are far from restricted to this ethnic group, such as domestic violence, poverty, drug addiction, low education levels and lack of skills—in sum, general impotence and helplessness (Manita 2005; Merry 2008; Poiares 2014). Nonetheless, while for many inmates the time spent in prison may be, perhaps paradoxically, a period of "protection" from aggression, from exposure to the risks and dangers experienced while in freedom, in the opinion of the correctional treatment staff this period should also serve to provide professional aid towards working on their self-awareness and self-esteem. The pep talks and lectures on specific topics that are usually provided are not sufficient to give these women the necessary tools, knowledge and skills they need to break the cycles that keep landing them back in prison. These are just a few of the topics that will be addressed in the next chapter, with a focus on the inmates' discourse regarding their own emotional experience of confinement.

Notes

1. Portuguese living in the Portuguese colonies of Angola, Mozambique or Guinea-Bissau before the democratic revolution in 1974.
2. Semedo Moreira worked for several decades in the Directorate-General of Prison Services and this explains his access to data otherwise not available.

References

Acedo, Sara Sama. 2015. A Way of Life Flowing in the Interstices: Cigano Horse Dealers in Alentejo, Portugal. In *Gypsy Economy. Romani Livelihoods and Notions of Worth in the 21st Century*, ed. Micol Brazzabeni, Manuela Ivone Cunha, and Martin Fotta, 68–87. Oxford and New York: Berghahn.

Casa-Nova, Maria José. 2009. *Etnografia e Produção de Conhecimento. Reflexões críticas a partir de uma investigação com ciganos portugueses*. Lisbon: Alto Comissariado para a Imigração e Diálogo Intercultural.

Gomes, Maria do Carmo. 2013. Políticas públicas de qualificação de adultos e comunidades ciganas. In *Ciganos Portugueses. Olhares Plurais e Novos Desafios numa Sociedade em Transição*, ed. Maria Manuela Mendes and Olga Magano, 81–92. Lisbon: Mundos Sociais.

Gomes, Silvia, and Rafaela Granja, eds. 2015a. *Mulheres e Crime. Perspectivas sobre Intervenção, Violência e Reclusão*. Vila Nova de Famalicão: Húmus.

———. 2015b. Trajectórias de vida e experiências prisionais de mulheres ciganas recluídas. In *Mulheres e Crime. Perspectivas sobre Intervenção, Violência e Reclusão*, ed. Silvia Gomes and Rafaela Granja, 47–65. Vila Nova de Famalicão: Húmus.

Liebling, Alison. 1992. *Suicides in Prison*. London: Routledge.

Liebling, Alison, and Amy Ludlow. 2016. Suicide, Distress and the Quality of Prison Life. In *Handbook on Prisons*, ed. Yvonne Jewkes, Jamie Bennett, and Ben Crewe, 2nd ed., 224–245. London and New York: Routledge.

Magano, Olga. 2014. *Tracejar Vidas "Normais"*. *Estudo Qualitativo sobre a Integração dos Ciganos em Portugal*. Lisbon: Mundos Sociais.

Manita, Celina. 2005. *A intervenção em agressores no contexto da violência doméstica em Portugal: estudo preliminar de caracterização*. Lisbon: Comissão para a Igualdade e para os Direitos das Mulheres.

Merry, Sally E. 2008. *Gender Violence: A Cultural Perspective*. Oxford: Wiley-Blackwell.

Mills, Alice, and Kathleen Kendall. 2016. Mental Health in Prisons. In *Handbook on Prisons*, ed. Yvonne Jewkes, Jamie Bennett, and Ben Crewe, 2nd ed., 187–204. London and New York: Routledge.

Moore, Linda, and Phil Scranton. 2014. *The Incarceration of Women. Punishing Bodies, Breaking Spirits*. London and New York: Palgrave Macmillan.

Poiares, Nuno. 2014. *Políticas de segurança e as dimensões simbólicas da lei: o caso da violência doméstica em Portugal*. Unpublished PhD thesis, ISCTE-IUL, Lisbon.

Rhodes, Lorna A. 2004. *Total Confinement: Madness and Reason in the Maximum Security Prison*. Berkeley: University California Press.

Image 3 Interior of a cell

5

The Effects of Imprisonment

This chapter focuses on inmates' narratives on confinement, its psychological and emotional effects. In *The Society of Captives*, Sykes (1958) characterized these effects, designating them "the pains of imprisonment", which roughly speaking, comprised the loss of liberty, absence of heterosexual relationships, loss of desirable goods and services, loss of autonomy and an absence of security within prison premises and inmate and officer relationships. Even though I do not aim to match Sykes's typology with the questions identified by the inmates in our conversations, it is in fact possible to find some resemblances as well as specificities.

Deprivation of liberty, loss of autonomy and freedom of choice—not having certain material goods or even activities to occupy their time—may be easily identified as common characteristics. The lack of sexual relationships was explicitly addressed as an issue by only one of the prisoners, who told me that "this is the first time in my life I miss it!" Though not a topic inmates addressed, there had been a case of a lesbian couple. The other women, however, minimized the subject, claiming that what they really missed while imprisoned is the absence of physical warmth and kindness.

© The Author(s) 2017
C. Frois, *Female Imprisonment*, Palgrave Studies in Prisons and Penology,
DOI 10.1007/978-3-319-63685-6_5

Directly as a result of this prison's very own characteristics—its size, the proximity and interaction between inmates and guards—not a single inmate expressed concerns regarding physical safety, much unlike what was usually pointed out to me as the main problem in male prisons. The feeling of insecurity, if we can use the expression, was connected with factors such as the uncertainty that came from lack of prospects regarding future life outside prison, in terms of work, residence, family, and so on.

There is yet another aspect that may diverge from the existing literature, and some interpretations of imprisonment, both male and female. As this chapter will show, for many inmates there is an underlying ambiguity to confinement. On the one hand, women say—especially recidivist offenders or inmates serving long-term sentences—"Now we are really feeling the prison", specifically referring to the endurance of a punishment, a penalty. On the other hand, though, they also find positive aspects in their suffering. For some, being in prison seems to be an opportunity—to change, to put an end to cycles of violence, poverty, exclusion, precariousness, others to detox from drugs—but it's also a place of stability, where they can enjoy a degree of autonomy within a set of limits. In other words, where they can afford to take decisions, make choices, even plan their future as they had never been able to, and had come to consider beyond their reach before imprisonment.

This reasoning raises questions that must be acknowledged, and they will occupy the next two chapters, addressing topics such as the idea of prison as a state care institution; prison time that breaks with mistreatments, violence, physical and psychological abuse; prison as a place where inmates may recover their individuality, while at the same time to certain women break with references from their past, from whom they were as persons before experiencing prison.

* * *

Throughout the months I accompanied inmates and officers, following a routine describing a pathway between the cell–courtyard–refectory–cell–hall–cell. Occasionally, and according to a plan scheduled previously, inmates were allowed in the administrative area, where the public phones were. I saw the women knocking on the heavy metal door separating the areas, most of them bringing a piece of paper with telephone numbers written down. On the phone they spoke in hushed voices trying to keep their conversations private, which was difficult because there was no separation between each phone and the officers were also around.

Many women showed signs of anxiety and in their daily experience within walls, provoked by their awareness of events that were occurring not inside but outside of those walls: waking up in prison wondering how their children had woken up that morning, if they had taken breakfast, gotten dressed; had they arrived to class on time? What they would eat for lunch that day? Had they done their homework? Who would pick them up, bathe them, feed them and put them to bed? This generated a permanent feeling that they were missing out on the daily routines of family life, constantly worrying, especially with their offspring everyday affairs. The only way to appease this sense of separation was by constantly finding things to remind them of their relatives in everyday trivial events, as if by talking about their children to other inmates or officers would somehow keep their presence more alive within the prison environment. Very few women came back from their daily telephone call with a "dry face". Usually they returned from these conversations drenched in tears, their bodies clenched giving expression to an introspective state of mind. Their silence was usually broken by other inmates' attempts to console them with words: "Don't be upset, I'm sure they're doing fine" or "Brighten up, everything will work out".

Concurring with the data obtained in national and international studies carried out in other female prisons, a large percentage of the imprisoned women at Odemira had their first child during adolescence, and at the time of their incarceration were single mothers with more than one minor in their care; some of these women's children were in the care of institutions or relatives (grandparents, aunts, cousins, godmothers). For these women, the privation of liberty was made more severe due to this separation and when asked what they most hated about being in prison, the inmates frequently identified this aspect as what was "truly hard" (Haney 2013). This point should not be disparaged considering that for some women the experience of prison would be made much more tolerable if they could have their children close during incarceration, even if it could only be one of them.

The delivery of mail and outside parcels was equally an emotionally charged event, often announced with an enthusiasm that sometimes verged on euphoria. It was not uncommon during those periods to hear exclamations and cries of joy echoing through the whole cell hall—"maaaail!" Besides the photographs, prison mail could mean receiving a voucher with credit to be used for personal expenses, drawings made by the children, or a love letter from a boyfriend or partner. In terms of the latter, it was significant that in the few cases of women who received this kind of correspondence, the relationships were maintained with men who were themselves incarcerated in other prison facilities. Despite never having been shown the content of these letters, I got to see that the outside of the envelopes were frequently decorated with romantic arabesques and "love you" messages, sharply contrasting with the heading for the sender, which usually read something like "Name; Inmate n°, Prison Facility, etc."

This type of intramural romance, apparently arousing passions whose strong bonds are nurtured on the idea of a shared fate, is aptly described by Megan Comfort (2008) and Natalia Padovani (2013). Thus, as with the telephone calls, the handing out of mail was always an emotionally moment, tension being derived from the fact that while it reminded inmates of an outside world which they were somehow missing out on, conversely it also introduced a breach in the routine of a secluded life that they have inevitably become used to.

Mariana, a 60-year-old woman, told me that the only thing that assuaged the anguish and revolt which surfaced when she thought about the abuses inflicted by her husband and his "well-deserved" death, as she described it, were the conversations on the phone with her kids, their visits, but above all the daily letters she received from them. These usually came with photographs taken by her daughter, who kept a visual diary of everything that went on at home, allowing Mariana to somehow keep up with her family's everyday life. Pictures of a little kitten adopted recently, of the new living room carpet, of a bedspread her daughter had put in her room; of the previous day's family dinner: "My daughter is doing very well, but it's my son I'm worried about, he's a little disorganized. She goes over when she can to give him a hand, but he's lost without me, to do the laundry, tend to the house, that kind of stuff".

Bearing in mind her personal history and the crime for which she was convicted, it was clear that a change had taken place in her life; prison time—despite the pain caused by being away from her children—had become much easier to manage at the emotional level than all the years of married life with a husband she had met as a teenager.

The abuse had started a couple of years into their marriage, while Mariana was expecting her first child. She remembered perfectly the first time she was beaten (a memory equally well preserved by other abuse victims I had known). One day Mariana's husband came home drunk from work, and after an argument triggered for some minor issue, he punched her in the belly. It was the first in a long line of aggressions that were regularly repeated throughout 40 years of marriage, most of which were hard to find a clear explanation for.

Besides those episodes that could be put down to his drunkenness, which became increasingly frequent along the years, jealous rages, possessiveness, the sheer exercise of dominance and subjugation were pointed out as motives for an ever more constant abuse. There came a point where Mariana's only concern was that he didn't "touch the children", that he focused only on her. She never tried to understand the motives that unleashed his violent acts. In her opinion, everything came down to her husband's meanness: "He was a bad man, a cruel man, who relished my suffering." Mariana gave me a detailed account of her past daily routine, of her job as an attendant in an old person's home, of how she concealed aggression marks on her body:

> I never told anyone, I was ashamed, afraid that he would beat me even more if I told on him; that he would make me pay for it. To give you an idea of what I mean, once he threatened me with a shotgun he used for hunting. I was terrified, so the next day I went to the police to hand in the gun and report what had happened, saying that he had threatened to kill me. Do you know what their reaction was? They called him down to the station to pick up his weapon, since it was registered to his name. I realized then that I was done for, that one day he would kill me and no one would do anything to prevent it.

The first time I talked with Mariana, she asked me not to tape record our conversation, she didn't want her children to "know about certain things". It took some time before she started to open up and reveal the details about her life, in what could almost be described as cathartic process. While on out first encounter, she spoke openly about the abuses inflicted during her marriage, how she often feared for her life and the lives of their children. At the end of some months of our talks, she felt confident enough to confide: "You know, what I did to him was not enough. He died too quickly; he didn't suffer nearly enough to pay for all the harm he did to me!"

The rage and hatred felt for that man were fresh in Mariana's memory, as in her body and in her gaze. It was as if she relived the abuse as she talked about it, but at the same time it seemed to bring her some relief, and finally she managed to bring herself to say out loud what she had never been able to tell either the judge or her children: "Yes, I wanted to kill him." Mariana had been sentenced to 12 years for killing her husband with a gun. Her description of that day was very clear. At that time they were going through a separation process; the son had already moved away several years before, her daughter was living in another apartment owned by the couple. That afternoon, the husband arrived home drunk and said he was going to kick her and her daughter out of the house, claiming that they were living off him, and were entitled to nothing, so they had to leave. During the quarrel, he threatened that if they didn't leave he would shoot both of them, and went out to his car to get his gun. Mariana then went into the kitchen to get a gun that she had found in the house a few days before and fired several shots, some of which hit him. When the police arrived, they found the man already dead, and Mariana waiting to confess her crime.

Mariana claimed that she never planned to kill her husband, that there had been no premeditation. When she found the gun a couple of days before, she pondered turning it over to the police. But she had already tried that once and it was useless, so this time her thinking was different: "He might use this gun to kill me, so I'm going to hide it in case I come to need it."

Not regretting his death, she regretted instead how swift and painless it had been. These feelings and attitude sharply contrasted with the friendly and cordial woman I found in prison, whose days revolved around her work, just as it had always been before imprisonment. She claimed to have been always highly regarded by her colleagues and by the director at the old people's home where she was worked for several years. In fact, she was allowed to await her trial in freedom because she was considered neither a threat to society nor a flight risk. Now she helped in the prison kitchen, and on her days off she would ask for permission just to "lend a hand". She couldn't stand having "nothing to do". When we were together, Mariana showed me the letters she had received from her previous colleagues at work, saying how much they missed her, asking for the recipe of a cake she made which everyone loved, and assuring her that her place would be "waiting for her" when she returned from prison.

Even though at that time Mariana was still on the second year of imprisonment, she expected to be released with an electronic bracelet midway through her sentence. She couldn't envisage any reason to be kept in prison any longer than that; she was well loved in her community, she had the support of her children, and they also needed her. Mariana would never admit to the sentencing judge that she didn't regret killing her husband, but intimately believed that she didn't need to be in prison to "change". Her criminal activity had begun and ended on the day of the murder. Mariana was guilty and accepted her penalty, but thought that it would be excessive to serve the totality of her sentence, since the actions were caused by the abuse she suffered. In sum, she was a victim before she was a criminal—a point that will be developed in later chapters.

"Feeling the Prison": Shared Solitude

Inmates do not all maintain this kind of regular contact with the outside world; neither do all of them experience freedom deprivation in the same way. In Odemira there were many different situations. There was a small percentage of women who received regular weekly visits and "almost always" had mail, but there were many who had absolutely no contact with anyone outside the prison besides the relationships maintained after imprisonment (as in the case of romantic liaisons with fellow male inmates), and others yet who had not received any visits from family and friends since their conviction, either due to the nature of their crimes and their relatives' rejection, or simply because Odemira is "far from everything" making visits there too expensive or impracticable.

For these women, we could almost say that the solitude caused by prison is doubled, to the point where many find it unbearable. When the ties with the outside are severed, they have no alternative but to turn to the inside, and to the relationships that can be forged there. Carla, who used to say that she was "following her daughter's footsteps", was finding it increasingly harder to withstand loneliness. I found it curious that someone whose movements were severely limited would claim that she was following the movements of someone outside, but I soon found out how Carla managed to achieve this:

> I applied for transference [from a central prison she was before] because my daughter moved to the Algarve to study, and so I wanted to come down here to be closer to her. Later she moved back up north and I applied to be transferred again, but meanwhile I was offered a working position in the kitchen and I started benefiting from home leaves, so I decided to cancel my transference request. It might be a good opportunity to apply for temporary leaves and even be eligible for parole. Now I only get to see my daughter and family every so often, because they are all very far away.

Carla's demeanor during our conversations was typically calm, giving a lot of thought to my questions, building her arguments carefully as she described her personal life history before and after imprisonment—now her second conviction for drug trafficking. Carla started using heroin and cocaine at the age of 19, after she had already finished her secondary education. Her first contact with hard drugs was made through her former husband, also a consumer. Working as a cook in her parents' restaurant, in the 15 years that elapsed between her initiation in drugs and our first interview, she managed to maintain what she described as a "stable life, raising two children" while she dealt drugs in a small city to the interior of Portugal.

She explained that the decision to deal drugs was a deliberate and "calculated" risk arising from her increasing drug use and its concomitant financial demand. In other words, it was the means she found to support her habit. Through contacts made with acquaintances, she put together a scheme whereby she bought the drugs from a supplier, transported and sold them, putting aside a part for personal use. Carla explained how, notwithstanding her illegal activities, she always strove to be what she called an "exemplary mom", and managed to keep these two apparently incompatible spheres of her life completely separate:

> I was always a dedicated mother, despite my addiction. I don't suffer from any mental disorders, and the drugs didn't disturb me, so I always led a normal life apart from the drug dealing and personal use. I was always a very dedicated mother, and my daughter was well-looked-after and educated. I used to live with my mother, but more recently [before prison] I had moved in with my grandparents, who used to help me out.

This family network proved essential to ensure that the oldest daughter (the one she was following around the country through her requests for transference from one prison to another) could finish her education and go on to college. Despite her awareness of how "wrong" her behavior was (to use her own words) she still claimed that it did not affect her role either as a mother, daughter or granddaughter. The paradox underlying her narrative is evident. Carla's case resembles many other cases of male or female addiction with similar histories, who despite their drug habit (in this instance coupled with its distribution), manage to maintain a steady job, to keep schedules, daily routines and behaviors that are absolutely unrelated to their drug problem (Frois 2009). This means that for Carla, the apparent dysfunctionality implied when considering the lives of two children who are brought up by two parents with active drug habits—and later also simultaneously imprisoned—was not acknowledged as such.

On her first conviction, Carla was caught with 10 grams of cocaine and charged with possession and intent to distribute. Sentenced to six years in prison, even today she could not understand why the judge had been so tough. Carla complained that "she [the judge] didn't even give me a second chance, after all I was a first-time offender", even though strictly speaking it wasn't the first time that she had been arrested for drug possession. She served only half of the six-year sentence, and in that period she went through detox, she worked, and benefited from home leaves before being released on parole.

Regarding this first stay in prison, Carla commented that it was not so severe, because there were fewer rules than nowadays: "We could have all the food we wanted brought in, we could use the phone for as long as we pleased, and the visits were also more frequent, it was different." She added that the experience had little effect on her, since it was "a short period, so I didn't take it too seriously, besides which I was younger, so I didn't feel it so deeply. It was almost just a good chance to get cleaned up and recover, it was a breeze."

Shortly after being released, Carla resumed her drug use. In less than a year she was also back dealing drugs. She blamed the "bad companies" for her behavior, admitting that she had thought she was cured and could control her drug use. As for the trafficking, Carla explained that she was aware of the danger of being arrested again at any moment. Nevertheless, she was willing to take the risk: "It was the thrill of the whole thing—finding the supplier and then doing the transport—it just stirred something deep within in me!" With another son born in the meantime, her time of freedom did not last long. Two years into her parole, she was tried again for drug-related crimes, this time having been caught with 15 grams of heroin. Her case file implicated 12 other people, and besides the conviction for this new offence (five and a half years), she accumulated the time of her parole violation. Thus, she was now serving a total nine years of imprisonment at Odemira. Her partner was also convicted (serving a 10-year prison sentence on charges of theft and robbery), so they were back once again in the same situation, now with another child left to care for, with both parents in prison.

This time, the most difficult aspect of being imprisoned was the feeling that she had no one to confide in, no one that was "close" to her. Occasionally she talked with her mother on the phone or wrote her a letter, but there was no one that she felt she could share her daily life with. On the one hand, Carla claimed to be glad of being in a small prison such as Odemira: it was relatively quiet and safe; there was a good atmosphere with the prison officers; there was work, and it was a drug-free environment, which protected her against relapse. But despite all these arguments and articulated discourse aimed at bringing out positive features which she found necessary to bring meaning to her experience, in the course of my visits to Odemira, I witnessed a transformation in Carla's spirit. As months went by, she gradually became more and more subdued, and even guards would comment: "Sometimes we even forget she's here." As her sentence progressed, Carla realized that she was changing as a person, to the point where she claimed not to recognize herself any longer.

Stroving to perceive this transformation as somewhat beneficial, at the same time she could not help feeling that something inside her "was dying". She assumed that before imprisonment she used to be "suborn", "cranky" and "impulsive", but after all these years she had changed: no longer imposed her will on others permanently, because now she could admit perhaps she might not always be right about something; no longer questioned rules because she knew that she would not get her way. Now she preferred to stay in "her little corner", talking as little as possible, because the lack of trust and bonds she felt to exist amongst inmates told her it was the best she could do. Carla summarized the effect of her long imprisonment in one sentence: "Now I am a submissive person. If they [referring to prison staff] tell me to do something, I do it and I don't ask why."

Thus, her apparent calm, passiveness, and obedience were the visible outcome of incarceration combined with the absence of face-to-face contact with outside friends or relatives. Even though she had voluntarily applied for transfer to Odemira, she had not seen her daughter, or anyone else, in over two years. Distance and economic impediments dictated it, so all she could do was to wait for her sentence to trickle away. The last conversation we had was precisely about this apathy and how she felt she was living what she considered to be a "psychological limbo". She had already served the whole term of her first sentence, and had just begun her second. This process had had an almost anesthetic effect on her. She could finally start to envisage the "end", even if it was still far off. Time could now be counted down, and the feeling that something had been finally set in motion seemed to introduce an extra element of anxiety, which was starting to have an effect on her. The way she described the relationship she had with the woman who had been dividing the cell with her for over a year is revealing of the kind of *shared solitude* she experienced:

For instance, there are two of us in the cell, and we are both alike, so we do not talk much. We get along fine, but there's not much need for talking. She likes to escape into her books, or watching TV, and I have my radio, and my books too... We've gotten used to our routine, to our rhythms. When there's something to talk about, we sort it out and go on with our things. In the morning we both leave the cell together—I go to my work in the kitchen and she goes for a shower—and we only see each other again at the end of the day. Sometimes we'll talk a little bit, but pretty soon we'll be in our beds.

This management of everyday cell-life, of an intimate cohabitation made up of silences, routines and respect for the other's space, very typical of the life in total institutions such as it was described by Goffman (1961), was in many respects replicated in other prisons (male and female) that I had already visited (Frois 2016). In fact, it can be described as a kind of forced intimacy through cohabitation, significantly different from voluntary intimate cohabitation in that it is not based, nor does it imply, maintaining or fostering bonds of friendship and trust. A poem written by one inmate for the prison newsletter expressed these feelings of solitude, longing and grief:

> ...*Thoughts*...
> Between walls and bars/my life is spent/at the prison of Odemira/the stage of torment/where my life is spent/my soul draining out/from the day I walked in/ nothing left to do but endure/ for how long I don't know
> The accounts I have heard/I will confide to you/ The pain withstood/is ours to tell/Our freedom lost/is nothing new/But it's the distance that consumes us//
> In visits and letters/we drown our sorrow/and find our strength/from those who treat us with love//
> Anxiety and grief/in all gazes/turned into smiles/to help them bear/ obliviousness/separation perhaps/ from loved ones who sometimes/erase us from their hearts//
> It's very tough I can assure you/to be in reclusion/it's a story in our lives/ much more than a lesson.

In the case of recidivist inmates, the effects of imprisonment were, if anything, even more severe. They usually referred to now being "really feeling the prison", meaning that as a result of their past experience, added to the fact that they were older now and thus physically and psychologically less resilient, they had gained an awareness and ability to anticipate, which made them dread the path ahead—the strictness of rules, or the solitude and distance from relatives, for instance. Deolinda, with a story of drug use that started at the age of 18, and now on her third prison term, illustrates this particular experience of imprisonment. Deolinda starts by recounting the crimes she committed, the trial process and sentence applied in her first "sojourn" at Odemira:

> My first time in prison I had 72 counts of theft, and I got four and a half years here at Odemira. I didn't have children back then, and my partner wasn't into drugs. We had been together for many years, and on my first home leave we decided to have a child. Eventually I was granted an early release half way through my sentence. I was pregnant, and I left prison shortly before my son was born. After some time, I started doing drugs again, and soon I was back stealing, swindling, trafficking, and so on. These crimes gave rise to several criminal charges: first a two-year suspended sentence for a minor offence, and later a three-year probation for something else. Finally, after the last charge, which was for drug trafficking, the court added all the convictions, and the resulting cumulative punishment came down to an eight-year sentence.

Deolinda was 40 years old at the time we spoke, and as she tried to explain what had changed since the first time she had been imprisoned at Odemira, she specifically mentioned how "easy" the first time had been when compared to how much she was "feeling the prison" now:

> The first time around I didn't feel the weight of prison, it was easygoing; I had visits from my family, from my friends; I took courses, I worked, it went by in a jiffy. Now it's very different. I didn't have children then, and that's one of the things I feel terrible about, because my boy really needs me. I don't have my mother, and there's no other woman who can care for him. And also the prison system is different now, it's stricter. Beforehand any friend who came to visit would be let in, whereas now only family visits are allowed. When it's not immediate family, a distant cousin for instance, it can't be on weekends, it has to be on a weekday. We used to be allowed 2, 3, 4, 5 phone calls a day, whenever we needed. Not now. We can have one call a day and only for five minutes… so gradually we also start losing touch.

5 The Effects of Imprisonment

Some changes introduced nationwide in Portuguese prison facilities in 2013 were having strong impact on the daily lives of the inmate population, especially for recidivist inmates, who went back into a system that they found to be much stricter by contrast to their prior experience, prison now really emerged as "a punishment".

For first-time inmates, who had no point of comparison—and knew about those changes only through the accounts of other inmates—the increased seclusion from the outside world was felt as a negative, but on the other hand they had no expectations otherwise; they had been "introduced" to their status as inmates with those limitations, rules, and schedules. One of the inmates commented, "In here we are like children again, with a time to eat, a time to bathe, a time for bed". Deolinda's discourse is well worth our further attention. After all, if those changes were so negative, why would she say "this suffering will do me good"?

> One day we'll have to go back into society, to freedom, and if we ever think of committing a crime again, we'll think better. Right now I'm really feeling this time in prison; feeling the distance from my family; there are many more rules, but in a certain sense that's just as well. Even though my suffering is greater, it will help me when I go back free… I haven't had any problems. I can go up to an officer, get things off my chest, and they listen to us. We have more empathy with some people than others, but there are several officers whom I can to talk to about my life, and they listen to me, give me advice. Besides, it's a tiny prison, so we get more opportunities, and it's easier to reach the warden.

Despite Deolinda, like Carla and several other inmates, having not built bonds of friendship in prison (Odemira confirms the dictum reproduced in other facilities that "in prison there are no friends, just good comrades"), she faced the separation from family, the solitude and grief, as an opportunity to reach the psychological and physical stability that she had been unable to find on the outside. This is perhaps one of the most paradoxical aspects of Odemira prison, considering the smallness of the environment in which its residents live. I gradually became aware of the phenomenon by observing how inmates interacted or, inversely, how they avoided each other, within the spaces available to them. In other words, sharing reclusion does not in any way result in greater proximity or sense of community.

> We rarely have any quarrels here; whenever something does arise, it comes as a surprise. There's the adage women don't get along well, but it's not the case here. I share a cell with four other women, and we all get along fine. It's not a matter of liking or disliking any of them; I just have to accept them. I wouldn't like to be by myself, it makes me uneasy, but maybe I'd prefer to be in a cell for two. In here we forget each other's crimes, what any of us have done; we eventually forget about it. At first, there's always going to be some gossip, or the odd remark, but after a while it stops, and we end up losing sight of certain things. Who am I to judge anybody? I also made mistakes. The fact that we are a small group also helps to minimize squabbles.

Regardless of expressions of solidarity or camaraderie that may manifest itself at certain moment, the preservation of privacy is overwhelmingly more present in the discourse of inmates regarding their interaction with others in this living space.

The pain and suffering marking their life experiences do not become a source of bonding or empathy with fellow inmates, even in cases where they claimed to have strong friendships (here we have to exclude those cases of inmates who are also relatives, which in Odemira applied only to the gypsy women). It becomes clear, for instance, that while committing a crime is the common denominator among all those locked up in a prison—"If we're here, it's because we've all done something"—nevertheless, it is kept in the background of topics discussed.

Criminal activities are rarely told in the first person (as in "I did this or that"), but instead arise indirectly in conversations about related topics, such as the discussion described in the previous chapter around the judicial process, the trial appearances and the legal counsel. There were very few occasions on which I witnessed inmates openly discussing their crimes, their motivations or the circumstances of their imprisonment amongst themselves. During our conversations (where the majority disclosed these very same past stories) they explained this was somehow a forbidden subject, and said that their enquiries never went beyond the initial question: "What are you here for?"

One of the women, convicted for having strangled her partner with an electric cord during a fight, claimed: "I revealed the reason for being sent to prison, but I didn't go into the details, you see? It's nobody else's business!" Stigma and shame, on the one hand, and on the other hand self-protection from criticism and judgement, dictated the general attitude towards other inmates' pasts.

There is yet a more profound reason for this closure than merely avoiding the comments and gossip of others. While we may interpret this silencing around the criminal deed as a means of managing one's identity and the stigma attached to crime and imprisonment (Goffman 1961), it is also a means to forget the past, or at least to obviate its overwhelming presence. In other words, refusing to talk about their crimes, or sharing their past with other inmates, enables them to bring normalcy to an everyday life that requires a constant effort and is inevitably disturbed by contact with outside interference—whether in the form of visits, telephone conversations or any situation left pending outside but which they feel a responsibility to solve.

More than the criminal deed itself, what these women have in common is their confinement, their impotence to deal with situations and decisions occurring beyond their reach, and for which they have to rely on the meddling of others. Bearing this in mind, it becomes clearer that as much security, stability and predictability prison routines may bring to everyday life, there is always going to be an underlying source of anguish and distress, which may surface at any moment, triggered by a letter from a relative bearing bad news, or by a visitor who didn't show up, or a fight with a companion over the telephone, or by a lawyer delivering an adverse court decision.

Virginia was another woman who admitted this time around prison was "taking its toll". At 45, she had been transferred to Odemira from a central women's prison where she had been sent three years before for crimes of theft and robbery perpetrated with a male partner. Having married at 20, and having only a primary education, she had been employed in several factories doing unskilled work. During her first years of marriage, and while her children were little, she also took on jobs as a cleaning lady in an old people's home. She was already in her thirties when she started to use drugs occasionally, and had left the father of her children.

When I met her at Odemira, she was already on her fourth prison term; this time convicted for assault, robbery and aggravated theft:

> My husband and I got separated eleven years ago. Then I met another man and I lived with him for two years. He was a cocaine user, and after a while I started using as well. He asked me to start "dating" [prostitute herself], and I did it for him. That's when we both got arrested for other things and sent to prison. I was sentenced to three and a half years, served two and was released on probation with a suspended sentence. After four months I hooked up again with the same crowd and I started stealing again. At the time I was living at my mother's house, and I was doing ok; I don't know what got into me.

The crimes that led to this fourth sentence were in line with her previous convictions, following a similar modus operandi, this time with a new partner who was also a drug user. Virginia described how together they held up stores, coffee shops, gas stations, robbed old pensioners; but she made a point of telling there was never "any blood or violence." Once inside a grocery store or a small supermarket, for instance, Virginia would "ask the lady at the store [usually a single employer or owner] for some sliced ham or cheese, and I would follow her to the cold meats section. Meanwhile my partner took the money from the register, cigarette cartons or liquor bottles or whatever was at hand at the counter". They used this method for several months before they were finally caught by the police, presented to a pre-trial and identified by victims and witnesses. This fourth conviction (which, in her opinion, resulted in a heavier penalty due to her recidivism in the same crime and method) was added to the probation period she had violated for previous crimes.

> I am very ashamed of it all. If I wasn't in here my son wouldn't have died. I'm quite down, and I have no one to confide in. Sometimes I talk with the guards, but I am a very reserved person. Before my son's death I was more lively; I worked, I took pride in my cell, not any more. Now I can't be bothered with any of it. Over there [the central prison she had been transferred from] we were over 500 women, and here we're only 50 or so; it's different. I'm only waiting to be released. I hope this time I'm leaving for good, and never return to these houses. I live with my pain.

Totally clad in black, she imbued our conversations with the grief for the death of one of her sons, an incident that occurred after she had been imprisoned. The boy had been found missing, and his body was later found in an advanced stage of decay. The circumstances of death were never fully explained, and it was never established whether it was accidental or criminal. The news came as a tremendous shock to Virginia. She blamed herself, believing that if she had not been in prison, she would have been there to watch over him and he would never have met his death that way. At the central prison where Virginia was held it was decided she should be transferred to a smaller facility, where she could be more closely followed, both by prison staff and even other inmates. When she received the news of his death, Virginia had made two suicide attempts, and posed a great risk given the prison's single-cell policy. Since she had already served a previous sentence at Odemira, therefore familiar with the prison and its working—she actually met up with inmates she had known from her first stay—she was transferred there. Now she shared a cell with three other women and felt "more accompanied".

During our first conversation, which took place shortly after her transference, Virginia went over the same thing again and again: "I still can't believe it, Miss Catarina, I can't believe this has happened. In my mind he is still alive, and they're all lying. I've never seen the body, never seen it with my own eyes, so I just cannot believe it." Virginia almost never mentioned the crimes she had been convicted for, even as she recounted that she had never had any formal job, and her life had been spent from place to place, staying with her mother—who was now incapacitated—or with one of the partners with whom she did her robberies. From her previous stays at Odemira she recalled knowing some of the "older" inmates, but found the prison "very different", with "many new rules". It was a very small prison when compared to the central prisons she had been in: "You come across all sorts of people here, but it's nothing like the place I was in before: people who had killed their grandparents, their parents, their children! Everything…there was little bit of everything there."

As the months went by, Virginia began to accept what had happened to her son, and it became the focus of her conversations; her absence while he was alive, the fact that she couldn't follow the events leading up to the discovery of his body. She tried to remind herself she still had another son, and a granddaughter, and she would join them when she got out. This other son, who worked as a mechanic, was "very sensible", and almost as a way to strengthen her resolve, she recalled how he had already warned her: "Mum, if you get into trouble again, I don't ever want to see you." On her part, Virginia stressed how hard this sentence was on her, "I'm never again letting drugs into my life."

At Odemira, and only a few days after admission, she had started working in the prison kitchen, and whenever she felt depressed she recurred to a guard to confide in, although she was also being treated by a psychiatrist and medicated for depression. Her plans for release were to go and live with her son and stay home to look after her granddaughter: "I've learnt my lesson, I've suffered enough."

The "Benefits" of Imprisonment

Rules, procedures and routines were apparently valued by inmates as important in bringing order to their everyday life. The predictability, or even monotony they promoted seemed to give inmates the necessary time to think about their past, their family, but more importantly, about themselves as subjects endowed with an agency. In their words, they explained how the deprivation of freedom gave them a chance for self-awareness, which had been impossible beforehand. They rediscovered their personal preferences—what they actually liked or didn't like—learning to make their own decisions, taking care of their belongings, and all of it "freed", as they put it, from the interference or pressure of others—spouses, children, state institutions (as social workers, for example). As Helen Codd confirms, "for women who are using drugs or living chaotic lifestyles prior to their incarceration, imprisonment can give them a form of 'time out' or breathing space." (2008: 130).

Despite the limited offer, many inmates considered the available work, education and free-time activities as opportunities meant for their own benefit improvement. Some of the accounts testifying to this diversity of possibilities were written down by the inmates themselves (or written for them in some cases) and published in the 3rd edition of the prison newsletter *Between Margins*:

> As soon as I arrived I was employed in the laundry room, where I still work. For a while I also did a part-time "packaging". Meanwhile I went back to school, to finish 4th grade [...] working is very good for me; it keeps my mind occupied and distracted from the way my life has turned out, but it also allows me not to rely on money coming from the outside.
>
> Two months after I arrived I was called to work in the boxes [...] A few months later, I was given the chance to work full time doing the cleaning, but I also kept my part-time. With these two jobs I can put more money on the side in my savings account, for when I get out. I am also studying, finishing 9th grade.
>
> I started work in packaging 10 days after I arrived. For a while it was all I did, but in the meantime one of the inmates in the sewing service was released and given that I had experience in the area I was offered to replace her. The work in packaging brings me some extra cash, but it's the sewing that really fulfills me, because I love this kind of work. I also love cooking, so I enrolled in cooking course.

As these vignettes illustrate, to the majority of women the activities they engaged with in prison were a range of opportunities: being able to study again (in some cases for the first time) was something that for different reasons had been impossible outside. For many of them, the work they did in prison (and even the wages they earned) was the first they'd had in years, and even the free time they now enjoyed was almost a kind of liberation from the demands and concerns they were subjected to while in freedom. In other words, the privations, solitude and anguish went hand in hand with the possibility of a different life opening up to them. In this context, the prison officers, rather than embodying an extension of the authoritarian roles personified earlier by the family, companions or husbands, were actually considered as accessible, understanding women, ready to listen and give counsel.

This perspective on the benefits of prison cannot be properly interpreted unless we consider the material and psychological conditions in which these women lived prior to their imprisonment. For those women who did not have a drug addiction, the interruption of their former lives could be said to have been less stressful precisely due to its predictability. The focus on work, on saving money to rebuild their lives once they were returned to freedom, was part of the discourse assimilated. Though not explicitly declared in political, legal or penal spheres, prison's assistentialist function is unquestionably present in the lives of inmates, not only of the women at Odemira, but of many other male and female prison facilities across the country.

Following this line of thought, when Thomas Ugelvik discusses the extension and amplitude of what is commonly described within the context of the penitentiary world as the "northern exceptionalism", claiming that "Nordic prisons and correctional systems are understood as integrated parts of the strong, inclusive and ambitious Nordic welfare states" (2016: 389), we realize that this case confirms the perceptions of inmates and officers themselves concerning the positive aspects of prison.

In the context of her study on inmates' families, Megan Comfort's findings also unequivocally demonstrate the absence of care and assistance mechanisms for women facing financial problems while their male partners are in prison. With this frame in mind, the author explains the "collateral-consequences perspective and the integrative functions of the prison-as-peculiar-social-service coexist, and indeed operate distinctively in different domains of a woman's life, depending on her socioeconomic standing and relationship circumstances" (2007: 18).

Hence, for example, inmates with a problem of drug addiction considered that Odemira didn't merely help them through the withdrawal process—unlike most other prison facilities Odemira is free of drug contraband—it also provided them with proper medical care (a methadone program is available), and all the necessary conditions for full recovery: clean shelter, wholesome food and hygiene facilities. When these women express their repulsion for old habits such as smoking the cigarette butts discarded by others, or recall the things they used to do for money (prostitution, robbery, etc.), they are acknowledging the transformation taking place within themselves, even if involuntarily.

In other words, while initially imprisonment is something they would all wish to avoid, it soon seems to develop into an opportunity for detox and as time goes by, it starts to be considered as a chance to break with the need to live according to the demands of their addiction (Frois 2009). Although prison cannot take the place of a therapeutic community, some women even considered it to have an additional advantage: they could not escape or simply choose to walk out the door, as they had done in previous treatment care facilities. In here, they explain, they would spend one, two, five years, away from drugs, the necessary time to really have a chance at starting over.

On this particular problematic, we should note that most Portuguese prison facilities fail to provide successful drug rehabilitation programs. Notwithstanding drug substitution treatment programs are available in most prisons, few of them have specialized therapeutic support, the exception being those prisons that have the so-called drug-free wings (usually small units separated from the main cell-blocks). The lack of specialized staff to follow up on the initial withdrawal process, results in high levels of relapse. Even inmates who spend several years without any contact with drugs are easily drawn back to their old habits soon after release, both to their drug use as to their criminal activities. This is what happens in Odemira, and one of the cases causing more outrage among the inmates was related precisely to a widespread perception that "some people don't learn anything from prison [and] blow all the chances given to them".

Marina, a 35-year-old inmate on her third prison term, was one such example. With a history of drug abuse started at the age of 16, she was convicted twice for possession and armed robbery. On both occasions she was held in remand at Odemira for nine months before being released on probation with suspended sentences. During those periods in prison she would detox and manage to stay clean, and as far as the prison's directing board and correctional treatment staff could tell, was apparently committed to "start over" a new life—working in the prison, maintaining healthy habits and overall showing good behavior. Even so, after the first release many predicted her relapse, so the second time she was sent to Odemira for the same crimes, almost everyone was positively baffled to see her being released again after another more nine months.

I followed part her second term at Odemira, and I also witnessed her return, when during one of my visits there she came up to me cheerfully exclaiming, "I'm back!" In a period of just over two months, Marina had left and returned. In the time she spent outside, Marina resumed her drug use, went back to dealing drugs and was arrested by the police a few hours after holding up and assaulting a shop owner. Marina stated she was "a person with a disease", distressed by the fact that even though she seemed to be doing well while in prison (meaning she managed to stay clean) "as soon as I find myself out there I go back to the same." When Marina's case came to trial, as usually occurs in such situations, she would now have to serve both her suspended sentences, which added up a total of eight years, in addition to the sentence set for her latest conviction. The other inmates were shocked and appalled to see her return. Their sneers—"she must like it here, coming back all the time!"—conveyed the idea they thought Marina did not value the prison or the "freedom" she had been granted. In other words, Marina represented all those who don't "learn" anything from being imprisoned and should therefore be kept there until they really started to "feel the prison" and the transformations that only a long period without freedom can bring.

In the same line of thought, one of the officers confided in me how frustrated cases like this made her feel, and she didn't mean Marina's drug relapses or behavior patterns but rather the courts' repeated decision to order her release. Some guards even considered such short-term convictions as ineffective and could not bring about the necessary transformation in a person's behavior. They claimed that less than five years of prison time was virtually useless. On this point, they seemed to concur with most prisoners' own recollection of their first convictions, and how little impact it had on their lives, mostly due to their shortness. Nevertheless, it is precisely this first-hand experience which raises the questions one may ask: Firstly, why is prison the place where some women find stability? As we confirm this circumstance, and considering prison as a kind of end-of-the-line solution, we are led to question the role and performance of the institutions that should have come between these women and such an extreme outcome. Secondly, and related to this, we may conversely ask to what extent can imprisonment be conceived as an extension of the welfare state system?

References

Codd, Helen. 2008. *In the Shadow of Prison. Families, Imprisonment and Criminal Justice*. London and New York: Routledge.
Comfort, Megan. 2008. *Doing Time Together: Forging Love and Family in the Shadow of the Prison*. Chicago: Chicago University Press.
Frois, Catarina. 2009. *The Anonymous Society. Identity, Transformation and Anonymity in 12 Step Associations*. Newcastle upon Tyne: Cambridge Scholars Press.
———. 2016. Close Insecurity. Shifting Conceptions of Security in Prison Confinement. *Social Anthropology* 24 (3): 309–323.
Goffman, Erving. 1961. *Asylums: Essays on the Social Situation of Mental Patients and Other Inmates*. New York: Anchor Books.
Haney, Lynne. 2013. Motherhood as Punishment: The Case of Parenting in Prison. *Signs: Journal of Women in Culture and Society* 39 (1): 105–130.
Padovani, Natália Corazza. 2013. Confounding Borders and Walls: Documents, Letters and the Governance of Relationships in São Paulo and Barcelona Prisons. *Vibrant—Virtual Brazilian Anthropology* 10 (2). Brasília: ABA. Available at http://www.vibrant.org.br/issues/v10n2/natalia-corazza-padovani-confounding-borders-and-walls/
Sykes, Gresham. 1958. *The Society of Captives. A Study of a Maximum Security Prison*. Princeton: Princeton University Press.
Ugelvik, Thomas. 2016. Prisons as Welfare Institutions? Punishment and the Nordic Model. In *Handbook on Prisons*, ed. Yvonne Jewkes, Jamie Bennett, and Ben Crew, 2nd ed., 388–402. London and New York: Routledge.

6

Tension, Authority, Rights

Although inmates may find daily life in prison frustrating—"It's always the same, days are all alike"—it seems to be precisely this cadence that brings the stability and predictability which ultimately help to make the experience of prison more endurable. Everything is structured and planned for in order to follow a certain order determined and imposed by the institution (thus largely inhibiting subjects from their autonomy and agency). For someone who is just an observer of this movement, ignorant of its underlying motivations and intentions, the image that transpires of life in prison resembles a wave-like pattern, swaying to an apparently unprompted and natural rhythm.

When this movement is broken for some reason, the unyielding force governing it reveals its rationale, since usually it is only summoned to deal with antagonistic movements arising from relationships established under its umbrella, in the form of complaints, protests, conflicts, instability, frustration, and anxiety. As Foucault (1995) notes, prison is a place where bodies are disciplined, habits are shaped and where the "wanting" and the "having" are ordered.

Bearing in mind the overwhelming function of monotony within prison environments, revealed in the perpetuation of habits and movements, it was with increased interest I witnessed two different events, which developed over the course of one of the weeks I was staying at Odemira, and which somehow disrupted the normal order of things. At an initial moment, I noticed something was slightly different from usual, although I could not identify its cause. The only recent change I could see were the two new admissions—one woman who had entered on remand two days earlier after being caught at the airport smuggling drugs, and the other convicted of the homicide of her male partner—but both of them seemed to have adjusted very quickly to their new environment, and I saw them mingling with their fellow inmates and going about their daily chores uneventfully. Thus, the feeling of unsettlement I perceived could not originate from any disturbance introduced by the presence of recent entries—a phenomenon which is not uncommon when a new inmate is admitted or when remand and convicted inmates are brought together in the same facility, as was the case here.[1] Something was definitely off-balance, and it was both audible and visible. The women seemed angry, their semblance stern and somber. There was a droning sound of constant mumbling in the halls, coming from inmates clustered in small groups of three or four by their cell doors, and talking in hushed voices.

This week I witnessed a scene I had never seen before, and I wasn't even sure of its development. At first I was even perplexed by the inmates' joyful outburst when the chief of guards entered in the cell hall carrying a load of toilet paper rolls. One of the inmates grabbed one of the rolls and held on to it with delight, pretending to be stealing a valuable treasure. Immediately the word spread around, summoning all the women from the courtyard to come inside. One of the officers sat behind a small table and started calling out each inmate by name to the line of inmates that had formed before her. Toilet paper was being handed out; and each person was entitled to two rolls, for which they had to sign a form confirming reception. Some of the women in line collected their own rolls, but also signed off for fellow inmates, either because they were unable to attend—caught taking a shower at the time, for instance—or simply because they were illiterate. It was a swift and orderly process, and everyone seemed quite contented.

Addressing no one in particular, I asked around if the two rolls were distributed weekly, to which the women reacted with some surprise and veiled smiles. The prison officer in charge of this duty immediately replied: "Monthly!" They must have read the disbelief in my expression, because another officer immediately cut in: "They can buy more if they need". To me, two rolls of toilet paper for a whole month seemed by any standards insufficient for anyone's daily needs (woman, man or child), and at that moment it didn't yet occur to me maybe some of these women could not afford to buy more (Frois 2016). I'd have thought a volume for each (approximately 10 rolls) was probably more reasonable, but it wasn't my place to make any comments, especially taking into account that these matters were decided by the Directorate-General for Prison Services. In other words, all prison facilities had to comply with the standards it set down regarding basic necessities, such as the number of meals, essential items for inmates with no financial means (clothing, hygiene products, etc.), and so the director and guards at Odemira had no responsibility or interference in the criteria determining how much toilet paper inmates were entitled to.

A few hours later—mid-afternoon—the women lined up again and more signing was done. This time around the prison guard was assisted by another staff member, the treasurer, who had an Excel spreadsheet with several columns and numbers; it was time for money withdrawals, the canteen. Each inmate could request a sum to be deduced from their personal accounts for "shopping" expenses for the next fortnight. Requests varied within €5 to €20, according to each woman's budget, but all of them seemed to have the same question: "Is the money here yet?" The treasurer gave the same reply each time: "Not yet, but you can ask the director if she can grant you a voucher".

Noticing my ignorance, another officer explained me how this procedure functioned. Inmates have different sources on income—work, pension, family contributions. From the salary they receive from prison work, half is put aside into a reserve fund made available on release, and the other half is put into their personal account for current expenses, which they can access every two weeks. On this day, the prison administration was facing three different situations: a small minority of inmates had money from their pensions or saved up from the previous weeks, another group had the salary (or not, as we are going to see) from their different prison jobs—cleaning, laundry, kitchen, and so forth—and there were still those who had money due from their work with exterior firm entities, namely, from the fruit packaging and labeling working protocol.

The question "Is the money here yet?" ensued from a problem that had already occurred in the payday a fortnight ago, when the prison warden realized the money from inmate's salaries had not been duly transferred to its account. In order to purchase needed items—coffee, cigarettes, shower gel—inmates had to rely on an exceptional authorization from the warden to withdraw a voucher from their own reserve fund, a situation that legally required special permission. As they put in their requests on the day I was there, some inmates seized the opportunity to question the treasurer about their savings, trying to know how much money they had saved.

From those who managed to obtain an answer, I realized this savings account depended largely on the kind of work each inmate did, but also on their prison time—the most veteran naturally having more savings. As the treasurer tried to answer everyone, she entreated inmates to sign their own documents rather than ask others to sign for them, while she protested "If you go to school here, at least you should have learnt how to spell your own name already!" A certain frustration was perceptible throughout this process on every side. However, for a mere outside observer, the proceeding seemed to be ordinary and simple enough, and I could not fully understand why the officers seemed so apprehensive, and the inmates so upset.

The general tension continued to build up as the day progressed. Inmates didn't understand how it was possible that their salaries had not been transferred to the prison bank account, and as they discussed the matter amongst themselves, gradually became more outraged with the situation. In the period between dinner and lockdown, there was a noisy atmosphere in the cellblock. Inmates joined in groups, and for once I couldn't hear the usual laughter or see anyone playing around. Not even those women who were known for their good spirits seemed to escape the general impatience.

When I asked one of them what was going on and why everyone was so upset, she replied: "No smokes, doc, and when smokes run out, this whole place goes nuts!" In other words, inmates were worried and it wasn't just about that day. They were becoming aware of what was at stake. The money hadn't arrived, and while some had run out of cigarettes, everyone had something they needed to buy, and the only chance for it in the next two weeks would be the following day. They expected payment and, if it didn't come, they would be dependent on a less than certain permission from the director to withdraw a new voucher. In the event that none of these solutions came through, there was another 15 days to wait, which some of these women clearly refused to consider as an option, since it would mean two weeks without cigarettes, coffee, chocolates, or hygiene products. Moreover, this was not an isolated event, and over the past few months had been increasingly frequent. Inmates employed directly by the prison facility felt particularly cheated and resentful. The underlying question seemed to be: how could the "State" fail to pay them?

The following morning, the treasurer returned to the cellblock bearing not just another Excel spreadsheet but bad news as well: the only money to be distributed came from those payments "the firm" had sanctioned by phone. The Directorate-General, however, had not released the funds to the inmates' salaries. In other words, anyone depending solely on this income would be left helpless, since the prison warden had not given permission for further withdrawals from the reserve funds. Inmates in this situation would thus be unable to buy anything until further notice. This was shocking news. The persistence of these problems in recent times had left even the more prudent inmates (who manage their money cautiously) in a difficult situation. To know that money belonging to them was being withheld for administrative reasons was frustrating, especially considering that some of these women had considerable savings (one inmate had saved up to €3000 during her time in prison).

I remained nearby listening to the conversation between the inmates and the treasurer, who calculated the meager sums each one was entitled to (in most cases even less than one euro). One woman, Diana, was particularly furious. The previous day she had been in a terrible mood. She was having her period and had run out of sanitary towels; she had been waiting for this day to buy more.

Without money, she had to ask the officers to dispense her some, an even more humiliating situation because instead of a box they would give her a couple of towels, telling her "to make them last" as if it was something she could control. "It's very embarrassing" Diana said, not believing how the Directorate-General, the *State*, could be three months behind paying the salaries of working inmates.

She found this inadmissible, and said so openly to the treasurer, who was clearly bothered by this confrontation while trying to explain: "You are absolutely right, but there is nothing I can do, it's not up to me", or "You have to wait, you'll just have to be patient".

Diana got increasingly agitated, interrupting the explanations, raising her voice louder each time and making her case more forcefully. At one point, the guard who was present decided to intervene. She told Diana that "everyone there" (meaning all the guards and administrative staff, including the director) were aware that Diana was "going through a difficult time" since she had received an unexpected sentence conviction whose seriousness had not gone unnoticed. The officer argued that, nevertheless, she was way out of line and could not address a member of the staff in such terms, and she was only doing her job. Diana was not convinced, and continued quarreling, but eventually took her distress out to the courtyard.

I found out later that the treasurer had returned to her office quite shaken up by the affair. She kept pointing out that it was not up to her to decide when those sums were released, and did not understand why inmates could not understand it, saying to herself: "The money didn't come, and I'm sorry but they'll just have to wait."

In any case, none of this concealed the more serious budget problems the prison was facing, unable to pay inmates who were ultimately their own responsibility. In fact, at the same time the director was dealing with a different, though related problem. The prison had certain funds allocated for specific expenses that had to be unfailingly applied before the end of the week, namely on the repair and maintenance of the vehicles used by the services, from the prison transport vehicles to the warden's official car. I asked myself why the money could only be spent on one particular department (considering these were not urgent expenses), instead of using it to solve a more pressing problem which was having such a serious effect on the prison's overall atmosphere.

It was only months later that I grasped the full extent of the significance of this day's events, and the frequency with which it happened, not just at

Odemira, but in most (if not all) Portuguese prison facilities. When the new Director-General of Prison Services took office in 2016—a position he resumed after some years of working as a court judge in the south of Portugal—there was a Parliament hearing held by the Committee on the Constitutional Affairs, Rights, Freedoms and Guarantees. The Director-General testified to the "most urgent" needs his team had identified within the Portuguese prison system, having reached an overpopulation of 130 %. He specifically mentioned the serious degradation of its facilities, with a list that went from collapsing roofs and electrical problems, to broken down bathrooms and doors with no locks. He gave the members of Parliament what he called a "bleak portrait" of the situation in which prison facilities were finding themselves, as well as the budget constraints faced by the Directorate-General itself to solve those same problems.

He also focused on a problem that reminded me of the episode I had witnessed in Odemira: the shortage of human and material resources afflicting the everyday running of these institutions, leading prison wardens to resort to ad hoc expedients—as in fact he had also needed to use in his capacity as Director-General—to solve unforeseen problems requiring immediate solution. These strategies to circumvent bureaucratic obstacles sometimes resulted in having the wardens themselves sit in the defendant's chair having to prove proper conduct, or in other words, to fight charges of fund diversion.

Therefore, it became clearer as to the kind of choice Odemira's director had to face on the day of the events described above. Either she ignored procedure to assuage the tension amongst her inmate population, or she followed the rules and risked an unpredictable escalation. For some weeks she had managed to avoid major trouble, but after three months she had run into a dead end. At the time the system was at a very delicate juncture, coinciding with the tenure of a new management team, and the implementation of some changes in regulations, which implied the suspension of bank transfers to several prison facilities. Consequently, all inmates whose revenue came from internal prison work were affected by this transitional phase while new rules were put into place. The existing money had to be used exclusively to cover those expenses and items already budgeted, and no exceptions—such as the one that arose during those past few weeks at Odemira—were to be made.

Returning to the day Diana decided to confront the prison treasurer, there was a moment at which the latter, running out of other explanations, finally said, "There's nothing we can do. The firm has already confirmed they would make the transfer today before 2 p.m., so those who do the fruit boxes will get paid, and the rest will not. Have you ever considered what it would be like if the Directorate-General simply stopped paying? It can happen, you know?" With this remark, Diana became even more indignant and upset: "That cannot happen! How can you say you don't know if they will pay? They have to! No one works for free; all workers are entitled to their salary. Do you work for free by any chance? I know my rights, lady!"

When the officer decided to interrupt this argument, she went up to Diana, and both of them stood chatting next to me for about 20 minutes. The officer said they all (referring to the prison staff) understood Diana's frustration, but she needed to see that it wasn't the treasurer's fault, since those kinds of decisions were not hers to make. The officer also advised Diana to moderate her tone; she had problems and everyone was trying to do their best to help her, but they couldn't allow her to take that tone, not with a staff member, guard, or fellow inmates for that matter. Seeing me there, the guard asked me if I would mind having a chat with Diana, "to see if she calms down a little bit, to let off some steam. It's actually lucky you're here. If you can have a word with her, it will probably do her some good."

The officer's request caught me by surprise—similar entreaties were more common coming from inmates—but I acknowledged the invitation. At this stage of my fieldwork, I was certain both guards and inmates were clear on the fact I was neither a psychologist nor social worker, but still inmates often sought out my help. When they wanted to "blow off steam", I seemed to be as good a confidant as anyone else, or perhaps in their eyes even a better one considering they used to say it was "good to talk with an outside person", someone who was neither a "colleague" nor an officer. Later on in the day, another guard would explain to me that Diana needed all the help she could get, considering the recent news of her conviction, which had been quite unexpected. In order to put this episode into perspective, and understand it wasn't an isolated event, it is important to provide a little background on Diana's case history. Perhaps this will give us a better idea that Diana's interaction with others (outside and inside prison) seemed almost to follow a kind of pattern.

Diana was a 40-year-old woman of Spanish nationality, who had been living in Portugal for over a decade. During this time, she had given birth to two children, one of which was now in a child care state institution (where he had been put at the age of seven), and the other (a three-year-old) was with the father, who had actually lived with Diana for a while. Having finished her secondary education in Spain, she had gone to Portugal "in search of adventure, without any plans". When her oldest son was four, he was flagged by his pre-school teachers and social workers as showing signs of parental negligence. Over the next two years the minor was institutionalized on three different occasions. Diana claimed that these evaluations had been the work of "malicious people" who, in her opinion, had wrongly interpreted certain facts as signs of neglect:

> I used to go out for a little drink at the end of the day, like everyone does, right? I knew if I left the kid home alone, it would be considered as mistreatment, so I always brought him along with me. They say [the neighbors who gave testimony during the trial] I used to get drunk, but that is a total lie. They made up that I bit him; how could anyone say that of a mother? It's all false. Later, one day the social assistant came to my house and took the boy. I called the home and they told me I could not speak with him, and I said to the social worker there: "Listen to me, lady, I'd do anything for my boy, even kill if necessary." So they charged me, and here I am. But I'm going to appeal, he's my son and no one can take him away from me.

Without a stable job and living as a single mother with her son, she didn't see anything wrong with her behavior, and thought that the whole affair was a scheme plotted by the social workers, the children's home and even the neighbors who testified against her. In the course of a trial lasting several months, and in light of her own son's declarations to the judge, she was subjected to psychiatric evaluations to establish her competency to stand trial.

The descriptions made by the social assistant who followed the case—the same one Diana threatened on the phone—as well as the minor's testimony, were confirmed by the medical reports. They revealed a history of physical and psychological abuse including things such as:

"several bite marks on the forehead, legs and buttocks", "attempts to asphyxiate the child holding a pillow over his face and sitting on it", besides various episodes described by neighbors, who saw Diana coming home drunk with her son having to help her home. The court had absolutely no doubt as to her guilt, and sentenced her to six years' imprisonment, as well as prohibiting her from contacting the minor until he reached the legal majority (a decision based on the child's own request to avoid any contact with his mother). During this period and since the child had no other known family besides Diana (the certificate registered him with father "unknown") he would be put in the care of state institutions.

During my visits to Odemira I had followed Diana closely, and therefore I already knew her to be constantly angry with everyone and everything, especially towards figures of authority, having now substituted the social workers who had taken away her custody of her son and the "mean" neighbors who testified against her, for the prison guards, correctional treatment staff and other inmates as the target of her rage. In other words, she thought no one understood she was being the victim of a tremendous injustice that seemed to have no end. Thus, depending on the day, I would find her either more actively anxious and annoyed, or a little more subdued and cooperative.

On the day she had the outburst against the treasurer, I went with her away from the prison block so we could talk privately in the room where I usually held one-to-one interviews, in the prison's administrative area. As we came in, she seemed to be slightly tearful, but as soon as we got talking, she quickly changed her countenance, remonstrating, telling me all the things she found were "wrong with the prison". She said that albeit I had been "inside", I could not see what was really going on: "It's not all smiles and contentment as you think. Yesterday you were there [in the refectory] and the warden showed up all cheerful, but it's not really what it's like". Even though I recognized the director's presence, whether during meals, prison block or courtyard, could induce some degree of formality, I had been there long enough to tell that the atmosphere in the refectory had been exactly the same as any other time. With or without the warden, there had been nothing unusual (either positive or negative) in that day's meal.

Diana didn't want to talk about the outcome of her conviction, and she indeed dismissed the subject, repeating once again the arguments about the social worker's malice. Instead, she preferred to take the opportunity to say that she had me there to complain that the prison wasn't offering her the "minimum conditions". That week she had her menstruation, and had to ask the guards for sanitary towels. Given that she had no money to buy toilet paper (and since she had quickly used up her two free rolls), she saved away the paper napkins at meals to use later when she went to the toilet. She protested that she had "started to work in the cleaning duty so she would not have to depend on anyone", and that she never asked other inmates for anything.

That was why she found it so unfair not to receive her salary. She claimed for dignity, arguing that she knew her rights; that she'd been living long enough in Portugal to know the law. The argument with the treasurer had been a result of frustration from having worked to afford her own things and was now being cheated out of them. Since Diana had cut off all relations with her family since she left her home town in Spain, and didn't want any kind of contact with the father of her other son, she could not even rely on any help from the outside. In short, Diana was set on making sure she "didn't need or depend on anyone", holding on to her autonomy and refusal to accept her precarious situation. Regarding the sentence, she was going to file an appeal to regain custody of her son, once again asserting that she would "even kill" for him.

Inmates' Rights

The events I had witnessed explained the tension of the atmosphere inside the prison block, especially evinced in the difference between the countenances of those who had managed to do their shopping and those who would have to wait another two weeks. In fact, the unrest caused by the problems with the treasurer not only did not subside, but actually became even more acute when some inmates had money to buy the items they needed, while others had to stand there patiently as they watched their mates taking the chocolate pie they had just bought to eat out in the courtyard.

The guards themselves could not avoid commenting on the situation, going as far as questioning how the whole affair had been handled. To begin with, they considered that no distinctions should be made between the different forms of payment, even if they did came from different sources. Secondly, they also distinguished between the different tasks performed by inmates, admitting that some work was "heavier" and more demanding, especially for those on kitchen duty, who had longer working hours. Without any pay, they couldn't be forced to work. They claimed that if the same thing happened to them, they would have already "turned everything upside down" and would refuse to work a single more minute until they got paid, while pointing out that the situation might give rise to problems they would be unable to control, such as debts amongst inmates and the resulting conflicts and arguments.

The officers even admitted that this kind of event might actually be harmful to the institution itself: "We are lucky because in here they are quiet, but in another prison this could lead to a riot, to serious problems in the population." Therefore, it was essential to take some action to prevent the current discontentment from going any further. This did not mean that they ignored the depth of the problem and how difficult it was to solve: while all the inmates who worked should certainly be entitled to a salary, in no way could inmates get the impression that outrage was an effective way to achieve their goal. Therefore, the officers had to impress upon the inmates that they could not "force" the warden to issue vouchers on their savings accounts as had been done other occasions. They knew that since this time the decision came directly from the Directorate-General, their only option was to maintain order inside the prison as best as they could.

That evening, in the queue for dinner, I saw one of the chief officers accompanying an inmate to her cell. When she came back and joined her colleague who was supervising the meal, she told us what had happened. The inmate had put in an "urgent request" to the warden asking for shampoo and soap. The officer went with her to check if the matter was really so urgent. She asked the woman to show her the bottle of shampoo, "which was still half full", and the soap, which was "still biggie and firm", leading her to conclude that it didn't merit an "urgent request". In other words, the chief officer judged and decided on the inmate's need to buy any more supplies of those products within the next few days, or if she could wait a couple of weeks. In this instance, and since this particular inmate shared a collective cell with other women, I couldn't figure out if she was worried that her shampoo and soap would run out, or if she was making the request on behalf of her cellmates, given that some of the women were amongst those who had not received any salary.

The officer's appraisal, and the act of checking itself, seemed to denote either a certain form of patronization, or at least a way of showing that she would not give in to what she considered a mere caprice—given the importance placed by the prison on its inmates "learning to manage their own resources", as the guard put it. She claimed not to understand these continual complaints and requests: "They have everything they need here: food, hot water, shelter, medicine, work. People with money can afford other luxuries, but prison assures them every necessity. If someone living outside doesn't have money for coffee or cigarettes, they can't buy them either, right?" The guard was implying that the prison was not obliged to provide for anything beyond what it already supplied for free: lodging, food, medical care, education and work. Everything else was superfluous. People should learn to administer their belongings and live sparingly, and she believed that only those who had "vices" usually gave way to that kind of unruly behavior.

The comparison with the "people outside" was fairly common discourse amongst some of the officers, who contrasted the comforts enjoyed by inmates in prison to the hardships faced by a segment of the general population outside, especially in the period following the economic and financial crisis of 2008 with the increasing rates of unemployment and poverty it produced (Lima 2016; Narotzky 2012; Rogan 2013). This comparison, between the "benefits" and "luxuries" enjoyed by inmates on the "inside", and the loss of rights and cutbacks faced by people on the "outside", despite less frequent in Odemira than in other prison facilities I visited (where the material and living conditions were severely worse), nonetheless gave expression to a very particular distinction between what should be considered necessity or accessory, between basic needs and what inmates can/may be deprived of besides freedom.

In addition to all the misconceptions at the root of such a comparison—insofar as inmates, just as anyone entrusted to a public institution (prison, hospital or school) are at the responsibility of the state—in this particular case inmates were not asking for anything more than overdue salaries. The prison institution was in breach of the "contract" it had made with the other party, and so their claims were, in their perspective, perfectly justified. Moreover, if we turn our attention to the episode of the toilet paper, or Diana's quarrel over the sanitary towels, we can see that the issue is not as straightforward as the chief officer presented it. While smoking and drinking coffee might be a matter of taste, there are other first necessity items besides a warm bath, three square meals and a bed to sleep in. Nothing could explain, for instance, that inmates were given household soap when their shower gel ran out, or that they had to use saved-up paper napkins when they didn't have any more toilet paper.

Before dinner was over, another inmate went up to one of the officers, saying she also needed to make an urgent request for personal hygiene products. The guard (a male) told her to put the request in writing and hand it in the next morning for processing. Next, he turned to me half joking, half serious, and commented: "Well, here's the kind of request I never got in 20 years of duty [in a major male facility in the north of Portugal]". Then he added, almost to himself: "When I come to think of it, men never ask us [officers] for anything. They just go up to another inmate and take what they need from them; even if it takes a little fighting, they sort it out by themselves!"

Exercising Authority

Next morning the routine was slightly different from what I had gotten used to so far. Despite having handed over my identification and checked my bag at the entrance locker, as always, I was made to wait at the front desk while a raid that was being conducted since 8 a.m. was concluded. This seemed a surprise; the previous day I had left the premises around 9 p.m. and no one had warned about that morning's event. Obviously I didn't expect to be notified of such procedures—being an outsider to this institution—but nevertheless it was odd that none of the guards with whom I'd been talking the previous evening had mentioned it, bidding me good night as usual with a simple "See you around". Their shift ended at 7 a.m., and so I wouldn't be seeing them again for the next couple of days. This was the first time I saw all the officers together in the prison; those who were just ending their shift stayed on, those were coming to replace them arrived a little earlier.

Accompanied by the nurse who had not been warned either, I waited at the front desk for the raid to end. In a short while the inmates would be leaving their cells and going out to the courtyard as usual. I saw some officers coming out from the cellblock, and as they removed their latex gloves I heard someone comment: "The place is so dusty! I really don't know how they can bear it". There wasn't much talking, but I didn't sense any kind of secrecy or any doors shutting at my presence. Apparently, the only unusual object found in one of the cells had been a portable radio, which should have been turned in. In this respect, it was a far cry from the typical raid in most large prison facilities, which usually produce an array of illegal products—shivs, cellphones, handmade batteries, hashish, and so on.

Given that this was a place where the presence of officers was so constant and the daily monitoring of cell conditions and tidiness so regular, I wondered what might justify this morning's "surprise inspection". In a small controlled environment such as Odemira—where guards and inmates alike were keen on orderliness and worked closely together, it seemed highly unlikely that anything unexpected would turn up that hadn't already been immediately reported by the inmates themselves—as had actually already happened in a previous episode, when an inmate smuggled a small quantity of hashish into the prison. I waited until all the cells had been put back into order and prison life returned to its usual routines before I was allowed into the cellblock.

The atmosphere was very different from the scene on the previous night. Everything was calm and quiet. All the tension and chattering that had filled the space a few hours before seemed to have abated. One might say that "order" had been restored. Despite the warden's assurance that this kind of procedure was "normal and strictly routine", I distinctly felt—unjustly or not—that that morning's intervention had been meant as a display of authority in response to the recent events. In other words, this space was governed by rules which had to be followed, and the atmosphere building due to the problems with salaries needed to be immediately subdued. Frustrations, outrage and claims against the institution should be relegated again to a secondary role. This was the moment to give inmates a clear indication that they were in no position to make demands and there would be no tolerance for insurgency. The best way to achieve this was to stop the course of events, and most of all to prevent inmates from appropriating and dominating the prison's emotional atmosphere.

That day, the overbearing presence of prison officers from the first hours of the morning, substituting the usual "good morning ladies" with which inmates were usually greeted as they were let out of their cells by a much starker "you must clear the cell for inspection now", had a tremendous impact all on its own. The two or three guards who were normally on cellblock duty were now over 15, and instead of one officer on each floor, there were now two or three for each cell. The full inspection thus amounted to a clear show of force, reminding inmates that they were not in charge and had to conform to the rules. I didn't question anyone about the nature of this intervention, trying to act with the same normality that everyone showed me.

There wasn't the usual hustle and bustle. Instead of laughter and conversations, as inmates finished ordering their cells, they started coming out to the yard. They kept unusually quiet, but was difficult to discern any kind of indignation in their expressions, and they abstained from making any comments whatsoever about the event, either to me or amongst each other. Even though in later visits when I returned to this point and inquire about such inspections prison staff and inmates would unanimously tell me that such interventions were "routine procedure", in my mind this particular episode had unquestionably been triggered as a direct response to the atmosphere built up over the preceding days.

The tension that surfaced inside the cellblock revealed that daily life in prison could just as easily take the guise of a well-oiled system, where everything seemed to operate with an almost clock-work precision—morning cell-opening, breakfast, showers, medication, activities, supper, lockdown—or as a hotbed for restlessness, tension, and latent conflict. More than the life within walls, it was the pressure coming from the outside (and in that sense, of the elements they had least control over), which seemed to have a much deeper impact on the state of spirit of those in reclusion. And why was that? Because outside events confronted inmates more acutely with the impotence of having to act within the boundaries imposed on them, and therefore revived in them precisely the reactions and ways of dealing with problems that had marked their lives before reclusion: arguing with an officer, for instance, trying to force their own way; refusing to work as a form of protest; covering for a relative who was going through some problem; rushing into a decision in the face of some unexpected news received on the phone, and so on.

Hence, it is as if when the world outside permeates the sphere of prison exerts a pressure that makes its walls close in even further, making the constraint of reclusion harder to withstand. In this respect, reflecting on the multiple personas inmates embody while in reclusion (as a means to gain some degree of agency and autonomy) we can see how the conditions which make it so hard for inmates in Odemira to find similar strategies of resistance and imperviousness, ultimately expose their fragility against the setbacks of everyday life.

Whether out of submissiveness, acceptance, or lack of choice, the fact that at Odemira inmates cannot "hide" behind the kind of "schemes" or forms of "evasion" usually found in prison facilities, where inmates develop alternative forms of interaction—bargaining, selling, exchanging favors—renders those situations where the system fails them all the more distressing. The shortage of money for cigarettes, coffee or any other personal items—which ultimately is felt as an acute loss of power—becomes even more oppressive than any other rule or regulation imposed on them by the institution to which they are committed. On the other hand, at no time can the prison allow inmates to forget that they were persons deprived of liberty, and to overtly express discontentment or act upon it. If we were to interpret the manifestation of disagreement as an act of resistance, in the sense defined by Ugelvik (2014), we understand that it was precisely those attempts that were being thwarted with the unannounced inspection carried out that day. As Ugelvik also points out, resistance and confrontation "involves showing that you are a person who can resist, someone who has not been deprived of all their autonomy and authority even if you have been put in prison." (2014: 11).

Thus, what happens when inmates, who (at least apparently) accept their conviction, trying to integrate the prison setup and meet the expectations they believe to be required of them, revolt against decisions that they consider unjust? This was the case with Virginia, whose story was described in the previous chapter. Virginia was one of the women who sought me out most assiduously throughout my stay at Odemira. Even knowing that I wasn't a psychologist, Virginia often wanted to "have a quick word". In one of these conversations, which took place a few days before the events just described, she asked my opinion about her chances at a furlough request she had filed for and which she was confident would get approval since it met all the necessary requirements.

When Virginia was transferred to Odemira, she had already served more than half of her sentence, and would therefore now be in a stage where she could prepare for her first temporary leave. Nevertheless, Virginia had questions that were not easy to solve. In the case of being granted, the most natural thing for her would be to spend the three days of leave at her older son's house in the north of the country. On the one hand, this would involve a four-hour journey (by public transportation), which entailed a considerable cost. Would it be worth her while to go all the way there, seeing as it would take her just as long to return? On the other hand, she didn't feel emotionally prepared to visit the grave of her other son, who had died while she was in prison.

This process seemed to be very painful, and so she had come up with an idea—an alternative solution—that she wanted to share with me. Instead of travelling up north, she would stay right there in the village of Odemira, taking up a room at a local inn which was sometimes used by the relatives of inmates on their visits. In her understanding, the purpose of furloughs was to prepare inmates for their future life in freedom. Virginia knew she would be moving in with her son upon release, and that she would not start working straight away, only after settling in. The major problem Virginia could foresee was having to face the reality of her younger son's death. Therefore, she wanted to benefit from her rightful furlough—it was important to start getting used to "free life"—but she believed it was possible to do just that right there in the village, and didn't need to spend all the time and money on a trip up north.

Virginia still hadn't brought up the idea with either the correctional treatment supervisor or the prison warden, and even though she had already submitted her request to the sentencing judge, Virginia told me, "Since you were here, I thought I would run it by you first". A little disconcerted, I tried to convey to her that I was in no position to provide answers to her doubts, but that I was sure the prison staff would understand her concerns and make sure all the proceedings were duly handled so that her leave would run as smoothly as possible.

I would only find out months later that Virginia had been denied her three-day leave, and that the plan she devised and discussed with me would never have been possible or accepted by either the warden or the sentencing judge. The idea of "preparation for freedom" implied an inmate's return to the community of origin and contact with the family, and never staying alone in a hotel 500 meters away from the prison.

The evaluation of Virginia's emotional and psychological condition had great bearing on this decision: her fragile state of mind was evident, and the risk of flight or relapse into alcohol and drug abuse was considered very high. Even in the event of being granted a parole leave, Virginia would need constant supervision. Though I didn't witness Virginia's reaction to the denial of that first petition for leave, when three months later she was once again denied a similar request, Virginia was openly insurgent with the prison guards, the warden and the other inmates. She claimed that the decision was "inadmissible", that they had to let her out: "It's in the law; you can't keep me locked up for the whole of my sentence!" In her view, this second rejection was wholly inexplicable. Not only she considered to be a fully integrated member of the prison community, but she also participated voluntarily in all prison activities. There didn't seem to be any plausible motives to prevent her leaves, and she repeatedly claimed that she was entitled to them.

On that afternoon, Virginia was not her usual calm and reserved self, and she was clearly angry. She warned other inmates in the yard: "As of tomorrow I'm refusing to work [in the laundry]. What have I got to lose? Nothing…I'm three months away from completing my sentence, what do I care?" Some women tried to calm her down, telling her not to make any rushed decisions. If she missed work, she wouldn't have another one so soon. Virginia became increasingly enraged: "They say I'm still not ready for life outside. That there is a risk of flight; but I've done everything right; I behave, I've never been punished, never even so much as stepped on the line… What is going on here?" Other inmates nodded in agreement. What "they" were doing was unfair, and Virginia was totally right.

The guards didn't attempt to assuage Virginia too forcefully. They kept at a distance, and only occasionally they offered advice, telling her to "take time to think it over"; that "right now you are very nervous" and should not "ruin everything now", specifically referring to Virginia's resolution to refuse going back to work. But the truth was that the chief of guards had voted negatively to her application for furlough. It wasn't a matter of Virginia's behavior inside the prison, which everyone acknowledged to be cooperative, but rather their assessment of Virginia's volatile emotional frame of mind. As an inmate they had known from previous stays in prison, they considered that with the years, her drug consumption and the recent death of a son had contributed for an underlying instability which revealed itself in small details of everyday life, as when they would find her crying on her own or isolating herself from others. Inside the prison she had supervision, and even if she wanted to she could never shut herself out completely. If she found herself outside, there would be nothing to prevent her from doing so. Her son had expressed his own concerns to the warden. He preferred that his mother was not released, considering that the longer she remained there, the better it would be for her.

In the chief officer's perspective, Virginia's reaction to the news only served to confirm that she had made the right decision in writing the report. Obviously it had not been the only determining factor in the final verdict, but nevertheless the moment Virginia declared her refusal to keep performing her duties and cooperate with prison activities, putting her rage out in the open, the prison officers interpreted it as proof that they had been right in their previous assumptions: "This woman is not ready to go out. If she reacts this way to 'negative' when she's in a protected environment, what will it be like when she's on her own outside? Life is full of rejections and we must all learn to live with adversity!"

A few weeks after this episode, Virginia was suffering serious consequences of her actions in the remaining months of her sentence. Her money had quickly run out and she was not allowed to revert her decision. Besides, the job she quit had already been taken up by another inmate. Without money for tobacco or coffee, Virginia turned to the son whom she had planned to live with. He didn't receive the news of her attitude well, and refused to help her with money. For him, this was a sign that his mother had gone back to her old habits, and that she had not changed at all. In a phone call Virginia described to me as "very tough", they had an argument, which ended up with her telling him he "was a good for nothing and never wanted to hear of him again".

Virginia then turned to her own mother, who was living in a home. She wrote a letter describing the hardships she was going through. Meanwhile, the despair from not having any money led her to start robbing tobacco from other inmates, and trying to trade shampoo or bath gel for cigarettes. This behavior was reported to the guards and resulted in a written reprehension. According to the prison warden, Virginia was being "a victim of her own choices"; the arrogance she had shown was demonstrative of her emotional immaturity. Despite all her years of imprisonment, the prison staff considered it highly likely that she would go back to committing crimes once she was released. The fact that her own son refused to help her only confirmed their theory. At this time, Virginia could only rely on the help of her mother, who sent money after receiving her daughter's letter, and told Virginia they would move in together and live on the money from the old woman's pension. Virginia described these last months of prison as "fraught with errors and suffering".

Episodes of tension such as we have been observing in this chapter give us an insight, even if only glimpsed, into the nature of the relationships that are built inside a prison: the outrage of inmates and their acute experience of impotence; the caution exercised by officers and correctional treatment staff as they confirm assessments that often rely on suppositions on whether the apparent change taken place in an inmate is real or not. This does not mean they are impervious to the outcome of a given situation or to the difficulties inmates have to face. Nevertheless, the fact that some inmates are unable to deal with the decisions imposed on them, and chose to break the commitments they had made with the institution, adopting a defensive and even combative attitude, was seen as a clear indication of a non-conformity with rules and regulations, and therefore as a sign that the desired process of change had not been fully achieved.

Notes

1. The integration of a newcomer, who goes through a short period of observation in solitary confinement—usually no longer than 24 hours (which at Odemira may even be dispensed with if the inmate specifically asks not to be left on her own)—is subject to previous assessment by the chief of guards and close monitoring by both guards and fellow cellmates. The "support" they lend each other (to use their own term) is crucial, in their perspective, during this phase of adjustment, and save for very rare exceptions, seems to be effective. The most veteran inmates take charge of explaining the routines and duties to newcomers, showing them how to make their bed, for instance, or reassuring them when they seem "scared".

References

Frois, Catarina. 2016. Close Insecurity. Shifting Conceptions of Security in Prison Confinement. *Social Anthropology* 24 (3): 309–323.

Lima, Antónia Pedroso. 2016. Care as a Factor for Sustainability in Situations of Crisis: Portugal between the Welfare State and Interpersonal Relationships. *Cadernos Pagu* 46: 79–105.

Narotzky, Susana. 2012. Europe in Crisis: Grassroots Economies and the Anthropological Turn. *Etnográfica* 16 (3): 627–638.

Rogan, Mary. 2013. The Irish Penal System: Pragmatism, Neglect and the Effects of Austerity. In *Punishment in Europe. A Critical Anatomy of Penal Systems*, ed. Vincent Ruggiero and Mick Ryan. London and New York: Palgrave Macmillan.

Ugelvik, Thomas. 2014. *Power and Resistance in Prison: Doing Time, Doing Freedom*. London and New York: Palgrave.

7

The Rule, the Letter, the Spirit of the Law

November, December, January, February, March. For months I returned to Odemira and for months routines were the same. Every time I resumed on conversations with the women I had already talked to, occasionally someone would come up to me asking bluntly what I thought of prison life, if I found it at all "strange". Usually I would lie, or at least hide some of my thoughts, though inwardly it could not be denied that the experience of enclosure was in fact having a sensory impact, which seemed to put a strain on everyday routines, leaving me more exhausted than usual. The periods not spent inside the prisoners' area, during lunch break, for instance, I would take the time to talk with the guards and other staff or to consult the inmates' records. These case files were of interest to me, not so much in terms of the bureaucratic details they contained, or as a means of comparison with the versions given to me by the inmates (Granja 2015), but rather as a useful source to understand legal or even biographical aspects, which sometimes inmates themselves had difficulty in explaining or remembering.

I sought to clear up some misunderstandings or questions left unanswered, as for example in Gina's case, a 32-year-old Mozambican woman I had interviewed. In view of all she had told me, it was difficult to understand why she had been sentenced to an additional deportation penalty besides her prison sentence at Odemira. Gina was living in Portugal from the age of 17, having joined her mother and sisters, who had come over before her. Having finished her 6th grade in Mozambique, she decided to go to Portugal to complete her education. Of her immediate family, only her father and brother had stayed behind. Upon arrival, however, she didn't find much encouragement from her family to pursue her studies. Seeking employment was considered a more useful endeavor, and so they helped Gina find work in the hospitality and hotel sector, where her mother and sisters already worked. In her typically reserved demeanor, hefty constitution and beaming expression, she assumed that I was a social worker or a psychologist assigned to "help" her (as she put it) deal with her crime. In this frame of mind, she was quick to make it clear that she was not a newcomer: "I don't like to speak about the past. I have been here for a while now, almost six years, and I've had plenty of time to think about it. After all this time, I just want to forget and to leave this place."

Actually, we had already crossed each other several times in the prison's administrative area, since that was where she worked, and she used to see me talking with guards, or the prison warden or even other inmates. After I explained my role there, and once she understood that our conversation did not involve any kind of therapy, but that I just sought an account of her story prior and during her imprisonment, we met on several occasions just to go over her everyday life and her expectations. She also delved into those very things she sought to forget and which she had dismissed with the formula "I don't like to talk about the past". While avoiding an explicit self-recrimination for her criminal actions, she was categorical when it came to declaring the efforts made to erase these memories throughout the years spent in prison.

A short while after she left school and began working as a cook, she started getting into trouble, going behind her family members' backs and dealing drugs with her friends around the neighborhood. Her eyes betrayed exhaustion and disappointment looking back on those years following her move to Portugal. In retrospect, she now considered that her drug trafficking venture had been a major mistake, saying that at the time she was "blind and totally clueless" both to the risks and dangers it entailed. Despite her succinctness when speaking about these activities, she described how she had started hanging out with other dropout youths in the neighborhood that had turned to drug dealing, albeit on a small scale, selling drugs on the street. Having been caught twice during police raids, on both occasions she was carrying drugs on her. Since she was tried separately on those two indictments, she was given two separate prison sentences of six years, and five and a half years, and in addition a deportation penalty was appended.

Gina explained that the hardest thing when she first arrived in prison was her family not knowing of her whereabouts: "I didn't tell them; I was afraid they'd turn their backs on me." Even though she often spoke with her mother and sisters on the phone, for the first two years of her sentence she never revealed the truth about where she was: "If there was any background noise that might raise suspicions when we were on the phone, I would hang up." Eventually, someone from the neighborhood told them the truth, and Gina was surprised that they didn't react all that badly, "they were just disappointed that I hadn't told them, because after all we are family." Gina's daily routine in prison was different from most other inmates. Her work in the officers' cafeteria meant that spent most of her days in the prison's administrative area, meaning that she had little contact with other inmates during the day, but on the other hand developed an even closer relationship with members of the prison staff:

> My schedule is always the same. I leave the cell at 7:30 a.m. to go to work all day and return to the cell at 8:00 p.m. In the cafeteria I make the breakfasts, then sometimes cook lunch; it's like my own little restaurant. [laughs] All this time I've had has allowed me to think a lot. I was totally deluded about life, and I never even had time to figure it out. Maybe today I could be having a steady life; I could be working as a cook, like I do here. Everything could be different; prison can only help us to correct our mistakes; all this time spent here feels like an eternity gone to waste.

Gina was thus caught in this conflict: on the one hand her prison experience constantly reminded her of a past she struggled to leave behind, while on the other hand she could not come to terms with the severity of her conviction, which she considered too harsh for a first-time offender. She would ask me why no one had given her "a chance", and why did she have to be expelled from the country: "Going back to Mozambique after all these years…What for? Why? My whole family is here!"

Despite assuming she had committed errors and that her sentencing was "deserved", she was obviously frustrated with her conviction, and even more so with her deportation. The decision to send her back to her country of origin, where she virtually had no remaining family ties, seemed disproportionate to Gina. She also believed that the lawyer who had been assigned by the court had proved incompetent or at least not totally committed to her case, revealed amongst other things in his unpreparedness and subsequent untimely reaction to move against what came to be the court's ruling for deportation without any further appeal.

The deportation penalty bore consequences on what would be the usual execution of the prison sentence itself. Typically, on completion of the terms established for a similar prison sentence, any person would already have been eligible for temporary home leaves; that is, at this moment Gina would have already had the chance to visit her family on the sentencing judge's and the prison board's discretion, were it not for the deportation penalty that pended upon her sentence. However, this option was not open to her.

The law states that home leaves seek to promote the strengthening of bonds with family and community as a means to "prepare the future" after release from prison. The sentencing judge found "no legal grounds for its exercise", in view of the fact that Gina was eventually going to be deported. As a result, Gina had to face serving the total remainder of her sentence, after which she would be sent to Mozambique where she could "start her life afresh". In this particular case, given that most of Gina's family lived in Portugal, that she had a permanent residence visa, and additionally, that the quantities of drugs involved in her conviction were relatively small, this decision seemed especially hard to comprehend.

All things considered, consulting Gina's personal file emerged as a potentially essential element of clarification. The file wasn't very extensive, basically containing the court ruling, the Inmate's Individual Correction Plan, a clemency plea and the supervisory judge's statement regarding a request for home leave. In the court decision we find the following:

> Drug trafficking is punishable with a prison sentence from 4 to 12 years (Article 21, n° 21, Law-Decree 15/93). General preventive measures are imperative attending to the frequent occurrence of this kind of crime in

our country. Considering the (small) quantity, the quality and type of substance involved (both heroin and cocaine are in the category of "hard drugs", due to the health risks they pose and the dependence they cause, in comparison to the so-called "soft drugs" such as cannabis), aggravated by the fact that the defendant had the intent to distribute, we are led to consider this act to be of medium gravity.

In this short excerpt, we are presented with a number of relevant elements. Law-Decree 15/93, named by some authors "the new drug law", sets the penalties for drug trafficking but does not embody the spirit of another law that was passed later (in the 2000s) regarding the decriminalization and depenalization of drug use and possession. Therefore, the judges' admission that Gina was carrying a "relatively small amount", explains why they do not put her crime in the category of serious or very serious offences. Her sentence, however, seems to be a clear response to a phenomenon that far surpasses Gina's particular circumstance, thus the reference to the recurrence of similar cases—namely those of drug dealing and drug use. They emphasize the intent to distribute as an aggravating factor, which in another part of the ruling is used to determine "the defendant's intentionality", and thus her culpability, especially considering that since she was not an addict, the drug was not for personal use, which could be a mitigating circumstance. The ruling continues, passing judgement specifically on Gina's responsibility and history:

> She was previously convicted twice on drug trafficking charges (the last of which resulted in a five years and six months imprisonment), having committed this offence *sub judice*, subsequently to her other two condemnations, revealing a high proclivity to commit such crimes, as well as an inability to learn from her previous punishments. Moreover, the defendant does not acknowledge the seriousness of her actions, and neither does she demonstrate repentance. On the other hand, the defendant does not have a professional occupation. In light of these facts, positive preventive measures are strongly advised.

The sum of this information explained, at least partly, some of the rationale that hadn't made sense in our previous conversations. Remember how Gina had said that she was a first-time offender and thus she didn't understand the rigidity of her sentence. After reading this documentation it was obvious that by "first-timer", Gina had meant that it was her first prison term, but not the first time she had been convicted of a crime. Her first conviction had resulted in a suspended prison sentence, and her second had led to a prison sentence that she was not yet serving when she committed the crime for which she was now being accused. The considerations made by the judges about her attitude and her "inability to acknowledge her own crimes" seemed to fit with the complaints made by other inmates about the counsel given by attorneys to "withhold potentially incriminating statements", even those they thought might defend them. In the court's eyes, this was someone who not only repeatedly committed the same crimes, but also showed a lack of repentance, or even admitted to verbally recognize the seriousness of her actions. Her lawyer ultimately appealed the additional penalty of deportation, arguing that the "the defendant is a legal resident along with all of her family. Expulsion from the country would result in the breakup of the family and cause great harm to all its members." This appeal was denied, and the court ruled that "there is no reason to risk the defendant causing any more damage to Portuguese society, especially considering the likelihood of the defendant's need to go back to drug trafficking given her incapacity to find other means to provide for her own subsistence."

When Gina was already serving her prison sentence, she sought the help of a prison officer to file for a clemency plea regarding her deportation, and in both of the correctional treatment staff opinions contained in her file, the institution's assessment was similar. Contrary to the court's ruling, they found that Gina "exercised a self-critical view of her own criminal acts", complied with prison rules, and had "assimilated the punitive purpose of her sentence".

As mentioned earlier, the additional penalty of deportation prevented Gina from applying for home leave schemes, which are usually denied in these cases on the grounds of flight risk. In spite of this, she made the plea to the supervisory judge, using the recurrent argument in these cases: "wished to spend some time with her mother, sisters and remaining family". The response was categorical:

The inmate has been condemned to an additional deportation penalty. On release, she will have to leave Portuguese territory and will be forbidden from returning for a five-year period. The inmate will thus have to make a new start in a different country. In light of this, and considering that the purpose of home leaves is to promote the strengthening of family and social bonds to the community with a view to preparing the subject for life in freedom, it is clear that this request lacks valid grounds for approval.

Antónia's case had also remained unclear to me before reading her file. If she had already been given a sentence, what could she mean by claiming she "didn't know" when she would be released? A prison sentence must necessarily set a definite date to start and at least several possible dates to "end", whether it is set at a mid-sentence release, five-sixths into the sentence or the full sentence. The law was very clear on that, given that in Portugal neither life imprisonment nor indefinite sentencing exists.

Antónia's situation fell under a different category: "relatively indefinite sentence". This means a "sentence applied to the author of an intentional crime, for which the prison sentence must be more than two years, as long as its author has previously already been convicted for at least two other intentional crimes with sentences also of more than two years, as well as a general assessment of the defendant's personality establishing a definite proclivity towards committing illicit criminal acts." (Article 83 Penal Code).

This procedure was explained to me by one of the prison administrative staff, since Antónia's file was extensive and contained many different parts. In the course of the various hearings that resulted in this latest conviction for drug trafficking, the judge had found that Antónia's behavior had been "inadmissible and inappropriate". When confronted with the crimes she was accused of—including a charge for being the ringleader of a criminal organization—Antónia had insulted the judge, cursed in court, lashed out against all the people present, including policemen, court officials and witnesses. Therefore, if in Gina's case we verified that the inability to show regret had a crucial influence on the court's ruling, it is easy to see how Antónia's behavior was interpreted as disrespect for the justice system, for rules and even more generally for any figure of authority. Having been repeatedly convicted for the same crime—a "recidist" as she put it—there were no attenuating circumstances, and not even her advanced age would be taken into account. And this was not a minor circumstance—Antónia was now over 70, just like her sister Rosa, who "estimated" she was 74.

The case of these two women was especially interesting as examples of the trajectory "from neighbourhood to prison" described by Cunha (2002), a path usually trailed through drug trafficking. Studying the case reports of these two inmates, their life histories, as well as the annual activity reports submitted to the Directorate-General of Prison Services, I managed to trace some of these women's imprisonment records. In an activity report from Odemira prison for the year 2001, I discovered that four women who were currently serving their sentences had already been there 15 years before. Two of them were sisters—Antónia and Rosa—and their daughters had also been convicted.

At the end of 2015, each of the sisters had been once again sent there along with their daughters. A few months later, they were joined by other daughters, who in turn were imprisoned along with their own daughters. Thus, the same prison was holding three generations of the same extended family—grandmothers, mothers, aunts, cousins, sisters, and even mothers-in law. Some of these women had spouses and sons serving sentences in male prison facilities, but also other relatives in different female prisons around the country. Moreover, only recently I had come across at least one of the matriarch's daughters and granddaughters (as well as a grandson) now in prison, while they were only visitors to Odemira.

Even though in this instance I was dealing with members of the gypsy community, we should be careful not to describe this kind of situation as a purely ethnic feature, but rather as a matter of jurisdiction and local residence. The modus operandi followed in drug trafficking arrests at the end of the 1980s gave rise to the kind of situation found in Odemira, as in many other prisons throughout the country: the simultaneous arrest of several family members due to their presence at the scenes where police raids were conducted. The profiling and targeting of specific types of neighborhoods for police raids followed the same patterns set in other European countries.

As Cunha explains in her several works on the subject (2002, 2008), even though we may find certain areas around large urban centers with a higher concentration of particular racial and ethnic groups, mostly dwelt by low socioeconomic groups, equivalent to the North American ghettos or the French banlieue (Fassin et al. 2013; Wacquant 2009) in Portugal these areas concentrate such a broad and varied population (ethnic, religious, nationality) that it would be misleading to narrow it down.

Assigning Identity: Guilt and Responsibility in Court Rulings

The court rulings included in the inmates' prison files became an important tool, not only towards understanding how an individual is held accountable for a criminal act in light of an existing legal framework, but also to complement an analysis of subjective and moral aspects underlying these decisions. While the accountability factor is at this point evaluated through the formal elements that establish factual authenticity, including some and discarding others, the testimonial evidence, the reports and expert opinions that contribute to the case's appreciation also inform the court's final decision. The judgement of the act itself is contained in that final statement, measuring the impact of the specific crime on society as well as its author's character and degree of responsibility—including the subject's personal history and record—thus providing a kind of moral profile on which his/her judgement must be based. The biographical relevance does more than provide a context for judging an isolated act that is being attributed to a particular person. It inevitably leads to that person's definition within a fixed category—indigent, outsider, delinquent, and so forth—rather than as a person, in this case as a woman.

In other words, the process of crystalizing a trajectory through the records and reports obtained from an array of sources—social assistants and institutions (e.g., juvenile care homes, courts or correctional services), courts, police authorities, prison facilities, and so on—provides a means to classify and situate the person in question in order to evaluate their present conduct and even envisage their future. As Michel Foucault so aptly observed: It is these shadows lurking behind the case itself that are judged and punished. They are judged indirectly as 'attenuating circumstances' that introduce into the verdict not only 'circumstantial' evidence, but something quite different, which is not juridically codifiable: the knowledge of the criminal, one's estimation of him, what is known about the relations between him, his past and his crime, and what might be expected of him in the future. (1995: 17–18)

It is important to question and problematize how such cumulative knowledge influences the judgement of authorities—from the court judge to social workers, prison guards, supervisory judges, and so forth. We may ask ourselves, for instance, to what extent does this method, and its potential for anticipating future behavior, not become a self-fulfilling prophecy, insofar as it seems to neglect that its own interference may in fact condition the agency of the subject under evaluation, providing the script for a story that has already been somehow "officially" written, and thus contradicting the primary goal of reintegration, which these same institutions supposedly work to achieve?

This kind of questioning becomes all the more important if we consider that this process of assigning what we could consider to be an institutional identity becomes one of the most influential elements at the moment of applying a sentence—justifying its purpose and calculating its extension. In other words, it is in the course of a trial, and specifically when a ruling is deliberated, that the subject's detrimental conduct is pointed out, and his/her shortcomings attributed to specific social and personal traits. That is the moment when the trial becomes a moral judgement; when all the attenuating and aggravating factors are weighed. A person and the sum of all his/her actions are, in many cases for the first time, brought together and inspected to produce an objective and distanced evaluation, based on pieces of information that are sewn together in the shape of a figure, a character. The problem is, as Roux underlines, that "since the reports [from social workers, psychologists] are submitted to the magistrate, they must remain 'informative' without the agents ever questioning the nature of the information they provide or the effects produced by this neutralization within the judicial process." (Roux 2015: 185).

Institutional narratives are thus created and supported alongside numerous sources, which are, a priori, already formatted according to what seems to be a bureaucratic device—following a predetermined script—rather than an assessment of all the encompassing elements that could otherwise be considered relevant. What is more, in their contribution towards the calculation of a sentence, these judgements have two goals in mind, defined in the Portuguese judicial system as *general prevention* and *special prevention*. On the one hand, an individual's action affects society in general with an impact that must not only be assessed but also interrupted, and on the other hand, the same action implies deliberate infliction of damage on specific victims. It is precisely this willfulness that a person must be held accountable for, not only for the practice of an act but also for the inability to restrain from practicing it; it is on this point that a person's agency is measured and evaluated. In the words of philosopher José Gil:

> At the heart of penal responsibility we find the definition of a common negative behavior: restraining want...It summons the intervention of common sense and its assessment of the possibilities open to common person as a measure for the transgressor's responsibility: if the average person can avoid infraction, thus so should the accused...What the former "can", the latter "should": the difference between what a normal person can do and what the person who practiced the action in question didn't do, gives us the measure of accountability. (1999: 203)

The following pages present some of the specific characteristics of female punishment-imprisonment, namely those corresponding to some of the topics considered in the existing literature, such as the inmates' socioeconomic condition, the presence of children and the role of inmates as their primary caretakers, the experience of abuse, drug habits, the prior history of contact with the justice system, and so on. The accountability or mitigation of sentences applied to female inmates implies an appraisal that includes objective as well as subjective elements. The roles of "womanhood" and "motherhood" are clearly brought to bear, whether as aggravating circumstances in conduct, or as a factor to ponder at the time of applying a sentence as we can see in the following excerpt of a court ruling:

> The defendant had six children from three different relationships. The education of the children was essentially entrusted to their respective paternal families or care institutions, revealing the accused's shortcomings in terms of her parental abilities. The defendant reveals a reduced cognizance of her

own delinquent life history, furthermore revealing a tendency to underestimate the damage caused to her victims and the society in general.

The reference, apparently strictly factual, to this woman's maternity to six children from three different partners, is surely not an irrelevant part of this ruling. Even if only implicitly, the judgement being made is that the person in question does not match the model of the (Portuguese) woman, who typically bears one or two children from a monogamous relationship, on average starting her motherhood around the age of 25. In the case of this particular woman, who was 45 years old at the time of her trial, having six children could be interpreted as a sign of irresponsibility or lack of pre-natal education, especially since she was still a teenager (16 years old) at the time of her firstborn. An additional sign of promiscuous behavior was implied in the enumeration of the children's different fathers, a circumstance that clearly fell out (at least to the magistrates responsible for this case) of conventional standards.

Therefore, as a woman she was being portrayed as betraying her role with her promiscuous, futile and even sinful behavior. But this normative evaluation also judges her "motherhood", once more pointing out the same signs of negligence, and the same failure to live up to expectations and responsibilities, insofar as the children's education was left up to the father or their families; the main offence here being against the female role as main caretaker and provider. In the cases where the fathers did not take the children into their care, she gave them up to institutions, demonstrating—as the court ruling implies—her absolute failure as a woman and a mother. Thus, we can see that the court is not judging this person solely for the act that brought her before them in the first place, but is indeed making a moral judgement based on the appraisal of her performance in a series of social roles.

Woman, Wife, Mother

The next case concerns a 35-year-old woman, mother of five children aged between 2 and 17 years old at the time of our conversation. Having two children from her first marriage, Joana had three more during her second engagement, characterized (like the previous one) by a conflicting relationship, with recurrent physical and verbal confrontation between the couple. Throughout this second union, the main targets of her companion's abuse were Joana and the children from her first marriage, whom her partner seemed to reject. Joana explained that the court procedures began with a domestic violence complaint against her husband she had formally presented to the police after having been assaulted with a knife.

Apparently the narrative lacked sense. How did a domestic violence complaint where, allegedly, the assailant was the man against the woman (as Joana initially described) result in both being convicted and sentenced to six years' imprisonment for acts that bore no relation to it—in this case, child maltreatment? Her answer was simple: over a period of several years she had witnessed the partner inflicting personal injuries to her eldest sons, through punches, kicks, death threats, physical and psychological abuse. Even though she was present at those occasions, she never acted or reacted by trying to defend the children. She was arrested by the police because on the day she made the domestic violence complaint, her mother—to whom, meanwhile, the grandsons told what was happening— decide to expose the situation, even if that meant her own daughter being imprisoned. The court considered her responsible and up to a certain point, an accomplice. She said that during these violent episodes she was afraid of being subjected to retaliation against herself. But added one more reason: "cowardice".

Explaining how, During those years of marriage, she lost her self-esteem and self-respect, believing in the rationale that alone she was not able of raising five children.

The judicial ruling told a story that it was not very much different from what Joana told me but it was underlined that she had had a direct intervention in the children's maltreatment. She was accused and convicted of insults and verbal attacks inflicted on the children, such as calling them "sons of a bitch" and forcing the older ones to take care of the toddlers, including feeding and bathing them; of menaces and punishments; and of tying the children to a chair if they didn't have "manners" at the table. Three years after these events, she said she had reflected on it and was self-critical: "I wasn't raised this way, my parents always went along. They had fights but nothing like this."

Gradually, she was realizing that her actions (and her passivity regarding her partner attitudes) had severely hampered her children who "lived in terror, they were not happy kids". But at the time, she continues, she had neither that perception, nor did she understand the gravity of the actions. Only after imprisonment and being "by herself"—that is, without being under the partner's direct influence—had she started to understand her past, and how her life and her conduct had been prejudicial to herself and her five children.

Joana also explained a procedure that currently happens in similar cases: going to the authorities to seek legal recourse is more to "make him afraid", to "scare him", and not necessarily to put an end to their union. This was the third time she presented a formal complaint of domestic violence, and her husband had been convicted and received two suspended sentences for similar acts. What does this attitude mean? That there are occasions when, due to a domestic violence episode, to call for police intervention is a way to retaliate against and intimidate the offender and not necessarily a measure to make him accountable for his actions. This is one situation the judicial system does not have the capacity to overturn. Classified as a public crime since 2000—that is, any person may denounce the crime to the authorities and it will always be prosecuted—the victim can no longer try to interrupt these proceedings. What happens in cases like Joana, who only wanted to "spook him"? The victim does not testify in court and the magistrates see their action curtailed, unable to attest the authenticity and the criminal value of the charges. As Joana explained: "It was effective for a while, but after that he resumed his behavior."

Tampering judicial action to her advantage, during these previous interactions she never mentioned the assaults her children were subjected to. And that was why, this third time she filed a complaint for physical abuse, her mother intervened and denounced the grandchildren episodes, who presented visible marks of mistreatment. She was given immediate custody of the elder children; it was only after the parents' conviction that the court assigned her responsibility for the younger ones. The court's ruling in Joana's case was very explicit in its moral evaluation of both her and her companion's behavior:

> In this concrete case, we consider that not even all the goodwill of this court could find this sentence sufficient punishment. Indeed, the defendants' notoriously perverse personalities make them unfit for the most basic rules of family life. We are certain that they would be a source of trouble and harm to any community. They are bad parents, bad neighbors, and absolutely impervious to any kind of admonition.

The "goodwill of the court" in this context would be synonymous of the benevolence and understanding that could decisively influence the sentence applied, thus revealing the extent to which it is a choice made in a particular instance. As the ruling states, on the counts of physical abuse inflicted on their children, a monetary fine could be applied, which might ultimately be converted into community work. But the tribunal considers that such a solution would be largely "insufficient" or, in other words, would not be a proportional punishment to the damage inflicted by the acts under consideration. It is, therefore, based on specific features of the crime, which the court values in subjective terms when it describes the defendants' personalities as "notoriously perverse" and incompatible with the conventional rules of family life.

This case presents us with a situation in which the testimonies of the children about their daily life at home is almost as important as the physical and psychological injuries inflicted on them: the reference to their parents' regular alcohol consumption, abusive language, threats and aggressiveness. The ruling also includes evidence from outside sources, namely the description of a disturbance with neighbors, involving the exchange of insults and threats, and which the police were called in to intervene. The judges once again appraise this conduct in subjective terms: "bad parents and bad neighbors", whose presence is a negative influence on any community. In sum, the court judges these two individuals as "bad citizens". The richness of the material found in these rulings gives us a very detailed view into the underlying reasoning behind the notions of *accountability* and *guilt* being pondered. The actions practiced on the children involved are censurable, but beyond that, there seems to be a general assessment of disconformity with society and the community, which goes to the defendants' standing as citizens, as responsible and self-determining individuals.

In light of this, the interpretation of culpability that defines personhood is informed by an individual's history. In some cases, socioeconomic precariousness and family instability may be used by the court to frame the subject within a given profile or category. In Joana's case, the situation is somehow inverted. Born into a stable and functional family, as a teenager finishing her secondary education Joana chose a path of transgression, rebelling against the rules she had been set. While in some cases a person's trajectory serves either as an attenuating circumstance or as corroboration of an almost inevitable outcome, as constituting a pattern, in other cases it is precisely its exceptionalism that is subject of appraisal, moral judgement and punishment, as an aggravating factor. Let us consider one more example of this assertion.

Contrary to Joana, Francisca did not acknowledge the crimes she had been charged with: she was also indicted for abusing her four children, all of them minors at the time of the crimes. She admitted to having beaten her eldest daughter (aged 14 years at the time), to having "slapped and pulled her hair" during an argument, but she denied all the other charges she was accused of. Francisca explained that even that occurrence with her eldest daughter had been the culmination of a problem that had been going on for several months, in a string of arguments that resulted from her daughter's persistent bad behavior at home and at school. She described herself as a good mother, in a stable relationship with her partner for two years: "This whole story was completely made up by the social assistant who claimed that I beat my kids, and all of this is the work of my Carla [her elder daughter] and my ex-husband."

Married at 16 due to an unplanned pregnancy, she had three other children before she and her husband separated, on the grounds that they "didn't get along with each other". Her youngest son was 4 at the time. She was 32 now, working as a hairdresser, and during this period she had twice entrusted her children to a home that accepted children from families in difficulty; once voluntarily, and the second time with direct intervention from the Child and Youth Protection Services, alerted to the children's condition of neglect and abuse by their school teachers, particularly as to their withdrawn and aggressive behavior towards other schoolchildren and visible signs of unexplained physical injury such as their constant bruising. Francisca classified the trial as a "farce", for despite her admitted conflicts with a teenage daughter, blame was assigned to the social assistant's unreasonable testimony of Francisca's inability and aggressiveness towards her children. In the social worker's report, partially transcribed into the court's decision, we can read the following:

> The defendant reveals traits of manipulative behavior, both towards the minors as towards the professional care providers, only recanting from her manifestly unrealistic discourse when confronted with direct evidence to the contrary. The defendant portrayed herself as a victim, continues to be in contact with the children, and is intent on keeping their custody and bringing them back to her household. In spite of this, the defendant is utterly incognizant of the unlawfulness of the practiced facts.

Despite her cheerfulness and expansive demeanor around the cell hall, whenever we talked alone, Francisca burst out in tears. She didn't understand why her daughter was doing this to her and why the ex-husband was corroborating the aggressions, "when he doesn't even live with them anymore." She asked herself why the judge was falling for that version of events and dismissed the family medical physician's opinion, for instance, who testified that he had never detected any sings of maltreatment in her children. After the daughter filed a complaint with the police, all siblings were put into social care institutions, albeit at different locations. The oldest daughter had already been transferred to three different homes due to her aggressive behavior, drug and alcohol abuse, and according to Francisca, for resorting to prostitution (similar rationalizations on what the inmates consider to be the real nature of the crimes may me found, for example, in Ugelvik 2012; Frois 2016; Waldram 2007). One of the youngest sons had also been moved to a Secure Training Centre (for children from 12 to 16), after being convicted for auto theft, and another one had manifested suicidal tendencies.

During our initial conversations, Francisca claimed that the judge had overreacted in the decision to hold her in remand, and her lawyer was of the same opinion. After all, she was a first-time offender and had never been in trouble with the law; she "wasn't a menace to public order". The judge had a different opinion, and ruled that she should be physically restrained from having contact with the children to prevent any kind of interference with their testimonies or their lives after the charges had been detected and documented. Regarding her previous marriage, Francisca alleged having been a victim of abuse herself: "He controlled me, filming and recording our conversations. He spied on my Facebook account; I had no freedom whatsoever."

As to the oldest daughter, Francisca admitted to having "lost all control over her. She was a troublesome child, and perhaps instead of beating her, I should have sought help from the Child and Youth Protection Services." Her case report did not include any of the children's accounts about their father, who no longer lived with them, only the events involving their mother. Francisca presented a tendentious version of the whole affair: "I know what is behind all of this, but I can't prove it. My ex-husband wants to get back at me for having left him. He's never had the kids' best interest at heart."

The trial hearings were held over the course of several months. Francisca became increasingly impatient, and said that the situation seemed to be getting worse all the time. She raged against the private hearings the judge had held with the other three children (which were video-recorded for future reference). As Francisca put it, she had not consented to this, and would never agree for "her boys" to be harassed in that manner. "The judge manipulated the whole thing. Her questions were directed to mislead them into answering what she wanted to hear. The judge is also against me, they all are, and I can't understand why". In one of my later visits to Odemira, Francisca's sentence had already been decreed, and I found the prison officers were shocked with the news from the court. Not only had they now been made aware of the crimes she had actually been charged with, but also they had witnessed one of the court hearings and heard the children's testimonies accusing their mother. The aggressions consisted in threats and insults—"One of these days I'm going to fucking kill you" and "I'll send you back to the home you little fucker"—as well as physical abuse, including punching, kicking, slapping, putting knives to their throats while she yelled "One of these days I'm going to beat the life out of you".

During the hearings, the children described several episodes with their mother: how once she dragged one of the daughters out of bed when she was already asleep to make her wash the dishes from dinner; another time when she started kicking her son for not having scrubbed the floor like he had been ordered. They said that their mother's boyfriend witnessed these episodes and did nothing, but also that they loved their mother and didn't want to be go back to foster care; that they wanted to remain together at home.

Francisca did not accept the court's decision. At no point during her trial did she expect to be found guilty, much less that she would be sentenced to nine years' imprisonment and forbidden from having any contact with her children before they reached adulthood. Once in prison, she felt that she had time to reflect, to learn more about life and about coexisting with others. When I asked what she felt about her children being put into institutions, she said that it was "horrible", and that in those places "they don't get love or attention, no one to give them the cuddling they need". The court's final ruling includes an explanation of the reasoning behind the prison sentence and the termination of Francisca's parental rights for the period of six years (until the youngest son reached 18):

> Bearing in mind that the defendant is the mother of the five minors victimized by her actions for several years while they were growing up; that her way of relating with them was physically and psychologically violent, instead of providing the protection and care that befit a mother's responsibility towards her children; and ultimately the serious consequences of her conduct on the minors—namely causing them to develop suicidal ideas, self-mutilation tendencies and low self-esteem—this court is left with no doubts as to imposing an additional penalty to terminate parental rights over her children.

We verify once again that the role of mother is accentuated as crucial in the court ruling and judgement—as if the mother has increased duties regarding her offspring, being the caregiver and not the perpetrator. The mother who, as was made clear in Joana's case, has the particular duty of putting her children's well-being in first place and because of this, bears the utmost responsibility for the harms caused to them, directly or indirectly. We may also ask what the court evaluation was regarding the father, since there was no information on this subject in the court ruling, and what does that reveal to us about the gender framework regarding parenting? In sum, the woman-wife, women-mother seems to determine the tribunal attitude: more "benevolent", or more "punishing", depending on what their expectations are of that particular person.

Let us now turn back to one of the other cases. Matilde (who had been convicted for small-scale drug trafficking, and whom I had sat with in class, helping her to write down a number 5), cried every day with the grief of being separated from her children—in her mind the worst ordeal of being in prison. Since Matilde was a first-time offender, the judge had handed down a five-year suspended sentence. The court's decision took into consideration the same elements we have been discussing, but in this instance with a different interpretation and consequences:

> We find that it is still possible to make a favorable prognosis judgement, to the effect that the simple censure of the fact and the dissuading threat of prison are found at this point sufficient punishment and effectively ensure that the defendant will refrain from future crimes. In fact, it was proved that the defendant is socially well adjusted and has a stable family life—being the mother of three children, all of them minors; that the facts occurred in circumstances of dire economic need and unemployment, and that the defendant has no prior convictions. On the other hand, the defendant showed contrition and sincere repentance, so it is the court's belief that the threat of prison conviction and her present remand in custody, away from her children, allowed her time to reflect upon the demerit of her past conduct.

In this small excerpt we observe that several attenuating factors were considered: having family support, being a devoted mother of three underage sons—described as having "contrition and sincere repentance", who is suffering from being apart her children; the criminal acts being the result of financial difficulties due to unemployment—and not, as was evaluated in Gina's case, as way of life—and, lastly, for being a first-time offender without criminal background. In short: this is a woman, (and also a mother as underlined) who while in custody was suffering from being separated of her children and was remorseful of her illegal actions. It is also noted that because of having family ties and because she had experienced eight months in prison remand she "reflected upon" and "interiorized" the damages she committed. As if somehow the characteristics here underlined corresponded to what a woman, as well as a mother, *should* be.

References

Cunha, Manuela. 2002. *Entre o Bairro e a Prisão. Tráficos e Trajectos*. Lisbon: Afrontamento.

Fassin, Didier, et al. 2013. *Juger, Réprimer, Accompagner. Essai sur la Morale de L'État*. Paris: Seuil.

Foucault, Michel. 1995. *Discipline and Punish: The Birth of Prison*. Trans. Alan Sheridan. London: Penguin.

Frois, Catarina. 2016. Close Insecurity: Shifting Conceptions of Security in Prison Confinement. *Social Anthropology* 24 (3): 309–323.

Granja, Rafaela. 2015. *Para cá e para lá dos muros: Relações familiares na interface entre o interior e o exterior da prisão*. Unpublished PhD thesis, Minho University.

Roux, Sébastien. 2015. Discipline and Educate. Contradictions Within the Juvenile Justice System. In *At the Heart of the State. The Moral World of Institutions*, ed. Didier Fassin, 171–196. London: Pluto Press.

Ugelvik, Thomas. 2012. Prisoners and their Victims: Techniques of Neutralization, Techniques of the Self. *Ethnography* 13 (3): 259–277.

Waldram, James. 2007. Narrative and the Construction of 'Truth' in a Prison-based Treatment Program for Sexual Offenders. *Ethnography* 8 (2): 145–169.

Wacquant, Löic. 2009. *Punishing the Poor. The Neoliberal Government of Social Insecurity*. Durham and London: Duke University Press.

8

Institutionalizing Exclusion

In the early days of my visits to Odemira I was met with an atmosphere of "poverty" that only over time I gradually managed to interpret and put into context. Although it manifested itself differently throughout the inmate population, it was possible to identify common features—the generalized economic problems of their families (both their own as their family of origin), histories of alcoholism and drug use, parental negligence and other forms of maltreatment and domestic violence. Adult women in the 30–40 age range, with minors in their care, and often relying as their main support system on their own mothers, who in turn were in need of care themselves, but nevertheless were called upon to take care of grandchildren. The large percentage of inmates who had been teenage mothers, the emotional and financial dependency on relatives, whether in cases involving substance abuse, failed marriages or other emotional relationships (usually ending soon after the birth of a first child), frequently featured in our conversations whenever topics of emotional relationships and kinship were addressed.

Chapter 7 emphasized how different material elements combine to form an image and construct a narrative around the person who commits a crime and is taken to trial; in the pages that follow, the analysis will focus on another closely related aspect: the relationship involving these women and a wide range of public and non-government assistance and care institutions. The aim is to observe the problems faced by some of these women prior to incarceration, and show that these were largely endemic rather than merely circumstantial; that is, deriving from structural and wide-ranging characteristics of contemporary Portuguese society.

Besides the fragments gathered from interviews and conversations throughout the fieldwork, inmates' prison records provided additional information about their socioeconomic background and family history. The similarities and patterns found, after going through dozens of these files, speak eloquently of the instability and precariousness of their situation, of negligence and abuse suffered in childhood and adolescence, and of the same cycles being carried into their adult life. To illustrate this, let us take the example of Laura, and see how her life history is reviewed in the documents used by the court as the basis for imposing a prison sentence, and how this institutional narrative is complemented by the evidence produced by social workers and guards in the prison facilities that Laura went through:

> The defendant comes from a large family of low socioeconomic means. Her psychosocial development was occurred in a markedly conflictual family environment associated with her father's alcoholism, and the resulting negligence of basic parental responsibilities. At the age of 12, and following several runaway attempts, the defendant was committed to various child care facilities run by the Ministry of Justice [Secure Training Center], where she completed primary school and attended a training course in hairdressing.
>
> Later, the defendant started working as a hostess [prostitution in bars], thus gaining financial independence from her family. Later she moved in with her mother, and didn't have any professional activity, relying on the income from welfare benefits [Social Integration Income, RSI] and her mother's pension for subsistence.

This short summary identifies three key stages. Her childhood was spent in what is commonly characterized by social workers as a dysfunctional family with nine siblings, in an atmosphere marked by aggressiveness and uncertainty. As soon as Laura became more autonomous—at the age of eight or nine—she began to see the "street" as a safer place than her own home: "Whenever he [referring to the father] came home, he started beating on everyone, and the only choice I had was to run away." Since the family and each of the children were already signaled by social services as likely targets of state intervention, and the minors labeled as being at risk, all the siblings ended up being distributed around different children's homes. However, at the institution where Laura is sent, she adopts an attitude described as "aggressive and rebellious" towards both her colleagues and her keepers, and repeats this behavior as she is continually transferred from one institution to another in the same area.

Despite the many problems and difficult coexistence, Laura finishes primary education at the age of 14 and is enrolled in a hairdressing training course. Finally, when she left the children's home upon attaining the age of 16—full adolescence—it was not her parents' home she decided to go back to. Laura starts to live in rented rooms, or in shared apartments with friends, and takes up prostitution in bars as a means of subsistence, keeping almost no contact with her family. She is initiated into drug use while working in one of these bars, and eventually moves in with a man who is both her companion and her pimp.

Over the following two decades, Laura is convicted on more than one occasion for crimes of theft and robbery, perpetrated alone or with men with whom she maintains brief relationships. On completing one of these sentences, Laura links up with her mother again (her father had died in the meantime), even though the rest of the family rejects her on account of her drug addiction and criminal record. Currently nearing 40 years of age, Laura has three children: one of them was taken into care when he was still only months old, and the other two lived with their respective paternal families. Throughout her adult life, in the periods when Laura was not in prison, she never managed to become fully independent, continually leading an unstable life and relying on state support. She justified this fourth conviction with the need to go back to robberies: "My older sister came to get my mother, claiming that I spent her pension money on drugs, and took her to live at her house."

As we are able to attest following this brief overview of Laura's life, her interaction with state care institutions went back a long way before her first prison sentence. It started as early as childhood, in what could be described as a spiral of provisional solutions. Up to a point it was the state that took care of her, assuming responsibilities of protection, education, shelter, health care, and so forth, until the moment when she became autonomous and independent. All later institutionalization did not respond to a situation of "care", but rather to situations identified as law transgressions and punishment. That is, at a certain moment, Laura was no longer considered as a person in need of help, but as an outlaw. Nowadays, an additional element is introduced: Laura's experience of exclusion and institutionalization is extended to one of her own offspring, put into a children's home just as his mother had been before him.

This cycle of poverty–exclusion–institutionalization–violence was present in the personal experiences of several inmates, and was not restricted to their own families of origin but sometimes continued in the families they came to constitute. Coincidentally, as I was reading an edition of the prison newspaper one day, I came across a piece recounting one such story. Its author was Ana, a 30-year-old woman whose slender build and physical complexion bore the marks of a hardened life. "My Hell" a free assignment from the prison schoolteacher, is fully transcribed below:

> There should be some justice regarding domestic violence. They [the perpetrators] commit a crime and still remain free. And if it wasn't bad enough to be a victim, we are still made to leave our house, and the city we live in with our children, to avoid the risk that he will find us. We leave with nothing, and we have to seek help from the Victim Support Association to find us a halfway house where we can be safe and protected. We have to start all over from zero.
>
> But the most negative aspect in all of this is that the children increasingly suffer. It is not enough that they have to face the hardships of a financially and emotionally unstable life, they also have to go through this additional problem. Even after running away, the fear never goes away. We are always afraid that one day he will find us.
>
> My life has been like this, frightened that I will run into him. I lived with the dread of an impending tragedy. Both my daughter and I were very lucky, because this hell lasted for 12 years. It was a time during which I took beatings almost every day, and my daughter witnessed all of it. It was a life of suffering and fear.

I will never know exactly how deeply this whole disgrace will affect my little girl.
Between Margins, Odemira Prison Facility Newsletter, March–April 2016, no. 2, p.10

The honesty of this narrative provides a crude portrayal of pain and despair. Despite having talked with Ana on several occasions, I knew little about her life beyond the fact that she had been sentenced to four years and nine months for crimes of robbery and small-scale drug dealing. Like the majority of inmates at Odemira she worked in the fruit packaging industry. Until I read her text, so far we had talked about her everyday life in prison, but we had never really gone into her past in great detail. Even though the episodes of domestic violence—particularly of men over women in the domestic sphere—were fairly common in the narratives of many inmates, in the passage above, Ana addressed other less discussed issues.

Most notably, she referred to the influence of these episodes on her own daughter's development, and she identified a sequence of stages that in some way led up to her imprisonment and the present moment she was in. My curiosity was mostly triggered by the question she puts at the end of her essay: "I will never know exactly how deeply this whole disgrace will affect my little girl." I wanted to know more about Ana's daughter, Filipa, and retrace her steps after her mother's imprisonment three years before. The only way to do this was to study Ana's case file, picking up on the information Ana had given to me that her daughter, now 15 years old, was committed to a *Centro Educativo* (secure training center): "She had some problems, and got mixed up in some kind of trouble". In other words, despite being apart, both mother and daughter were at that moment in a situation of reclusion.

The information contained in the records amounted to a series of reports made by the Family and Juvenile Courts at the time of the inquiry, which lead Filipa to be sent to the secure training center where she was living now. Just as we saw in the previous chapter, these documents provide only a kind of fragmented portrait, in this case of an adolescent. One of the documents describes the family household: "Filipa, 12 years of age, is the daughter of a drug abuser…her relationship with both parents has always been permeated by acts of violence, recurrent separations and reconciliations, and overall instability. Neither parent had a professional activity. She revealed learning disabilities and problems of interaction with colleagues, whom she frequently attacked verbally and physically when she started to attend primary school." Even though the documents do not indicate the precise dates of this path, they allude to one particular year in which Filipa lived with her mother in the halfway house for victims of domestic abuse. It would have been after this period that Ana moved in with a boyfriend with whom she started to commit crimes, Filipa having been admitted at a children's home. At this institution, and "after an initial period of making an apparently good adjustment, Filipa started to have conflicts with other colleagues, to break the rules of the institution, and to make escape attempts."

With a hiatus in the timeline, the documents pick up Filipa's trail again at a later period, at which time her mother has already been convicted and imprisoned, and one of Filipa's paternal aunts has been granted guardianship of the girl. Alleging financial reasons to justify her inability to provide proper care for a pre-adolescent girl, the aunt decides to let Filipa continue to live at the children's home, and have her over only on the weekends. However, this arrangement doesn't seem to have worked out well.

According to her aunt's account—taken by the social worker that followed Filipa's case—"She disobeyed any rules set for her, fixing up dates with boys via the Internet, stealing items from the house, and resorting to aggressiveness as a way to resolve conflicts." Faced with these antagonisms, the aunt refuses to continue taking responsibility for her niece, putting an end to the weekends, or any other kind of tutorship. Without any family support, Filipa evinces what the social worker describes as "a spiral of self-destructive behavior".

Besides the practice, along with a group of schoolmates, of petty thefts from shops, she starts to "get involved in promiscuous relationships with older men, maintaining occasional sexual relationships in exchange for shelter, money and food". In other words, the children's home institution seems to fail at keeping Filipa within what is meant to be a structured environment, and to instill her a "balanced" social interaction, as is stated in the report. We find a large number of reports covering those months in which some explanations for the girl's trajectory are advanced: "After her mother's imprisonment, she [Filipa] perceives her relatives (father, grandmother, aunt) as unwilling or unable to provide her with the emotional or financial means to retrieve her from the children's home, strengthening her feelings of abandonment and self-depreciation."

Even though recognizing the problems, there didn't seem to be much choice left but to maintain the current situation: Filipa should remain in the guardianship of the state until her mother is released from prison and have means to secure the necessary socioeconomic conditions for their support. If these conditions are not met, the alternative is to keep Filipa in state care until she reaches the legal age provided she completes compulsory education or a professional training course that can guarantee her financial independence. It becomes obvious that the social workers involved with Filipa's case faced difficulties and legal constraints, making several attempts to overcome these obstacles by transferring the adolescent to other institutions where she might become better adjusted. Leafing through Ana's file, I come across a letter written by the Family and Juvenile Court identifying criminal charges brought against Filipa.

One year after her mother's incarceration, and after having been admitted into two different homes in the same area of the country, Filipa is charged with participation in robberies. One of the robberies she was accused of—involving a cell phone and €20 in cash—was carried out as part of a group, on two 14-year-old youths as they were coming out of a movie theatre. Besides a biographic account and family history, these court reports describe Filipa as "insensitive and incapable of establishing close emotional bonds...This behavior is reflected in her assessment of the criminal act for which she has been charged, displaying total indifference and lack of empathy for the defenselessness of the victims; incapable of any self-censure that might restrain her attitudes in respect for the existing legal rules and social norms." Regarding Filipa's experience in the different children's homes, the report also mentions that "institutional care did not prove adequate to grant her protection and instill a responsible behavior". We are thus faced with the repeated acknowledgement of the state institutions' inability to cope with Filipa's case. Her mother was in no position to help, and can only question herself about the effect that such a family environment might have on her daughter. The court therefore states its decision: "The unstable and unruly life history can only be reverted through an *intervention in a contained environment*".[1] In other words, Filipa is sentenced to two years in a secure training center. From being a neglected child, she has now grown into a young delinquent who needs to be reformed and rehabilitated.

As one reads through a report that attempts to portray a child (now an adolescent) over a 12-page summary of her life history, it almost feels as if we have been transported to a Kafkaesque account of how the wide array of support and care systems of a society (family, friends, child protection services and benefits) gradually become entangled as they successively fail in their goals, until being forced to give in to a final solution, "intervention in a contained environment"—incarceration. With each successive report, evaluation and verdict, an image of Filipa starts to emerge, and its profile pleads for all manners of "interventions" until eventually the conclusion is reached that effective action can only be ensured within a closed environment.

The history of these two women is intricate, and the contours of Ana's personal trajectory included many other aspects besides those highlighted in the reports about Filipa. Nevertheless, they allow us to isolate a common denominator—how the different state and non-government institutions intervened in the life of this mother and daughter. According to Ana, and regardless of her opinion on the final outcome, there had been a succession of problems which had gradually escalated. The first of these had been her daughter's exposure to the kind of relationship she maintained with her husband and the abuse and violence that characterized it. She blamed herself for allowing him to beat her and not having spared her daughter from witnessing these aggressions. Ana was not minimizing her own personal suffering; in fact it was enhanced as she took on the role of the mother who had been incapable of protecting her daughter. There was an underlying motive for the decision to abandon her husband, resulting from an episode that had the daughter at its core: "She witnessed everything, and always saw what her father did to me, although he never touched her. But there was one day when he was beating me—the girl must have been 10 or so—and she grabbed a knife and said she was going to kill her father. That day I decided it was enough, realizing that it was a matter of time before a greater tragedy occurred."

Neither Ana nor her husband had a steady paying job, and both lived on welfare benefits. Her husband's alcohol abuse had been a constant characteristic of their life together. Shortly after the day Ana saw her daughter reach for a knife to stab her father, she made contact with the Victim Support Association. She was immediately guided to a shelter home 300 km away from where they lived. Mother and daughter remained there for almost a year, during which Ana worked as a house cleaner, and eventually she decided to leave the shelter and share an apartment with a fellow colleague. The idea was to "share the apartment and expenses, and I honestly thought I was doing the right thing, but I made things even worse." However, a few months after this decision, the woman with whom she had chosen to start this new stage in her life decided to go back to her ex-partner, and Ana is left on her own; only now she is faced with additional financial difficulties. At this point she decided to contact other institutions that usually deal with this kind of situation: the charitable foundation Santa Casa da Misericórdia, which supplied meals; the local social services to find them a new dwelling, and social security to apply for minimum income benefit. In the course of these endeavors, Ana is visited by a social worker who inspects their home to assess their living conditions. Without money to pay the rent, they were risking eviction from a house that was already deprived of many basic commodities, since her housemate had taken almost all the domestic appliances and furniture with her.

The social worker suggested getting back in touch with Filipa's father to ask for child support, but Ana refused. To do so would imply letting her ex know their whereabouts and she feared reprisals. According to Ana, it was at this time that the Child and Youth Protection Services intervened, ordering Filipa to be taken away to a children's home, leaving Ana on her own, even though she was homeless and jobless. The boyfriend she had at the moment offered to put her up, and it was then that she started using drugs. Over the following year she commits several robberies and initiates her drug trafficking activities, the crimes for which she was later convicted. It is also at this time that her daughter's life goes through the series of events described previously.

When we talked about this sequence of events, and how she felt about their simultaneous imprisonment, Ana stressed that there were some "truly positive aspects" to the situation they were now both in. Regarding Filipa's transference to the secure training center, as opposed to living in a children's home, she claimed:

> This was the best thing that could have happened to her. At the home she got no attention, they let the children run loose, coming and going as they please. It's no wonder they soon start getting into trouble. At the secure center it's completely different, and she really likes it there. They can't do whatever they please, they have rules, they keep schedules, and they are followed very closely.

Referring to her own experience in prison, she added: "Prison is helping me a lot too. Now I have my life in order, I'm no longer scared, and I don't have so many concerns. I can plan our future for when we both get out. Just this weekend [benefiting from a furlough period] I was with her and she told me not to worry. When she gets out she's going to her aunt's, and when I get released the both of us will go and live together."

It is not difficult to understand why Ana finds positive aspects to their present situation of incarceration. Considering their history, one might conclude that only in a closed and controlled environment were they able to find some sort of organization for their lives. When Ana states, "I am no longer scared", we can appreciate the marks of the psychological damage left on her from years of domestic violence and abuse. This aspect is worth underlining, since it was recurrent in the testimonies of other inmates at Odemira. For many of them, the time spent in prison is somehow perceived as a period that allows them to "organize their lives" as if outside their lives had slipped their control.

Finally, Ana's case also helps us to reflect on the performance of state care institutions in this type of situation. Unlike most victims in the majority of cases of domestic violence against women, Ana took the initiative to come forward—usually the hardest thing to do—reaching out for help and acting on it by moving away from home. She put an end to a cycle of violence that was starting to give rise to similar patterns of behavior in her daughter. Nevertheless, something seems to have gone wrong in the process after a few months spent in a shelter home. The end result of her endeavors to seek help from other institutions—housing, food support, and other benefits—was having Filipa signaled as at "risk" and ultimately having her taken away. This is where we may consider that state institutions failed their purpose. The fact that these organizations focus on the welfare of the children was not enough to guarantee an actual solution for the problems in this case, splitting the family instead of finding a way to provide the conditions for their life together.

This circumstance obviously did not imply that Ana had no other choice but to fall back on drug abuse and criminal offences. In theory, any adult woman (or man) could have found a number of alternative solutions to deal with the problems Ana was facing. But the fact remains that Ana did not feel she had any other alternative, and she acted accordingly. This inability to help herself is precisely the type of shortcoming or fault that the social workers who evaluated Filipa's case imputed on her: profiled as the mother who neglected her child, who subjected her to poverty and exposed her to violence, and ultimately the woman who chose to commit crimes.

Crime as a "Last Resource"

There was another inmate at Odemira whose life history contained similar features to Ana and Filipa's, except that in this case the woman in question acknowledged the practice of crimes as a "conscious decision", or as she also put it "the last resource at my disposal". Camila explicitly asked to see me, several months past I started my fieldwork at Odemira. She had been advised to do so by other inmates, who had said: "Talk to the professor, it will be good for you". When she told this, I hurried to make it clear that I wasn't a psychologist, and that I was only gathering material for a book about Odemira. I explained that I was absolutely unqualified and powerless to interfere legally or otherwise in her judicial case, and that I had never done so with any other inmate. She said that had never been her intention, she just wanted to "talk".

She had been told that I "understood their problems". Camilla initially told me that she had been "feeling very jumpy and nervous" lately, and was needing to "get things off her chest" because she recently had a clash with another inmate who had been her associate in the past and had been arrested on the same day as her. This 46-year-old woman belonged to a group of gypsy women who had entered Odemira a few months ago on remand. At first her discourse was muddled and incoherent, but as she unraveled her story it gradually became clearer.

Camila started to talk about the problems she was going through at the moment and which had led her to come and speak with me. Two other women who had been arrested with her were accusing her of incriminating another person for crimes she had committed, and Camila claimed that this was totally "unfair". The group she belonged to was comprised of a dozen women charged with perpetrating small robberies in shops—clothes shops, supermarkets—and doing armed robberies in old people's houses, in some cases resorting to violence. She had taken part in many of the crimes she was being accused of, but wasn't willing to "take responsibility for other people's crimes".

In turn, the remaining members of the group did not accept this attitude; especially considering that one of the other perpetrators was a relative of hers. Arguments and rows between them were becoming frequent, in some cases even requiring the intervention of prison officers to mediate the dispute. This coexistence was becoming untenable for Camila, but she attributed the conflicts to a different cause, which was unrelated with the crimes they had perpetrated as a group.

The fact was that to the other gypsy woman, Camila was not a "true" gypsy since some of her attitudes and manners were openly disapproved of by women from this ethnic group, and this was a cause for suspicion and dislike. Camila wore her hair shoulder length, instead of letting it grow down to the waist; she smoked, which was considered utterly unacceptable in a gypsy woman; she could read and write (she had completed 6th grade), which was an impossible thing for most gypsies (male and female) of her generation; and she had a driver's license and her own car.

After this initial outburst, Camila told me she was "feeling much calmer" and started running me through the events—which for all purposes had taken place in the space of a few months—since she committed her first robberies until she was held on remand pending conviction:

> I started committing robberies in 2015. Before that I was a street vendor, and I also did cleaning on construction sites, I did several things. Then I

became unemployed, and when my unemployment benefits ran out, I applied to the minimum wage program, but that also ran out after a while. My husband left me and I was homeless; I was left with nothing. I went to the City Council for help, but they did nothing for me. There were some abandoned lots in the area, some of which I knew from my time doing cleaning work. What did I do? I moved into one, cleaned the place up, painted it, and fixed it up as best I could. I had no running water or electricity, but I moved in there with the kids anyway. I have a 15-year-old and a 13-year-old boy, and two girls aged 11 and 9.

It was hard to get them to school and everything, but I did all I could. I continued applying for a minimum wage extension, but then I took the children's father to court, and he was ordered to give €100 per month for child support. He never did. The court said they were going to send a social worker to inspect my house, and I asked the City Council services to find me some place, anything as long as it had water and electricity. A room would do. The court also contacted the City Council, and they told them I was a good mother, only needed to have proper conditions. Then the social worker came by and reported that I didn't have a "real" house, which I totally agreed with, and again I told them that all I needed was someone to help me. They decided they would grant me six months to solve the problem: either I found a proper place to live, or they would have my children taken from me.

I begged; I called on the social worker, I went back to the City Council over and over, I knocked on every door. I couldn't find work; I was illegible for unemployment benefits. I managed to struggle by, but when they told me that I had six months to find a house or I'd lose my children, I thought I was going to lose my mind. I know I did wrong, mind you, it was wrong for me, for my kids, for everyone...but I started to steal things—food, clothes, even breaking into houses, etc. I thought I could get the money to keep my children with me.

Just like Ana, Camila also tried to set the existing institutional mechanisms in motion, in what we perceive to have been a long and grueling process, with repeated evaluations and administrative proceedings. From her narrative, we must underline her uncommonly thorough knowledge of the different available options. In the overwhelming majority of cases, given the low education levels and scarce legal or civic education, women in similar situations have a hard time finding their way through the institutional meanders, understanding the often over-technical written language, or sorting out the necessary documents to "prove" their dire situation and eligibility for state support or other kinds of help. Added to the bureaucratic illiteracy, on the other side of the process they may find civil servants who tend to be overly strict in terms of paperwork and bureaucracy (see Herzfeld 1992), and as a result most of these procedures are dropped at an early stage.

What Camila means when she says that she "knocked on every door", is that her plea for help was comprehensive: City Council oversees its constituent's housing problems; Social Security has the means to deal with financial problems of families in need by granting family benefits or a minimum wage. By pleading to the Juvenile and Family Court so that the father of her children was made to comply with parental responsibilities, Camila also showed knowledge of her and her children's rights. In spite of this, at a certain stage of these diligences, Camila seems to have stumbled upon a conflict of interests. The ultimatum imposed on her—six months to find a new residence or lose her children—is a form of intervention that looks at the problem from the children's viewpoint as somehow detached from the mother's situation. Instead of considering maintaining the integrity of this family, the preferred option is to separate the children and put them under the care of the state.

Since Camila had no contact with her own family, she didn't consider turning to them for help. She claimed that, even though she was a gypsy, she had made her own decision not to live among her relatives on account of her "non-gypsy" way of life. She didn't recognize herself with the life styles and codes shared by her community—in view of which now we can understand the antagonism other gypsy inmates at Odemira had for her. Rather than reconsider her relatives as an option, the strategy she came up with to solve the obstacles facing her was to join a group of men and women who committed burglaries around that part of the country. She was a valuable asset to the team. Since she owned a car, she could perform the kind of task usually left up to men—transporting stolen goods to stash houses and reception spots; driving other members of the group around in search of new targets; act as a getaway driver, and so on.

Camila explained that she had a very precise aim: with the proceeds from the robberies she would be able to raise enough money to move with her children to a new place. When the time came for the social worker's visit, at least it wouldn't be on account of the house that her children would be taken away. Camila admitted that it only took a few months to see her plan fail. The group had been signaled by local police forces; wiretaps had been made; formal complaints had been filed. The moment she was arrested, her children were led to a children's home, something that deeply distressed her during the period when the court procedure was still underway. Camila had meanwhile rekindled the bonds with her family of origin, who had hired an attorney as soon as they discovered she was imprisoned and were applying to be the legal guardians of the children so they wouldn't have to remain in state care. Her future was uncertain and she was coping badly with the solitude of life in prison. Despite being treated by the prison doctor and taking medication for anxiety, she claimed she "needed a different kind of assistance, a psychologist to confide in."

Ana and Camila's cases are examples of women who seek institutional help and reach a point where they find themselves caught up in a bureaucratic circuit that not only does not solve their problem—indeed most of them desist very quickly—but rather actually seems to end up turning against them. As if these women, upon reaching a difficult situation of poverty and exclusion, were not *victims*, but *agents* of their own condition.

The Everyday Experience of Violence: Victims–Criminals

Throughout these pages we have been observing that one of the pervading features in the personal trajectories and life history of most imprisoned women is the daily experience of violent acts involving them and their children, whether as victims or even as authors. Physical and psychological abuse characterizes a large percentage of the conjugal, parental, and emotional relationships of inmates at Odemira. In some cases it implies a kind of endemic violence assimilated into of ways of being and acting: as an integral and defining part of relating and interacting. Slapping, punching, kicking, insulting, belittling, punishing, and so on, have been (at least at some moment of their lives) naturalized and even ritualized. The women who had this kind of experience somehow expected, and were prepared for, conflict and quarrels; they developed an ability to foresee it and knew how to react, in most cases adopting a passive strategy. This point is relevant since most of the women at Odemira convicted for the murder of their husbands/partners had been victims of physical and psychological abuse. This means that, despite seemingly having come to trivialize the violence under which they live, eventually its real consequence emerges, as one day they have a disproportionate reaction, taking their aggressor's life. And in these cases, the descriptions almost seem to make this outcome predictable: a row escalates to the point they fear for their life, and consciously or not, they defend themselves by reaching for something that may be used as a weapon (a kitchen knife at hand, or the same gun they have been threatened with), killing their partner.

There is a noticeable anger and outrage underlying the narratives of most women when they talk about the beatings endured throughout years of marriage. Whether out of jealousy, alcoholism, or simply because "that's the way it was", they had to take their spouse's or partner's physical and verbal abuse. In the cases highlighted in the previous pages and chapters, some women explained how their partner's attitudes rendered them impotent by making them feel intimidated and they then convince themselves (or be led by others to believe) that they would never be able to start a new life and take care of their children on their own. Thus, with time they learned to relativize the recurrent acts of violence as "occasional episodes", and entered a state of denial, which postponed decisions with the hope that the problems would eventually sort themselves out. The most important, they said, was to "keep holding on", finding ways to divert their spouse's anger as best they could. At the same time as they expressed rage when describing their past experiences, there seemed to be an underlying resignation and even conformism, as if somehow they not only still considered their experience as an inevitable "fact of life", but moreover as if this kind of problem ought to remain confined to the domestic sphere; not as something that should be resolved with the help or intervention of outside parties.

This acknowledging of shame, guilt and stigma provides an explanation to anyone who may ask why some of these women, who were victims, spent those years without going to the police to file a complaint; why they hadn't, for instance, reached out to the Victim Support Association, or simply left their aggressor. These decisions imply the endurance of complicated and often lengthy processes, which many women take as a personal humiliation; and, furthermore, when talking about this subject, one inmate asked me angrily: "Why did it have to me to give up my house, my things, when he's the one who should be punished?"

Her question ultimately raised a legitimate objection: under the present law on domestic violence, the solutions presented to the victims (to go to a safe house, for example) means—at least for them—it is they who are relinquishing their rights, and not the offenders. In addition, and even though the children were often witnesses (and subjects) of the same conflict and aggression, for most of these victimized women, making an official complaint or making the problem public in any way (telling family, friends, or colleagues at work what was going on inside their household) implied an exposure that they were unwilling to allow. In fact, they considered it humiliating and almost an admission of their own incompetence (as spouses and especially as mothers).

In their opinion, this scrutiny by third parties could be just as harmful as the aggressions they had endured, which seemed to come out of nowhere and often ended just as quickly—which might or might not happen at all. Making their situation public would definitely materialize a situation in which they would also have to expose themselves. Thus, they gradually choose to shut out any contact with their family, which they knew would only reveal their own weakness and might even turn against them. Friendships were also reduced to a minimum, to avoid giving their husbands a pretext for bouts of jealousy, just as at work their intimate sphere was likewise protected. A common expression in these women's discourse was "I was waiting for him to change or to grow old and tired". In other words, they had decided that one day the problems would solve themselves, and they did so even knowing that they ran the risk of not making it alive to see that moment arrive.

It is worth considering another case that helps us to understand the connection between the experience of domestic violence and the ensuing crime of homicide, even though one should be cautious in assuming that there is a nexus of cause and effect. Matilde, unlike Mariana (who admitted her only regret was that her husband had found a "painless death") claimed that not a single day went by that she didn't feel repentance for killing her partner, even considering the hardships she had been through living with a man whose long-term unemployment and alcohol and drug abuse had been at the root of many arguments and frequent verbal and physical aggressions against her.

Mother of two underage children who had been left in the care of relatives upon her conviction, Matilde was a serene, cheerful woman, whose suffering came not just from being imprisoned, but actually from having taken another's life. During our first conversation, she repeatedly declared that he was a "bad man" but that she was in love with him, and in any case, she had no "right" to kill him. Living with her action was a constant punishment, and prison was faced almost as an experience that allowed her to atone for her past deeds. Ultimately, she accepted that she deserved being incarcerated; that there was no other way to offer reparation for her crime. The courtroom decision revealed the paradoxes implied in passing a murder conviction on someone who had been subjected to prolonged, daily abuse and maltreatment.

On the same day that Matilde killed her partner, the police had been called in to intervene at their household, after some neighbors had reported a row between the couple, which resulted in physical assault. The police officers took evidence of multiple marks left on Matilde, and when they tried to talk with the offender, he managed to escape. A few hours later that day, and when Matilde was home alone, she heard her partner's cell phone receiving text messages from another woman regarding a date apparently planned at a bar that same night. Matilde said she felt a rage surge inside of her—not only did she take daily beatings, she also had to endure being cheated on. She headed out to the place in question with the idea of exposing and confronting both of them, and she took a kitchen knife with her. She was met by him with insults and more aggressions, but this time she decided to fight back, stabbing him.

The swift medical intervention called on the scene was not enough to prevent the man from dying a few hours later in the hospital.

The judicial hearing sentence is almost a transcription of what Matilde described to me: "The defendant did not intend to kill the deceased, convinced that the stab wound would only cause slight injuries, and her actions were dictated by a state of despair, her judgement clouded by the discovery that her partner, who was also her aggressor, was having a romantic relationship with another woman."

Matilde claimed that her motive had been jealousy, and rage, given the attacks she had been subjected to. At that moment she felt she could also cause him the same kind of damage she had endured. During the trial, the defense argued that the experience of domestic violence should be considered an attenuating circumstance, which should reflect on her sentence. However, the judges found that Matilde's actions could not be considered a direct response to the aggressions she had suffered, and neither did they constitute a "means to put an end to an alleged situation of domestic violence, since her actions in this particular instance had not been caused by said aggressions, but out of jealousy".

This is a particularly difficult case to consider, especially given that the events took place in such a short period of time. No more than three hours elapsed between the initial domestic incident, the intervention of the police, and the mortal stabbing at the bar. Nevertheless, what the court is being called upon to judge is not her husband's aggressive behavior, or even if there is cause for legitimate defense in view of such aggressions: "The existence of a present or imminent aggression on the part of the victim has not been proved, and is thus considered irrelevant as grounds for considering legitimate defense for circumstances that occurred a few hours before in a different context in which the defendant claims to have been attacked."

This means that the court distinguished between the moments in which Matilde committed a crime motivated by jealousy, and the previous situation in which she was a victim of abuse. In other words, at the moment of the crime it was considered that she was not under any direct threat, and furthermore there had even been an element of premeditation in her act, given that she had left home that day armed with a knife.

These several examples are relevant for a reflection upon the various aspects involved in the current discussion about domestic violence, whether between spouses or between parents and children. Within the Portuguese context, the various changes introduced in the laws that deal with crimes of this amplitude, reveal significant idiosyncrasies. Notwithstanding the countless number of cases of domestic violence registered over the past decades, the law that made domestic violence a public crime—meaning those crimes that do not require a formal complaint from the victim to open a criminal investigation and follow judicial prosecution—was only passed in 2001. However, the enforcement measures being employed as punishment for these offences, on the one hand, or the public campaigns for victim awareness (including initiatives by nongovernment organizations), on the other hand, still present shortcomings in dealing with the complexity of the situations at stake.

Cases in which a formal complaint had already been filed and did not prevent a fatal outcome are not at all rare; on the contrary, or for that matter, cases where the aggressor had been granted with several suspended sentences but was allowed to continue living with the victim before, during and after the trial proceedings. In sum, the only choice left to the victim is to move out (and in that case decide whether or not they can take the children with them, whatever the case may be), and look for a shelter home, taking care to cut off all contact from family and friends until the trial ends, and then accept or conform with the court decision, which may prove to be not entirely efficient (in terms of preventing further attacks) in the end.

If the victim decides to take another course of action, as, for instance, moving in with relatives or friends, they will be unprotected from potential run-ins with the aggressors, who in most cases are allowed to await trial in freedom, and may or may not be subject to a restraining order. Thus, the protection they need and the choices they are faced with are not considered (by most victims) sufficient to prevent the cycle of violence from continuing—quite the opposite. Any of these measures can actually trigger episodes of vengeance, and lead to undesired encounters in places where the victims feel they are less protected than they would have been in their own homes.

From all of this we can also understand a further aspect, underlined by the majority of the women with whom I came across at Odemira: leaving their home, their personal belongings, their life, is something that most of them are not able or simply not willing to do. They argue that they should not be the ones to be disadvantaged, almost as if they were being doubly punished. There is yet one more obstacle to consider, which has to do with the financial difficulties these women have to face if they decide to break out from their previous situation. Most of them are not financially independent, and cannot afford to be the sole provider of their families. In fact, this is one of the factors that most decisively contribute to the apparent resignation with which many of them stay on. The lack of choice or will to change is not solely due to fear or impotence, but also to economic dependence from the partner, especially when underage children are involved.

Notes

1. My emphasis.

Reference

Herzfeld, Michael. 1992. *The Social Production of Indifference. Exploring the Symbolic Roots of Western Bureaucracy*. Chicago and London: Chicago University Press.

Image 4 Inmates working in the "boxes"

9

"Getting in is Fast, Getting Out is Harder!"

Over the course of several months, prison routines underwent transformations that followed a seasonal rhythm, as both inmates and guards pointed out to me on several occasions. Besides various training activities that complemented regular school classes, between the months of April and October a protocol established with a local fruit packaging company transformed the prison and all its spaces into a kind of assembly line, and its inmates similar to factory workers, divided in groups according to the different tasks assigned to them. By mid-May, as the school year reached its end, very few women were left unoccupied. Rooms and hallways that remained empty and useless during the rest of the year were now furnished with workbenches. During this period, even those who already performed some kind of prison duty (cleaning, laundry, bar, etc.) combined both functions, using all their free time to "do a few boxes".

Prison schedules, including cell opening and lockdown (particularly in the evening time) were also adapted to extend working hours, allowing inmates to continue their work after dinner (the so-called "exceptional timetable") so they could meet the deadlines set by the business protocol. Given that this kind of work paid wages well beyond the regular prison jobs—for example, a cleaning job paid on average €60 a month for a

© The Author(s) 2017
C. Frois, *Female Imprisonment*, Palgrave Studies in Prisons and Penology,
DOI 10.1007/978-3-319-63685-6_9

three-hour day's work, while an inmate could (depending on individual production) earn between €400 and €600 a month doing packaging work—this post is financially very attractive. This was, in fact, a highly expected opportunity, several times invoked by the inmates during the winter months.

Both the warden and the head officer considered that professional activities were vital to instill a sense of the importance of being engaged in work (inside and outside prison), helping inmates learn to manage their income and plan ahead, and above all providing a source of empowerment and self-confidence in their abilities and autonomy. During this particular summer, besides the packaging and labeling of fruit boxes, the prison also held a two-month remunerated training course in cooking. Despite the higher wages in the packaging job, women divided their time between both activities. They found the cooking classes more useful in terms of their future: "We get a diploma, and learn things that can be useful to us when we leave this place." Many of them saw this course as a chance to gain skills that one day, when they reached the end of their sentences, would allow them to "open my own business, a little restaurant". All classes—both written and practical assignments—were held in the prison kitchen, and inmates attended the course in full cooking uniform; two hours in the morning and two hours after lunch.

All the inmates seemed to be in good spirits during those months. There was work, there was money, there was tobacco. The good weather also completed the congenial atmosphere. Days were sunny and there was always something to do—a major contrast with the monotony and chill that pervaded prison life over the previous months. In fact, Odemira resembled a well-oiled system. The only inmates that did not participate in all this particular activity were some of the gypsy women. One of the guards told me that many of them were "unable" to label the boxes. It didn't seem to be a particularly skilled work. Was it because they could not read or count? This might indeed present a problem, since the job required them to match the label with each kind of fruit box correctly, but other than that it seemed to be a purely mechanical work. I was told that the problem was related to the fact that the majority of these women lacked the necessary fine motor skills that are usually gained during childhood (a problem that also reflected in their writing disabilities, see Casa-Nova 2009; Gomes 2013; Gomes 2015).

While most inmates quickly discovered a method to hold the strands of label stickers between their fingers, slipping them along in an almost mechanical way that sped up the labeling process and made the work more productive, the gypsy women who stayed out didn't manage to put the labels on straight. Either the strands of labels get all tangled up and the stickers get all stuck together, or the wrong labels go on the wrong boxes. The inmates suffered a penalty for each box wrongly labeled, and they had to refund the company for these mistakes, an event that was taken very seriously by the supervisor, a 22-year-old woman, one of the youngest inmates at Odemira:

> When I left my parent's house, in a small city to the interior of Brazil, I moved to São Paulo, where I found a house at a *favela*, because it was cheaper. I shared this house with a friend. I had a job as a shopkeeper and I met a boy there. Meanwhile I became unemployed and he suggested that I do this 'transportation', persuading me that there was a lot of money in it, that many people he knew had already done it and there had been no problem. I was very dumb.

As in the case of so many men and women convicted for drug smuggling in Portugal, particularly foreign citizens (Matos and Barbosa 2015), Teresa was one of those inmates whose criminal activity started, to use her own words "unexpectedly but directly related with the personal and financial circumstances of the moment". Although over the past decades it has become common to find amongst the Portuguese inmate population different types of drug-related offenders, such as drug dealers or the dealers-consumers, in the last decade there has been an increasing number of foreign citizens convicted as drug couriers; people apparently with no direct link with its sale or consumption, and precisely in view of this being especially vulnerable to be explored by trafficking networks. In other words, when Teresa was lured by her boyfriend to transport narcotics from Brazil to Holland—with a stopover at Faro, the major city of the Portuguese southern Algarve region—she had no prior connection to the drug world, either as a user or distributer, and her decision to participate was taken simply as a means to solve the financial problems she was facing at the time. Teresa claimed to ignore both the origin and the final destination of the substance she carried in her personal luggage.

Living in a *favela*, unemployed and bankrupt in one of the country's busiest and fast-paced cities—especially compared to the quietness of her home town—as Teresa faced her failure to succeed in a big city and was hesitating about going back to her parents, she became the perfect target for this kind of venture, especially given her naïveté as to the real risks and dangers of the drug trafficking world. She was young and presentable, she needed the money, and she was credulous enough to trust those telling her "it was so easy that no one ever gets caught". Thus, it didn't take much persuasion to convince her to put the 3 kg of heroin in her travel suitcase. It took almost no preparation. Her boyfriend explained that she should act naturally to avoid raising any suspicions during the flight, and told her she would get $5000 for the job, enough to last her several months in São Paulo.

The information she was given was on a strictly need-to-know basis: she would board a flight from São Paulo to Faro, Portugal. Once there, she should check into a motel at an address they gave her previously and wait until someone instructed her on the flight she should board to Amsterdam, Holland—her final destination. The boarding at São Paulo airport went without any problems, and the flight was uneventful. As she disembarked at Portugal's Faro airport, she didn't seem to raise any suspicions either, so she was rather taken by surprise when she saw two officers from the Portuguese Polícia Judiciária approach her when she was already waiting in line for a taxi. They asked her to follow them back into the airport to carry out a search of her luggage.

Teresa confessed at once that she was carrying drugs, and she also immediately discovered that she had been exposed by a third party, even though she wasn't told by whom. The investigators who made the apprehension told her they had received an anonymous phone call identifying Teresa as a drug mule. From the airport she was taken before an investigating magistrate, who decreed that she be held on remand awaiting trial. A few months later she was condemned to a prison sentence of five and a half years, to be served at Odemira prison facility (the nearest from the airport).

For several months Teresa tried to conceal her predicament from her family back in Brazil, until she finally decided to confide in her mother, who agreed to keep up her story, telling the rest of the family that Teresa had found a job in Portugal's southern region. She described her parents as honest, hardworking people, who would "be deeply distraught if they found out the truth". Teresa's father had never been keen on her leaving home to study. He would have been shattered to discover where she had ended up. The whole affair had to be concealed so that she could also put it behind her when she eventually returned back home.

As she recounted her story, Teresa blamed herself for the situation and cried with regret. She recriminated herself for her "foolishness", for her candidness; she shouldn't have been so careless, but she needed the money desperately. Now that she was separated from her family, Teresa considered that she deserved this punishment, and that she was very well treated in prison; that both officers and fellow inmates had been extremely welcoming. A few months into her sentence, Teresa started to become conscious that cases like hers were all too frequent—not only in terms of the crime of drug transportation, but also of their exposure. Some inmates who knew her story told her it was a fairly common scheme: occasionally the drug ring would expose one of their mules in order to divert attention from other couriers, who might even be on the same flight without knowing about the others. Teresa had been "sacrificed" as she put it, and blamed herself for not even suspecting that she might actually get arrested.

A couple weeks after she had entered Odemira, Teresa was appointed supervisor in the fruit-labeling job, managing the work of her fellow inmates, overseeing their tasks, organizing the shifts and ensuring that deadlines were met. This position gained her an above-average wage, meaning that Teresa could earn around €600 a month for the period the protocol lasted. She saw this responsibility as an acknowledgement by the warden and prison officers of her abilities and reliable character, characteristic of someone who hadn't pursued crime as a professional career or lifestyle. While she lamented her mistake, she felt she had a different status as a worker in prison, making her consider that her time there was not totally useless, and she made a point of performing and keeping this post as she would have any other job outside. As she proudly exclaimed: "I am one of the youngest here and I'm already responsible for all these women!" Teresa didn't want to be deported and be made to serve the rest of her sentence in a Brazilian prison. She knew the prison conditions there to be much worse, and she didn't mind expulsion, if that meant cutting down the duration of the prison time she had to serve. She said that maybe one day in the future she would have a chance to visit Portugal, saying: "This seems to be such a lovely country, but I never got to know it did I?"

The Uncertainties of Sentencing

One afternoon, amidst the bustling atmosphere that pervaded the prison during this period of intense activity, I saw Matilde (whose story was already described in the previous chapter), coming into the cellblock waving a sheet of paper and excitedly announcing "I've been given the cut!" as she jumped around with joy. Some inmates ran up to her to read what was written on the paper, and I remember thinking that it must be good news, and that it was probably something like a reduction in her sentence. I was therefore rather confused at the time when the guard with whom I was chatting at the time called Matilde over and put a hand on her shoulder saying: "Matilde, don't be too disheartened. You haven't done anything wrong. You must understand that your sentence is long, that the crime was serious; it was just too early, but you did well to give it a shot. Four months from now you can try again".

After all, "getting the cut" was a prison expression that meant a temporary or early leave, such as a furlough or even probation, had been denied. All that enthusiasm had not been an expression of joy, as I initially supposed, but rather a performance put on to conceal the actual frustration caused by this rejection.

There are different moments in a sentence when an inmate can file for temporary or early leave from prison, and they are all inscribed in the Code of Enforcement of Prison Sentences and Imprisonment Measures. According to Chapter IV, "Prison Facility Exit Leaves", these can occur upon reaching the middle of the sentence, on completion of two-thirds, and finally when the inmate has served five-sixths of the sentence. When these periods are achieved, an assessment is made based on a report drafted by the chief of guards regarding the inmate's behavior, as well as on a report made by the social worker or correctional treatment officer following the case (determining whether the inmate in question has incurred disciplinary infractions, or whether she is well adapted and participant in prison activities), and finally on a report from the prison director. Once these documents are given over to the sentencing judge, the merit of the request is appraised taking into consideration other elements such as the ones mentioned by the officer at Odemira when she addressed Matilde: the length of the sentence and the time already served; the type of crime and its impact on the community; the support network that the inmate will find upon release (where she will stay and with whom, what reasons are alleged for release—maintaining family bonds are the most frequent); and how cooperative and motivated to "change previous behavior" an inmate is (see also Article 78° of the Code of Enforcement of Prison Sentences and Imprisonment Measures).

Considering Matilde's case, in a certain sense it almost seemed cruel to subject herself to a process that she knew from the start—as did the prison officers and correctional treatment staff—had very little chance of success. Actually, the real surprise would have been if her request had been granted. So why submit it? Well, firstly the law allows it, so inmates have a right to do so. Secondly, an officer explained to me that it was customary, and inmates filed these requests almost as a pro-forma they have to go through. It is usual for inmates to have two or three requests denied before they finally receive a positive reply—since in the meantime their sentence time has also elapsed. This practice seemed to be commonly acknowledged, and even those inmates who chose not to hasten the process, seeking to avoid early rejections or seeming overly anxious, were usually not spared the same initial denials. It was very rare for someone to go home on their "first attempt".

But even knowing that her chances of success were remote, all the same Matilde felt disappointed and frustrated. A rejection is always a rejection; hearing a "no"; being deemed unfit. In this context, these moments gain a particular significance. Even when an inmate manages to put her crime "behind her" as she goes through her everyday life in prison—closing that chapter on the day the judge reads her sentence, and becoming immersed in work and the daily routines and making a criminal episode seem like it has receded into a distant past—the fact is that it never really goes away. The paper Matilde waved around for all to see was a material reminder that she was really not free, neither from her crime nor even from her past. As much as Matilde tried to forget, ultimately the sentencing judge was there to remind her, or at least to ensure that her deeds were not forgotten by the community.

On that day two other women received identical verdicts. Throughout the afternoon, amidst the activity of the box labeling and cooking course, these episodes became a major topic of conversation amongst the inmates. In a way, they all tried to find explanations for these cases, and in doing so they were evaluating their own chances when their turn came to file similar requests. While Matilde's situation was almost self-explanatory, the other two candidates had nurtured some hope that this time they would be allowed to go out. Despite being recidivist offenders—and therefore penalized on that account—they were both past the middle of their sentence. One of the women, who stood by listening to these conversations, turned to me: "What will it be like when my turn comes? Getting in is fast, getting out is harder!"

The feeling was one of resignation, and the generalized opinion was that recidivist drug trafficking offenders were constantly more severely penalized than others. On this point, we are in the sphere of expectations and perceptions regarding what is fair and what is unfair, of what "prison"—considered as an institution which reifies justice through the walls, bars, guards, correctional treatment staff and directors that configure it—is expected to deliver to those it confines, based on their conduct. Thus, inmates displaying "good conduct" during imprisonment will expect their behavior to be rewarded (or at least acknowledged) by the judicial authorities when the time comes to evaluate them for leave. Insofar as there is no gradual system of privileges in place (although there is a system of penalties that includes being dismissed from work, or being put in isolation—something which at Odemira is only used to punish extremely serious breaches of prison regulations) and since inmates and prison officers work closely to maintain a cooperative and smooth operation of the prison, whenever someone "gets the cut" instead of what they supposed would be an approval, it is received with surprise and almost seen as a betrayal. In other words, given that inmates make a positive assessment of their trajectory in prison, striving to comply with all they consider to be expected of their behavior, when they see their claims denied, they feel as if they have been cheated, as if after all "it was all for nothing". Thus, early on in their reclusion every inmate learns to identify the decisive moments in their sentence, and to infer the chances they present.

Although inmates usually avoided discussing in detail the motives that led them to practice the crimes for which they were convicted, and were especially evasive on this topic amongst each other, in their conversations it is common to hear references to specific legislation and to the articles of the Penal Code that may apply to their case, comparing their sentence lengths with fellow inmates in similar situations, trying to make an estimate of their chances, and drawing up different scenarios. Despite the well-defined underlying arithmetic, these decisions contain significant imponderables, particularly as concerns those elements the inmates have no control over, such as the personal view taken by the sentencing judge appointed to review their case. In other words, while they are constantly trying to read into the attitude and comments of guards, correctional treatment staff and the warden, looking for some telling sign that may let them guess which way their report will sway once they file a request for leave, that is impossible when it comes to the sentencing judge.

There is obviously always an element of convenience in these relations, which all parties manipulate one way or another: inmates make an effort to become adjusted to prison life, acting according to what they believe is expected of them: conformity, obedience, cooperation. They know that "good behavior" is a key element, and more or less consciously they act upon this knowledge to approximate their demeanor as much as possible to purported expectations. In turn, the prison officers, the social workers and the directing board are constantly advocating cooperation, valuing and praising its accomplishment. In this environment, however, no one on either side ever loses sight of their purpose: inmates are intent on leaving as soon as possible, and prison staff are focused on ensuring the smooth operation of the prison (Carlen 1982; Crewe 2012; Tait 2012). The sentencing judge ends up being a somewhat abstract entity who reveals little about him/herself. Even so, inmates try to figure out—by his/her gestures, words, questions or comments—the kind of person he/she is, so they can later exchange opinions with fellow inmates: "This one is cool, he/she is all right" or "This one's long-faced, not the sort to cut any slack". While their everyday experience allow inmates to form a personal opinion of the guards and the correctional treatment staff, just as they also manage to build up an image of what the "lady director is like", it is harder to do the same with the sentencing judge, who is not only almost a stranger to them, but more importantly they are unable to influence on a daily basis, by exhibiting their "good behavior" or demonstrating how "changed" their attitude has become (whether genuinely or calculatingly). Therefore, it is as if this critical moment of evaluation is perceived as unpredictable, almost as a "wheel of fortune", actually inverting the legal precepts in which everything is supposedly well defined.

This uncertainty deeply affects the subjects in reclusion, because just as they compare sentence lengths, they are also constantly trying to foresee how their case will turn out in the end; what will be the decision the day of the hearing regarding their request for early leave. Notwithstanding the fact that furloughs granted by the prison warden, and in this sense not dependent on outside entities—a possibility also contemplated in the law—are fairly common at Odemira, even for these inmates the only thing that really counts is the moment they are told their prison time has come to an end, that the day for leaving has arrived, that they can go free.

The Value of Time, or the Purpose of Prison

Rita's case was illustrative of how difficult and complicated the wait could become for an inmate. Rita was one of the only two women at Odemira who had reached the level of higher education, having completed a degree in accounting. At 52, she was an affable and serene woman. It was December when our first conversation happened, and she was eight months into a two-year sentence for fraud and embezzlement. At the time, she told me: "It's almost over; it's actually not such a long time. When I came in, it was only a month before they gave some work to do, and so I became busy quite soon, and right now I'm very involved in the prison newsletter; the first number is just coming out."

Rita had been convicted for economic crimes she had committed over a decade ago. She admitted that during all this period it never crossed her mind that she might ever actually have to serve time in prison. Her crime was "so old", and so rare the cases of economic crimes that actually produced a prison sentence (legal actions were so slow that often ended up proscribing due to exceeding the statutory time-limit) that she never imagined this outcome. Additionally, throughout these years she had filed several appeals and proved her financial incapacity to make compensation for the debts resulting from her crimes.

Her history was identical to many other cases involving small-scale frauds. Rita explained that when she worked as a freelance accountant, she offered to act as a "fake manager" for several small construction firms, whose real owners did not have residence visas and could thus not legally operate their businesses in Portugal. As a married woman and mother of two children, her financial problems began precisely when one of her sons asked to be sent to university in one of Portugal's major cities, distant from where they live. As her bills increased, she decided to start forging the firms' accounts and use the money to pay for her family's expenses. Rita claimed that the amounts were not very significant, "Eighteen thousand Euros from one firm; twenty from another…" As these scams were scarce and far apart, "no one really noticed", but even so the businesses themselves were illegal. In fact, the problem only surfaced when the owners decided they wanted to legalize their firms, and the fraud was detected.

An audit exposed the forged accounts, and Rita was fired from her job. She was warned that if she didn't return the subtracted amounts, the owners would take the case to trial. That was precisely what happened and the judicial process ensued lasting several years, causing her to lose her family home, but also resulting in the attachment of assets belonging to her parents, who had acted as her guarantors in loans she had contracted during that period. For a while after that, Rita still managed to work at home doing freelance jobs, but soon enough, as other legal problems and convictions ensued, she had to rely on her unemployment benefits for sustenance.

The years went by, and with one appeal after another, she tried to "show the judge" that she had no means to pay the debts: "What could I do? My unemployment benefit had ended, and I had to resort to the social integration income, how was I supposed to pay all those debts?" In spite of all her allegations and documents to prove her difficult financial situation, after almost 10 years of trials, the two-year suspended sentence she had initially received, pending the restitution of her debts, was finally made effective. Her family and friends were shocked:

> We never thought I'd ever go to prison for this. I know what I did was wrong, and I regretted it as soon as I was found out, but I really never thought I'd go to jail for it. My husband even said how unfair it was that only I should have to go to prison, given that the money had gone to all of us at home…but it was my responsibility, wasn't it?

Without expecting it, and notwithstanding her lawyer's warnings that it might come to this, Rita was arrested one morning at home by the National Republican Guard officials: "You know that feeling of being pulled into a parallel universe? That's how I felt. One moment I was in my home, and the next thing I know I'm in here." Regarding the contrast between the idea she had formed of prison and what she actually found in her experience of it, she told me:

> You know, I imagined prison would be much worse. I'm starting to realize that this prison is a special case. First of all, there are no drugs. Secondly, there aren't even 50 women here, and almost all of us are over 30 years old, except for four or five girls in their twenties. Besides, since there are so few of us, there is always an officer guard there for us, so you don't find the kinds of stories you hear from other prisons where there are drugs, cell phones; all kinds of contraband. I haven't seen it for myself, but that's how the others tell it—I suppose it's because they are much larger places…

Notwithstanding the difference in the type of crime, there are features in Rita's case that are common to the trajectories of many other inmates: she was locked up for a conviction which corresponded to a specific period of time, two years in this instance, but at the same time she still had several pending judicial processes. That was the status of the situation when I first talked to her, so at the time Rita knew exactly how much time she had to serve. But the circumstances changed over time, following a development which the inmates interviewed by Didier Fassin (2015) describe very accurately when they complain for having been imprisoned for a given crime and later seeing their sentence grow while they are locked up due to the conclusion of trials for other crimes they had committed at a different time in their life.

Rita presented exactly such a situation. When she was "about to leave", having served over half of her sentence, she filed a request for a two-day home leave, which she was legally more than entitled to. She was preparing her release, just like Matilde, following all the necessary procedures. The reply that came back, however, was even worse than a mere rejection. Her request was put on hold pending the result of her other ongoing accusations. In contrast with what she presumed—and paradoxically, without anyone cross-checking all the information regarding her current penal situation—there was another case being tried against her, with a great chance of producing a conviction. The possibility of extending her time in prison had increased precisely because, since she was incarcerated, her ability to earn an income with which to solve the remaining debts for which she was being successively punished had correspondingly been diminished.

Until the final decision from the court judging this new case was announced, and until the conclusion of the sentencing judge's appraisal of her request, Rita would have to wait in prison for one of two possible outcomes: either she would have to serve her full sentence and then wait for the result of the second trial in freedom (and then be made to return were she to be convicted), or she could see her sentence extended while still in prison, and be made to remain in Odemira to serve the new term as well. Rita had been thrown into a kind of limbo, where she could no longer be sure exactly for how much more time she would have to be locked up. What she had taken for certain when entered Odemira—that she would spend two years in prison—had become unpredictable, and a permanent source of anxiety. She didn't know when it could be, nor if the court ruling would come out in time; she would have to wait until the last day of her sentence to find out whether she would be actually be going home, and if so, how long would it take before she might possibly have to go back inside. On one of the last occasions we were together, Rita told me:

> So you see, after all these months, at this point I had already convinced myself that I was about to get out, and now the end is not even in sight. I can't understand how the tribunal works; they turned one of their rulings, or was it an appeal, I don't even know any longer. I'm paying with time for what I couldn't pay with money. On top of the two years I initially had, maybe now another five will be added, and meanwhile there's no chance of

an early leave for me. I'm suffering, my husband, my kids, my parents, we all suffering with this never-ending situation.

The expression of "paying with time" what cannot be "paid with money" was an apt metaphor for Rita's particular situation, but if we think of Foucault reflections on this subject, it is even apposite to describe one of the main purposes of prison sentences—a portion of time is subtracted from someone as a way of retribution for an offence, as if somehow, a lifetime acquired a quantitative value which could be exchanged as a form of restitution to society for a damage caused to it by the "owner" of that life. However, many of these women found that a prison sentence was too heavy a punishment.

More than inadequate, it seemed ineffective to them. How would society benefit by depriving them of their freedom? What purpose could it serve if they had already repented; if they had already learned their "lesson" and would not commit any crimes ever again? This was Rita's thinking, as she reminded me how long she had gone after her initial blunders without ever committing any other similar crimes. Mariana and Matilde also followed similar arguments when they tried to make me see that their reason for committing their crime had been extinguished the moment they had killed their respective partners, and could never be repeated again. Similarly, these same issues were raised by some of the women convicted for drug trafficking—that they hadn't done it for greed or desire for luxury, but strictly out of need, as a matter of survival and the sustenance of their children.

For these women, prison was a punishment inflicted on them by a court, but it didn't serve any practical purpose other than depriving them of their family and separating them from their children. In short, to harm them even more. When they were released, their poverty and vulnerability would be even greater, in the same proportion as their chances of finding work or providing for their children had been diminished, given that now they would also be burdened by a criminal record.

The discrepancy between what is regarded as fair or unfair, between acceptance of an error, on the one hand, or accepting prison as a "deserved punishment" on the other—with all the implications that deprivation of freedom entails—reflects as well a divergence between an intended purpose and its practical achievements. Perhaps the best expression for this dichotomy is enclosed in the question posed to me at one point during my fieldwork by one of Odemira's inmates. It was after dinner, and the day was coming to its end. Some women were waiting in line for their night medication, while others were just hanging around the cellblock, waiting for the cells to be opened for the night. I stood with a small group, listening to their conversation, when a young woman of 30 or so turned to me and said: "But after all, what's the use of that book you're writing to us? What we need is to be given a chance, not a book!"

References

Carlen, Pat. 1982. Papa's Discipline: An Analysis of Disciplinary Modes in the Scottish Women's Prison. *The Sociological Review* 30 (1): 97–124.

Casa-Nova, Maria José. 2009. *Etnografia e Produção de Conhecimento. Reflexões Críticas a Partir de Uma Investigação com Ciganos Portugueses*. Lisbon: Alto Comissariado para a Imigração e Diálogo Intercultural.

Crewe, Ben. 2012. Prison Culture and the Prisoner Society. In *The Prisoner*, ed. Ben Crewe and Jamie Bennett, 27–39. New York: Routledge.

Fassin, Didier. 2015. *L'Ombre du Monde. Une Anthropologie de la Condition Carcérale*. Paris: Seuil.

Gomes, Maria do Carmo. 2013. Políticas Públicas de Qualificação de Adultos e Comunidades Ciganas. In *Ciganos Portugueses. Olhares Plurais e Novos Desafios numa Sociedade em Transição*, ed. Maria Manuela Mendes and Olga Magano, 81–92. Lisbon: Mundos Sociais.

Gomes, Sílvia. 2015. Trajectórias de Vida e Experiências Prisionais de Mulheres Ciganas Recluídas. In *Mulheres e Crime. Perspectivas sobre Intervenção, Violência e Reclusão*, ed. Sílvia Gomes and Rafaela Granja, 47–65. Vila Nova de Famalicão: Húmus.

Matos, Raquel, and Mariana Barbosa. 2015. Mulheres de nacionalidade estrangeira detidas em Portugal. Breve caracterização de trajectos de vida e envolvimento no crime. In *Mulheres e Crime. Perspectivas sobre Intervenção, Violência e Reclusão*, ed. Silvia Gomes and Rafaela Granja, 67–83. Vila Nova de Famalicão: Húmus.

Tait, Sarah. 2012. Custody, Care and Staff–Prisoner Relationships. In *The Prisoner*, ed. Ben Crewe and Jamie Bennett, 13–26. New York: Routledge.

10

Conclusion: Prison as a "Mirror" of Society

It's the Christmas Party. My last visit had been more than a month ago, and at that time inmates were already busy and excited with the preparations. It seemed like a very good way to make my "exit": to say goodbye to Odemira not as a scholar but as a guest. It was also an opportunity to get a sense of the place without having to be permanently analyzing the surroundings, and it would force me to make that effort of shedding my academic persona. I brought pastries and popcorn for the party, realizing that I too was rather excited about the event.

On the days leading up to my visit I often found myself anticipating this encounter, trying to decide what treats to take, imagining something the women might like on this special occasion. I tried to forget all the meanings and feelings usually attached to the Christmas season—the warmth of loved ones, or family life, for instance—since I knew that, ironically, these were precisely the kind of thoughts that can be very hard to bear in prison. Actually, the warden had more than once commented that she made an effort to make these parties as lighthearted as possible to ward off melancholy; it should be a celebration, a party.

Upon arrival I was met by a group of *cavaquinho*[1] players from town, who had been for some years now regularly invited to play at the prison's

Christmas party, seeing as they had the same music teacher; some of the prison officers also played in the band in their spare time. The group of about fifteen men and women, fully dressed in the region's traditional attire, gathered around the prison cafeteria for some tea and biscuits. One of the older members in the band asked me if I was also "committed" there. I laughed and explained that I was a scholar from Lisbon doing research on the prison, but the man went on:

> I was going to say 'a guest', but it didn't seem like the right term either! But you know, it's already the third year I come, and I really enjoy it. On my first time I was a little scared. I thought I would find...how should I put it? A dump! I remember what the prison in town used to be like when I was a kid; seeing the raggedy men and women with their arms stretched out through the bars begging from passers-by. I thought it was still the same. Now imagine my surprise when I come here and I find all these pretty women, all dressed up and made up, singing and dancing! It was the total opposite of what I imagined.

Despite its comical tone, the player's account was also very enlightening. Without knowing it, he had just given me a first-hand description of a place I had only read about in the archives of the Directorate-General of Prison Services. Odemira's first "prison" had been right in the center of town, in the same building as the courthouse. The men were confined in the basement and the women on the upper floor, both exposed to the gaze of the public, whom they used to beg for food and money. When they were moved to the new location where the prison currently stands—and which at the time was no more than a barren field—inmates were removed from the public eye and from the town's daily life. Although with Odemira's demographic and urban growth the prison no longer stands isolated and has somehow been assimilated into the urbanscape, it has nevertheless remained outside the town center and away from the spaces of public life.

Meanwhile, more "guests" arrived: town hall officials, the prison's schoolteachers, doctors and nurses, a representative from the fruit packaging firm, National Republican Guard police officers, directors from neighboring districts in the region. At one point I saw the prison van coming through the gates, and three men being taken out in handcuffs. I only realized what these inmates were doing there when the doors of the van were opened wide to unload a set of instruments—a drum set and electric guitars—they were another act for the party.

The prison block had now turned into a showroom, with chairs lined up all along the main hall, and the surrounding cell doors adorned with Christmas decorations. At the far end, blocking the entrance to the canteen, a stage had been set up, installed with speaker columns and microphones against a black backdrop lined with party decorations. For an instant, I almost didn't recognize the people sitting around in the room. All the women were as if transfigured, all prepped up in glimmering long evening dresses of silver and gold, high heels, and sophisticated hairdos. The inmates had used their own money to choose their special outfit for the occasion. This was their day, and it showed. For some years now, the prison director and one of the administratives had followed the same plan: they visited several shops in the area, taking pictures of the dresses on display and then showed them to the inmates so they could choose the ones they liked best, and they also bought all the accessories, make-up items, and so forth, which the inmates then paid for. All women, even those who chose not to "perform", participated in the party in some way—with the decorations, organizing and setting up the party, cooking, sewing, and so on.

The front rows of chairs were reserved for the guests, and the rest were taken up by the inmates, and for the next three hours we would all be presented with a show that included acting, karaoke singing, gypsy and African dances, *fado* music,[2] gymnastics and even poetry reading. The *cavaquinho* band and the male inmates' band also performed that afternoon. Closing the show, the director, administratives and prison guards, joined by the inmates who had performed, sang together onstage. For a moment, all distinctions seemed to fade. There were not many new faces, but I still asked around about some inmates whom I hadn't seen yet. Two of them, mother and daughter, had gone to trial that day. Virginia was now in Caxias prison, after she had committed self-mutilation and the psychiatrist had decided she needed psychiatric supervision, even after she was released, which would be anytime soon. Gina, whom I almost didn't recognize in her silver-spangled dress, was close to release, and she beamed with anticipation. After the show we moved to the refectory for the dinner party awaiting us. Long tables had been set up and arranged in two different sections; a smaller one reserved for the guests and a larger section for inmates, who besides being obviously jubilant and imbued with the party spirit, were also simply looking forward to a different meal.

As the evening wore on, and I observed these women, I could see not only how much the dresses, make-up, shoes, and accessories revealed their femininity, but also how even those usually more reserved and bashful were so genuinely being themselves in their singing and dancing. During that evening, neither prison, nor crimes, nor past were anywhere to be found. Nothing in the stories and confidences they had shared with me over the past months had led me to expect that they could possibly ever present themselves as they were now: the woman now acting in a play, singing in a tulle skirt, was the same one who had years before been the victim of domestic violence until she stabbed her husband to death; the *fado* singer in the long dress was the same girl who had a 15-year story of drug addiction. The gypsies who gracefully swirled around in a characteristic gypsy dance were those same women accused of burglary and assault, whose husbands were also in prison and their children institutionalized. Their past, and even their present life in prison, had not completely erased their wholesomeness, or their selfhood.

Methodological Dilemmas, Ethical Commitments, Political Implications

Several years ago, when doing research on a prison in the Lisbon suburbs (unanimously described by the prison officers and correctional treatment staff who worked there as one of the country's most problematic facilities, due to the violent nature of the crimes committed by the inmates who were imprisoned there) one of those guards told me: "The point is that prisons are a mirror of the society in which they exist. What you find in here is the exact same as what we have outside, both the good and the bad." I tend to agree with this statement, though not necessarily for the same reasons as the ones he alleged.

What he was trying to explain was that the inmates in his care were violent, unscrupulous men, with no regard for law or authority, and that outside those walls there were many others just like them: with little education, with no jobs or any kind of family support; who spent their lives stealing, assaulting and trafficking. His conclusion thus establishes a kind of directly proportional relationship, which I find arguable, since it is not hard to recognize numberless ways in which life behind prison walls does not necessarily replicate and neither does it represent the "nature" of a society. However, if we take the statement to mean, on the one hand that a prison system somehow embodies and stands for all a society has failed to accomplish, and on the other hand it represents everything a society is willing to accept and enforce on its members under certain conditions, then I believe it is possible to say that "prison mirrors society".

****

Throughout this book we had the chance to observe and interpret the histories of several women imprisoned at Odemira. Some of the inmates had already been convicted and serving a prison sentence for several months or years when I first spoke with them, while others were still either in their first stages of reclusion, or awaiting trial in remand. In the case of the latter, as the months went by and our interaction was maintained, many of them went through several trial hearings and were eventually convicted and received a prison sentence. The chance to witness these developments and changes in their status allowed me to gain a deep understanding of how these women experienced their reclusion; how in some cases their own narrative and account of the crime they had committed suffered inflections; how their perception of justice and the justice system fluctuated, and even, as we have seen, how their view on the victims and the consequences of their actions acquired new contours.

It was not uncommon to find examples of inmates who described their judicial process (including the charges brought against them) as unfair, claiming to be victims of prejudice and discrimination—whether due to their socioeconomic condition, their ethnic origin or even their own crime—which was motivated by a combination of the bad faith and bigotry of judges, police forces, social workers, ex-spouses, and even relatives, who all "turned against" them. The anger and perplexity at what they called "injustices" was always latent, and it occasionally brought out emotions and reactions that were in stark contrast with the composure with which just moments before they had been describing their personal situation.

Notwithstanding the profusion of empirical and qualitative works on the prison context and their contribution towards our knowledge and understanding of prison environments, some of these studies seem to leave out their interlocutors' reasoning motives and even the description of the acts which led them to prison in the first place. In other words, it is as though there had been a choice to ignore the role of crime in the lives of those persons prior to their confinement.

Rather than question this choice, I find it important to underline my concern with questions such as: How do those criminal acts and those criminal trajectories shape or influence inmates' experience of confinement? How do they frame inmates' discourse and determine their relation to others in this environment? In other words, I believe that in order to understand imprisonment, and the impact it has on a person's life—to learn how they view their past, experience their present and project their future—it is essential that we also understand how they arrived at this vantage point; the choices they made, how they rationalize their past actions and their own trajectory. It is clear that there is wide variety of existing studies in the field, which reveal all their relevance without having to focus on their interlocutors' criminal actions as their main subject, and obviously we cannot ignore that there are many other equally important perspectives and factors to consider. But the fact remains that it is precisely the act of committing a crime, and the set of circumstances surrounding this event, which ultimately led to a very concrete outcome—imprisonment— and furthermore, which decisively marks the identity and discourse of our interlocutors at this particular moment.

Taking into account that, as this book has shown, that Odemira prison stands out not only from the majority of Portuguese prisons but, we may add as well, the majority of prison facilities around the world, we must demand that decision-makers, the general publics, the prison staff should be interested in knowing—given that knowledge implies responsibility—who lives and work in prison and what that experience is like.

In order to understand the experience of daily life at Odemira (as in any other context where we intend to carry out an empirical study) it was essential to become acquainted, even if incompletely, with those women's life histories, and particularly with one of its most defining events—the moment in which they committed a crime—since it somehow both crystalized so much of their past life and identity as it shaped their life and identity from that moment on. In other words, their criminal actions are at the heart of their new relationship with the world—with the community, the authorities, the law, the legal and judicial system, and so forth. Regardless of whether an ontological transformation actually takes place in a particular subject—in the sense that the subject will from that point on identify him/herself with "the kind of person who would do those kinds of things", as inmates at Odemira sometimes described themselves—it inevitably marks a "before and after" which we must acknowledge and respond to in this kind of investigation.

Following this line of thought, it also becomes clear that talking with the same inmate on more than one occasion, and over an extended period of time, about such a defining moment, allows us to observe the inflections (and possibly the ambivalences or even contradictions) in their discourse. This becomes particularly noticeable in cases where the first contact occurs while the inmates have just been recently imprisoned, whether upon conviction or still on remand. As time goes by we can almost see how prison and confinement gradually impregnates their bodies, transforming how they present and represent themselves to others. The discourse suffers successive reconstructions as it incorporates new information and adapts to the daily coexistence with other inmates: as the circumstances and the reasoning changes, so too the outlooks gain new contours and words new meanings. It is as if upon their arrival in prison they are convinced of the uniqueness and individuality of their story. As their time of imprisonment advances, they discover a kind of communion with their peers which, whether desired or unwanted, introduces in their previously isolated and "original" actions a relative measure—one could say a context—framed by all the other stories, experiences and trajectories around them.

Another advantage of the formal and informal conversations maintained over the course of repeated visits is the relationship that develops between a researcher and his/her interlocutors; a degree of proximity allowing time for the revelation of certain details and pieces of information that are usually omitted—either deliberately (out of shame, inhibition or basic prudence with strangers) or simply because the opportunity did not arise. This addition of new information was a recurrent feature of my fieldwork at Odemira, whether intentionally, as for instance when an inmate voluntarily sought me out because she wanted to "explain better" some of the things we had talked about on a previous occasion; accidentally, as when we were casually hanging around in the courtyard or cafeteria; or even indirectly, by reference to something or someone else.

The choice of cases that are described in greater detail in this book does not correspond to the most representative or common crimes within Odemira's inmate population. Had that been the criteria it would necessarily imply selecting narratives that involved drug trafficking, and as much as I consider that each case is an individual story and that the type of crime is not a significant common denominator, I consider that this would inevitably constrain our view, influence our perception, and limit our understanding of these women.

The richness of ethnographical and empirical data results precisely from the possibility to provide the most faithful possible portrait of the daily coexistence and interaction between people who, besides the uniqueness and multiplicity of their life experiences, were also judged and imprisoned for different acts. It is with this diversity they have to live, and as such it made sense that this book would seek to capture it. There is an additional reason to include various types of crime and not just the most common, and this applies not just to Odemira, but also to the Portuguese female penitentiary system as a whole. Although this prison might be considered an exceptional case in many ways, with characteristics that are substantially different from the two other existing female prisons in the country, there is one feature, however, in which it does not distinguish itself, and that is the composition of its population. While drug-related crimes are by far the most representative among the female inmate population, in all prison facilities we find women convicted for murder, theft, fraud, abuse, debt, and so on. We can therefore claim that, regardless of the small scale we are working with, in this respect Odemira reflects the diversity of the female crime-scape in Portugal.

Despite highlighting and describing the stories of some women at greater length, this does not necessarily mean I kept a more frequent contact or developed a closer relationship with these women in particular (or that they became what we commonly designate as "privileged informants"). It also doesn't mean that I didn't contact or talk to inmates other than those mentioned in the book, and which for various reasons were not explicitly portrayed here. In fact, my inclination would be to lend a "voice" and find a place for every single inmate at Odemira, or possibly to give greater prominence to the prison officers with whom I shared many experiences. But if I was anywhere near successful in my intentions, what this book actually narrates and reconstructs is actually made up from all these presences—whether I am describing a typical meal in the refectory, or an afternoon spent in the courtyard. All those people—inmates, guards, technicians, administrative staff, nurses, teachers, and so on—are inevitably present all through this book; as we crossed each other in the hallway, in the permanent droning echoes around the cellblock because there is a telephone ringing somewhere, a gate being unbolted, an inmate singing, another scrubbing the floor, the siren of a prison van leaving for trial. At Odemira, time has been recalled, but it never stands still.

Notes

1. A traditional Portuguese string instrument resembling a ukulele.
2. Fado is the main Portuguese traditional music genre, listed by UNESCO as an Intangible Cultural Heritage.

References

Aas, Katja Franko, and Mary Bosworth, eds. 2013. *The Borders of Punishment: Migration, Citizenship, and Social Exclusion*. Oxford: Oxford University Press.

Accornero, Guya, and Pedro Ramos Pinto. 2015. 'Mild Mannered'? Protest and Mobilisation in Portugal under Austerity, 2010–2013. *West European Politics* 38 (3): 491–515.

Acedo, Sara Sama. 2015. A Way of Life Flowing in the Interstices: Cigano Horse Dealers in Alentejo, Portugal. In *Gypsy Economy. Romani Livelihoods and Notions of Worth in the 21st Century*, ed. Micol Brazzabeni, Manuela Ivone Cunha, and Martin Fotta, 68–87. Oxford and New York: Berghahn.

Adriano, Paulo Jorge. 2010. *Penitenciária Central de Lisboa. A Casa do Silêncio e o Despontar da Arquitectura Penitenciária em Portugal*. Unpublished Master thesis, Lisbon.

Baldursson, Erlendur. 2000. Prisoners, Prisons and Punishment in Small Societies. *Journal of Scandinavian Studies in Criminology and Crime Prevention* 1 (1): 6–15.

Barker, Vanessa. 2009. *The Politics of Imprisonment. How the Democratic Process Shapes the Way America Punishes Offenders*. Oxford: Oxford University Press.

Barreto, António. 2000. Crises da Justiça. em *Justiça em Crise? Crises da Justiça*, org. António Barreto, 13–28. Lisbon: Dom Quixote.

Bennet, J. 2016. *The Working Lives of Prison Managers. Global Change, Local Culture and Individual Agency in the Late Modern Prison*. London and New York: Palgrave Macmillan.

Bloom, Barbara E., ed. 2003. *Gendered Justice: Addressing Female Offender*. Durham, NC: Carolina Academic Press.

Bosworth, Mary, and J. Flavin, eds. 2007. *Gender, Race and Punishment: From Colonialism to the War on Terror*. New Brunswick: Rutgers University Press.

Bosworth, Mary, and Ema Kaufman. 2013. Gender and Punishment. In *The SAGE Handbook of Punishment and Society*, eds. Jonathan Simon and Richard Sparks, 189–204. London: Sage.

Bosworth, Mary. 2016a. *Engendering Resistance: Agency and Power in Women's Prisons*. New York: Routledge.

Bosworth, Mary. 2016b. *Engendering Resistance: Agency and Power in Women's Prison*. London and New York: Routledge.

Bosworth, Mary. 2016c. *Engendering Resistance: Agency and Power in Women's Prison*. London and New York: Routledge.

Boutron, Camille, and Chloé Constant. 2014. *Être mère en Pérou: droit ou double peine?* Champ Pénal/Penal Field. XI.

Bravo, José. 2000. Justiça Penal em Portugal: Crise para além do Ruído. In *Justiça em Crise? Crises da Justiça*, ed. António Barreto, 263–275. Lisbon: Dom Quixote.

Buondi, Karina. 2016. *Sharing this Walk. An Ethnography of Prison Life and the PCC in Brazil*. Chapel Hill: University of North Carolina Press.

Cardi, Coline, and Geneviève Pruvost. 2011. The Violence of Women: Suppressions and Narratives. Champ Penal/Penal Field, vol. VIII. Last time accessed 2 May 2017. http://champpenal.revues.org/8367

Carlen, Pat, ed. 1985. *Criminal Women. Autobiographical Accounts*. Cambridge: Polity Press.

———, ed. 2002. *Women and Punishment. The Struggle for Justice*. Devon: Willan Publishing.

Carlen, Pat. 1982. Papa's Discipline: An Analysis of Disciplinary Modes in the Scottish Women's Prison. *The Sociological Review* 30 (1): 97–124.

Carlen, Pat. 1983. *Women's Imprisonment. A Study in Social Control*. London: Routledge & Kegan Paul.

Carlen, Pat, and Anne Worrall. 2014. *Analysing Women's Imprisonment*. Devon: Willan Publishing.

Carvalho, Maria João. 2003. *Entre as Malhas do Desvio*. Lisbon: Celta.

Casa-Nova, Maria José. 2009. *Etnografia e Produção de Conhecimento. Reflexões Críticas a Partir de Uma Investigação com Ciganos Portugueses*. Lisbon: Alto Comissariado para a Imigração e Diálogo Intercultural.

Codd, Helen. 2008. *In the Shadow of Prison. Families, Imprisonment and Criminal Justice*. London and New York: Routledge.
Cohen, Stanley, and Laurie Taylor. 1972. *Psychological Survival. The Experience of Long-Term Imprisonment*. London: Penguin.
Comaroff, Jean. 2010. Anthropology and Crime: An Interview with Jean Comaroff. *PoLar: Political and Legal Anthropological Review* 33 (1): 133–139.
Comaroff, Jean, and John Comaroff. 2016. *The Truth about Crime. Sovereignty, Knowledge, Social Order*. Chicago: Chicago University Press.
Comfort, Megan. 2008. *Doing Time Together: Forging Love and Family in the Shadow of the Prison*. Chicago: Chicago University Press.
Costa, Eduardo. 2003. A Lei Escrita e a Lei na Prática em Portugal. In *Prisões na Europa: Um Debate que Apenas Começa*, ed. António Pedro Dores, 93–102. Oeiras: Celta.
Covington, Stephanie, and Barbara Bloom. 2003. Gendered Justice. Women in the Criminal Justice System. In *Gendered Justice. Adressing Female Offenders*, ed. Barbara Bloom, 1–20. Durham: Carolina Academic Press.
Crewe, Ben. 2009. *The Prisoner Society: Power, Adaptation, and Social Life in an English Prison*. Oxford: Oxford University Press.
———. 2012. Prison Culture and the Prisoner Society. In *The Prisoner*, ed. Ben Crewe and Jamie Bennett, 27–39. New York: Routledge.
Crewe, Ben, and Jamie Bennett, eds. 2012. *The Prisoner*. New York: Routledge.
Crewe, Ben, and Alice Ievins. 2015. Closeness, Distance and Honesty in Prison Ethnography. In *The Palgrave Handbook of Prison Ethnography*, ed. Deborah Drake, Rod Earle, and Jennifer Sloan, 124–142. London and New York: Palgrave Macmillan.
Cunha, Manuela. 1994. *Malhas que a Reclusão Tece. Questões de Identidade numa Prisão Feminina*. Lisbon: Centro de Estudos Judiciários.
———. 2002. *Entre o Bairro e a Prisão. Tráficos e Trajectos*. Lisbon: Afrontamento.
———. 2008. Closed circuits: Kinship, Neighbourhood and Incarceration in Urban Portugal. *Ethnography* 9 (3): 325–350.
———. 2010. Race, Crime and Criminal Justice in Portugal. In *Race, Crime and Criminal Justice: International Perspectives*, ed. Anita Kalunta-Crumpton, 144–161. New York: Palgrave Macmillan.
———. 2013. The Changing Scale of Imprisonment and the Transformation of Care: The Erosion of the "Welfare Society" by the "Penal State" in Contemporary Portugal. In *Ethnographies of Social Support*, ed. M. Schlecker and F. Fleischer, 81–101. New York: Palgrave Macmillan.
———. 2014. The Ethnography of Prisons and Penal Confinement. *Annual Review of Anthropology* 43: 217–233.

———, ed. 2015. *Do Crime e do Castigo. Temas e Debates Contemporâneos*. Lisbon: Mundos Sociais.
Cunha, Manuela, and Susana Durão. 2011. Os Sentidos da Segurança: Ambiguidades e Reduções. *Etnográfica* 15 (1): 53–66.
Dores, António Pedro, ed. 2003. *European Prison: Starting a Debate*. Oeiras: Celta.
Drake, Deborah. 2012. *Prisons, Punishment and the Pursuit of Security*. New York: Palgrave.
———. 2015. Finding Secrets and Secret Findings: Confronting the Limits of the Ethnographer's Gaze. In *The Palgrave Handbook of Prison Ethnography*, ed. Deborah Drake, Rod Earle, and Jennifer Sloan, 252–270. New York: Palgrave Macmillan.
Drake, Deborah, Rod Earle, and Jennifer Sloan, eds. 2015. *The Palgrave Handbook of Prison Ethnography*. New York: Palgrave Macmillan.
Duarte, Vera. 2012. *Discursos e Percursos na Delinquência Juvenil Feminina*. Vila Nova de Famalicão: Húmus.
Durão, Susana. 2008. *Patrulha e Proximidade. Uma Etnografia da Polícia de Lisboa*. Coimbra: Almedina.
Fassin, Didier. 2011. *La Force de l'ordre. Une anthropologie de la police des quartiers*. Paris: Seuil.
———. 2015. *L'Ombre du Monde. Une Anthropologie de la Condition Carcérale*. Paris: Seuil.
Fassin, Didier, et al. 2013. *Juger, Réprimer, Accompagner. Essai sur la Morale de L'État*. Paris: Seuil.
Fassin, Didier, et al. 2015. *At the Heart of the State. The Moral World of Institutions*. London: Pluto Press.
Fatela, João. 1989. *O Sangue e a Rua. Elementos para uma Antropologia da Violência em Portugal (1926–1946)*. Lisbon: Dom Quixote.
Fernandez, Fabrice. 2013. La discipline derrière les barreaux. Humanisation de la sanction dans le monde carcéral. In *Juger, Réprimer, Accompagner. Essai sur la Morale de L'État*, ed. D. Fassin et al., 167–200. Paris: Seuil.
Ferreira, Vitor Peña. 1999. Sobrepopulação Prisional e Sobrepopulação em Portugal: Evolução Recente, Situação Atual e Alguns Factores que a Explicam. *Temas Penitenciários* 2 (3): 7–38.
Fili, Andriani. 2013. Women in Prison: Victims or Resisters? Representations of Agency in Women's Prisons in Greece. *Signs* 39 (1), Women, Gender, and Prison: National and Global Perspectives (Autumn): 1–26.
Foucault, Michel. 1977. *Discipline and Punish: The Birth of the Prison* (A. Sheridan, Trans.). London: Penguin.

References

Foucault, Michel. 1995. *Discipline and Punish: The Birth of Prison*. Trans. Alan Sheridan. London: Penguin.
Frois, Catarina. 2009. *The Anonymous Society. Identity, Stigma and Anonymity in 12-Step Associations*. Newcastle upon Tyne: Cambridge Scholars Publishing.
———. 2011. Video-Surveillance in Portugal: Analysis of a Transitional Process. *Social Analysis* 55 (3): 35–53.
———. 2013. *Peripheral Vision. Politics, Technology and Surveillance*. Oxford and New York: Berghahn.
———. 2014. The Fate of 'Backwardness': Portuguese Expectations over Modernization. *Anthropological Journal of European Cultures* 21 (2): 89–113.
———. 2016. Close Insecurity: Shifting Conceptions of Security in Prison Confinement. *Social Anthropology* 24 (3): 309–323.
———. 2017. Privação de Liberdade, privação de dignidade. Violência em Contexto Prisional. *Etnográfica*.
Garsten, Christina, and Anette Nyqvist, eds. 2014. *Organisational Anthropology. Doing Ethnography in and Among Complex Organisations*. London: Pluto Press.
Genders, Elaine, and Elaine Player. 1995. *Grendon. A Study of a Therapeutic Prison*. Oxford: Clarendon Press.
Gil, José. 1999. Responsabilidade. In *Enciclopédia Einaudi*, vol. 39, 201–214. Lisbon: Imprensa Nacional.
Goffman, Erving. 1959. *The Presentation of Self in Everyday Life*. New York: Anchor Books.
———. 1961. *Asylums: Essays on the Social Situation of Mental Patients and Other Inmates*. New York: Anchor Books.
———. 1963a. *Stigma. Notes on the Management of the Spoiled Identity*. New York: Simon and Schuster.
———. 1963b. *Behavior in Public Places. Notes on the Social Organization of Gatherings*. New York: The Free Press.
———. 1967. *Interaction Ritual: Essays on Face-to-Face Interaction*. New York: Anchor Books.
Gomes, Maria do Carmo. 2013. Políticas Públicas de Qualificação de Adultos e Comunidades Ciganas. In *Ciganos Portugueses. Olhares Plurais e Novos Desafios numa Sociedade em Transição*, ed. Maria Manuela Mendes and Olga Magano, 81–92. Lisbon: Mundos Sociais.
Gomes, Silvia. 2014. *Caminhos para a Prisão. Uma Análise do Fenómeno da Criminalidade Associada a Grupos Estrangeiros e Étnicos em Portugal*. Vila Nova de Famalicão: Húmus.

Gomes, Sílvia. 2015. Trajectórias de Vida e Experiências Prisionais de Mulheres Ciganas Recluídas. In *Mulheres e Crime. Perspectivas sobre Intervenção, Violência e Reclusão*, ed. Sílvia Gomes and Rafaela Granja, 47–65. Vila Nova de Famalicão: Húmus.

Gomes, Silvia, and Rafaela Granja, eds. 2015a. *Mulheres e Crime. Perspectivas sobre Intervenção, Violência e Reclusão*. Vila Nova de Famalicão: Húmus.

———. 2015b. Trajectórias de vida e experiências prisionais de mulheres ciganas recluídas. In *Mulheres e Crime. Perspectivas sobre Intervenção, Violência e Reclusão*, ed. Silvia Gomes and Rafaela Granja, 47–65. Vila Nova de Famalicão: Húmus.

Gonnella, Patrizio. 2013. Italy: Between Amnesties and Emergencies. In *Punishment in Europe. A Critical Anatomy of Penal Systems*, ed. Vincent Ruggiero and Mick Ryan, 226–244. London and New York: Palgrave Macmillan.

Granja, Rafaela. 2015. Para cá e para lá dos muros: Relações familiares na interface entre o interior e o exterior da prisão. Unpublished PhD thesis, Minho University.

Gupta, Akhil, and James Ferguson, eds. 1997. *Anthropological Locations. Boundaries and Grounds of a Field Science*. Chicago and London: University of Chicago Press.

Haney, Lynne. 2013. Motherhood as Punishment: The Case of Parenting in Prison. *Signs: Journal of Women in Culture and Society* 39 (1): 105–130.

Hastrup, Kirsten, and Peter Hervik, eds. 1994. *Social Experience and Anthropological Knowledge*. New York: Routledge.

Herzfeld, Michael. 1992. *The Social Production of Indifference. Exploring the Symbolic Roots of Western Bureaucracy*. Chicago and London: Chicago University Press.

James, Deborah, and Christina Toren. 2010. Introduction. Culture, Context and Anthropologists' Accounts. In *Culture Wars: Context, Models and Anthropologists' Accounts*, ed. Deborah James, Evelyn Plaice, and Christina Toren, 1–18. Oxford and New York: Berghahn.

Jewkes, Yvonne. 2012. Autoethnography and Emotion as Intellectual Resources. *Qualitative Inquiry* 18 (1): 63–75.

———. 2015. Foreword. In *The Palgrave Handbook of Prison Ethnography*, ed. Deborah Drake, Rod Earle, and Jennifer Sloan, ix–xiii. London and New York: Palgrave Macmillan.

Jewkes, Yvonne, Jamie Bennett, and Ben Crewe, eds. 2016. *Handbook on Prisons*. 2nd ed. London and New York: Routledge.

Jewkes, Yvonne, and Helen Johnston. 2006. *Prison Readings. A Critical Introduction to Prisons and Imprisonment.* Devon: Willan Publishing.

Jewkes, Yvonne, and Serena Wright. 2016. Researching the Prison. In *Handbook on Prisons*, ed. Yvonne Jewkes, Jamie Bennett, and Ben Crewe, 2nd ed., 659–676. London and New York: Routledge.

Johnsen, Berit, Per Kristian Granheim, and Janne Helgesen. 2011. Exceptional Prison Conditions and the Quality of Prison Life: Prison Size and Prison Culture in Norwegian Closed Prisons. *European Journal of Criminology* 8 (6): 515–529.

Liebling, Alison. 1992. *Suicides in Prison.* London: Routledge.

———. 2008. 'Titan' Prisons: Do Size, Efficiency and Legitimacy Matter? In *Tackling Prison Overcrowding. Build More Prisons? Sentence Fewer Offenders?* ed. Mike Hough, Rob Allen, and Enver Solomon, 63–80. Bristol: Policy Press.

Liebling, Alison, and Amy Ludlow. 2016. Suicide, Distress and the Quality of Prison Life. In *Handbook on Prisons*, ed. Yvonne Jewkes, Jamie Bennett, and Ben Crewe, 2nd ed., 224–245. London and New York: Routledge.

Liebling, Alison, David Price, and Guy Shefer. 2012. *The Prison Officer.* 2nd ed. London and New York: Routledge.

Lima, Antónia. 2003. *Grandes Famílias, Grandes Empresas. Ensaio Antropológico sobre uma Elite de Lisboa.* Lisboa: Dom Quixote.

Lima, Antónia Pedroso. 2016. Care as a Factor for Sustainability in Situations of Crisis: Portugal between the Welfare State and Interpersonal Relationships. *Cadernos Pagu* 46: 79–105.

Machado, Helena. 2015. Genética e Suspeição Criminal: Reconfigurações Actuais de Co-produção entre Ciência, Ordem Social e Controlo. In *Ciência, Identificação e Governo*, ed. Cláudia Fonseca and Helena Machado, 38–55. Porto Alegre: Coleções Editoriais do Cegov.

Magano, Olga. 2014. *Tracejar Vidas "Normais". Estudo Qualitativo sobre a Integração dos Ciganos em Portugal.* Lisbon: Mundos Sociais.

Maguire, Mark, Catarina Frois, and Nils Zurawski, eds. 2014. *The Anthropology of Security. Perspectives from the Frontline of Policing, Counter-terrorism and Border Control.* London: Pluto Press.

Mahtani, Sabrina. 2013. Women and the Criminalization of Poverty: Perspectives from Sierra Leone. *Signs: Journal of Women in Culture and Society* 39 (1): 243–264.

Manita, Celina. 2005. *A intervenção em agressores no contexto da violência doméstica em Portugal: estudo preliminar de caracterização.* Lisbon: Comissão para a Igualdade e para os Direitos das Mulheres.

Martin, Thomas Max, Andrew Jefferson, and Mahuya Bandyopadhay. 2014. Sensing Prison Climates. Governance, Survival and Transition. *Focaal—Journal of Global and Historical Anthropology* 68: 3–17.

Mathews, Roger. 1999. *Doing Time. An Introduction to the Sociology of Imprisonment.* London: Palgrave Macmillan.

Matos, Raquel, and Mariana Barbosa. 2015. Mulheres de nacionalidade estrangeira detidas em Portugal. Breve caracterização de trajectos de vida e envolvimento no crime. In *Mulheres e Crime. Perspectivas sobre Intervenção, Violência e Reclusão*, ed. Silvia Gomes and Rafaela Granja, 67–83. Vila Nova de Famalicão: Húmus.

Medlicott, Diana. 2007. Women in Prison. In *Handbook on Prisons*, ed. Yvonne Jewkes, 245–267. Devon: Willan.

Melhuus, Marit, Jon Mitchell, and Helena Wulff, eds. 2010. *Ethnographic Practice in the Present.* Oxford and New York: Berghahn.

Mendes, Maria Manuela, and Olga Magano, eds. 2013. *Ciganos Portugueses. Olhares Plurais e Novos Desafios numa Sociedade em Transição.* Lisbon: Mundos Sociais.

Merry, Sally E. 2008. *Gender Violence: A Cultural Perspective.* Oxford: Wiley-Blackwell.

Mills, Alice, and Kathleen Kendall. 2016. Mental Health in Prisons. In *Handbook on Prisons*, ed. Yvonne Jewkes, Jamie Bennett, and Ben Crewe, 2nd ed., 187–204. London and New York: Routledge.

Moore, Linda, and Phil Scranton. 2014. *The Incarceration of Women. Punishing Bodies, Breaking Spirits.* London and New York: Palgrave Macmillan.

Moreira, J.J. Semedo. 1994. *Vidas Encarceradas. Estudo sociológico de uma prisão masculina.* Lisbon: Centro de Estudos Judiciários.

———. 1999. Ciganos na prisão: Um universo diferente? *Temas Penitenciários* 2 (2): 5–18.

———. 2011. Privação de liberdade: Uma aritmética da população prisional. *Ousar Integrar—Revista de Reinserção Social e Prova* 10: 63–84.

Narotzky, Susana. 2012. Europe in Crisis: Grassroots Economies and the Anthropological Turn. *Etnográfica* 16 (3): 627–638.

Ocaña, Mónica Aranda, and Iñaki Rivera Beiras. 2013. The Spanish Penal and Penitentiary System: From the Re-Socialising Objective to the Internal Governance of Prison. In *Punishment in Europe. A Critical Anatomy of Penal Systems*, ed. Vincent Ruggiero and Mick Ryan, 245–262. London and New York: Palgrave Macmillan.

Padovani, Natália Corazza. 2013. Confounding Borders and Walls: Documents, Letters and the Governance of Relationships in São Paulo and Barcelona Prisons. *Vibrant—Virtual Brazilian Anthropology* 10 (2). Brasília: ABA. Available at http://www.vibrant.org.br/issues/v10n2/natalia-corazza-padovani-confounding-borders-and-walls/

Palacios Cerezales, Diego. 2011. *Portugal à Coronhada. Protesto Popular e Ordem Pública nos Séculos XIX e XX*. Lisbon: Tinta-da-China.

Parnell, Philip. 2003. Introduction. Crime's Power: Crime, Law, and the State. In *Crime's Power. Anthropologists and the Ethnography of Crime*, 1–32. New York: Palgrave.

Parnell, Philip, and Stephanie Kane, eds. 2003. *Crime's Power. Anthropologists and the Ethnography of Crime*. New York: Palgrave.

Penglase, Ben, Stephanie Kane, and Philip Parnell. 2009. Interview: The 'New Anthropology of Crime'. *PoLAR: Political and Legal Anthropology Review* 32 (1): 105–123.

Pereira Bastos, Susana. 1997. *O Estado Novo e os seus Vadios. Contribuição para o Estudo das Identidades Marginais e sua Repressão*. Lisbon: Dom Quixote.

Piacentini, Laura. 2007. Researching on Russian Prisons. A Consideration of New and Established Methodologies in Prison Research. In *Handbook on Prisons*, ed. Yvonne Jewkes, 152–173. Devon: Willan.

Pina Cabral, João. 2003. *O Homem na Família: Cinco Ensaios de Antropologia*. Lisbon: Imprensa de Ciências Sociais.

———. 2010. The Door in the Middle: Six Conditions for Anthropology. In *Culture Wars: Context, Models and Anthropologists' Accounts*, ed. Deborah James, Evelyn Plaice, and Christina Toren, 152–169. Oxford and New York: Berghahn.

Poiares, Nuno. 2014. *Políticas de segurança e as dimensões simbólicas da lei: o caso da violência doméstica em Portugal*. Unpublished PhD thesis, ISCTE-IUL, Lisbon.

Pratt, John, and Anna Eriksson. 2013. *Contrasts in Punishment. An Explanation of Anglophone Excess and Nordic Exceptionalism*. London and New York: Routledge.

Rhodes, Lorna A. 2004. *Total Confinement: Madness and Reason in the Maximum Security Prison*. Berkeley: University California Press.

Rogan, Mary. 2013. The Irish Penal System: Pragmatism, Neglect and the Effects of Austerity. In *Punishment in Europe. A Critical Anatomy of Penal Systems*, ed. Vincent Ruggiero and Mick Ryan. Lonn and New York: Palgrave Macmillan.

Roux, Sébastien. 2015. Discipline and Educate. Contradictions Within the Juvenile Justice System. In *At the Heart of the State. The Moral World of Institutions*, ed. Didier Fassin, 171–196. London: Pluto Press.

Rowe, Abigail. 2012. Women Prisoners. In *The Prisoner*, ed. Ben Crewe and Jamie Bennett, 103–116. New York: Routledge.

Ruggiero, Vincent, and Mick Ryan, eds. 2013. *Punishment in Europe. A Critical Anatomy of Penal Systems*. London and New York: Palgrave Macmillan.

Santos, José Beleza dos. 1947. *Nova Organização Prisional Portuguesa (alguns princípios e realizações)*. Coimbra: Coimbra Editora.

Sarat, Austin, ed. 2014a. *The Punitive Imagination. Law, Justice and Responsibility*. Alabama: The University of Alabama Press.

———, ed. 2014b. Examining Assumptions. An Introduction to Punishment, Imagination, and Possibility. In *The Punitive Imagination. Law, Justice and Responsibility*, ed. Austin Sarat, 1–18. Alabama: The University of Alabama Press.

Smith, Peter Scharff. 2014. *When the Innocent are Punished. The Children of Imprisoned Parents*. London and New York: Palgrave Macmillan.

Scheper-Hughes, Nancy. 1992. *Death Without Weeping: The Violence of Everyday Life in Brazil*. Berkeley: University of California Press.

Schinkel, Marguerite. 2014. *Being Imprisoned. Punishment, Adaptation and Desistance*. London and New York: Palgrave Macmillan.

Semedo, José. 1994. *Vidas Encarceradas. Estudo Sociológico de uma Prisão Masculina*. Lisbon: Centro de Estudos Judiciários.

Semedo, José. 2004. *Relatório Estatístico 2004*. Lisbon: Direção Geral dos Serviços Prisionais, Serviços de Organização, Planeamento e Relações Externas.

———. 2005. *Relatório Estatístico 2005*. Lisbon: Direção Geral dos Serviços Prisionais, Serviços de Organização, Planeamento e Relações Externas.

Simon, Jonathan, and Richard Sparks, eds. 2013. *The SAGE Handbook of Punishment and Society*. London: Sage.

Smith, Peter Scharff. 2014. *When the Innocent are Punished. The Children of Imprisoned Parents*. London and New York: Palgrave Macmillan.

Solinger, Rickie, Paula C. Johnson, Martha L. Raimon, Tina Reynolds, and Ruby C. Tapia, eds. 2010. *Interrupted Life. Experiences of Incarcerated Women in the United States*. Berkeley: University of California Press.

Sousa Santos, Boaventura. 1990. *O Estado e a Sociedade em Portugal: 1974–1988*. Porto: Edições Afrontamento.

Sykes, Gresham. 1958. *The Society of Captives. A Study of a Maximum Security Prison*. Princeton: Princeton University Press.

Tabbush, Constanza, and María Florencia Gentile. 2013. Emotions behind Bars: The Regulation of Mothering in Argentine Jails. *Signs: Journal of Women in Culture and Society* 39 (1): 131–149.

Tait, Sarah. 2012. Custody, Care and Staff–Prisoner Relationships. In *The Prisoner*, ed. Ben Crewe and Jamie Bennett, 13–26. New York: Routledge.

Torres, Anália, and Maria do Carmo Gomes. 2002. *Drogas e Prisões em Portugal*. Lisbon: CIES/ISCTE.

Torres, Anália, et al. 2009. *Drogas e Prisões: Portugal 2001–2007*. Lisbon: CIES/ISCTE.

Ugelvik, Thomas. 2012. Prisoners and their Victims: Techniques of Neutralization, Techniques of the Self. *Ethnography* 13 (3): 259–277.

———. 2014. *Power and Resistance in Prison: Doing Time, Doing Freedom*. London and New York: Palgrave.

———. 2016. Prisons as Welfare Institutions? Punishment and the Nordic Model. In *Handbook on Prisons*, ed. Yvonne Jewkes, Jamie Bennett, and Ben Crew, 2nd ed., 388–402. London and New York: Routledge.

Ugelvik, Thomas, and Jane Dullum, eds. 2012. *Penal Exceptionalism? Nordic Prison Policy and Practice*. London and New York: Routledge.

Wacquant, Löic. 2000a. *Prisons of Poverty*. Minneapolis and London: University of Minnesota Press.

Wacquant, Loïc. 2000b. The New 'Peculiar Institution': On the Prison as Surrogate Ghetto. *Theoretical Criminology* 4: 377–389.

Wacquant, Löic. 2002. The Curious Eclipse of Prison Ethnography in the Age of Mass Incarceration. *Ethnography* 3 (4): 371–397.

———. 2007. *Urban Outcasts. A Comparative Sociology of Advanced Marginality*. London: Polity Press.

———. 2009. *Punishing the Poor. The Neoliberal Government of Social Insecurity*. Durham and London: Duke University Press.

Waldram, James B. 1998. Anthropology in Prison: Negotiating Consent and Accountability with a 'Captured' Population. *Human Organization* 57 (2): 238–244.

———. 2007. Narrative and the Construction of 'Truth' in a Prison-Based Treatment Program for Sexual Offenders. *Ethnography* 8 (2): 145–169.

Waldram, James B., and U. Saskatchewan. 2009. Challenges of Prison Ethnography, *Anthropology News*, January, 4–5.

Wall, Karin, ed. 2012. *Famílias em Portugal*. 2nd ed. Lisbon: Imprensa de Ciências Sociais.

Wall, Karin, and Lígia Amâncio, eds. 2007. *Família e Género em Portugal e na Europa*. Lisbon: Imprensa de Ciências Sociais.

Wall, Karin, Vanessa Cunha, Leonor Rodrigues, and Rita Correia. 2015. Famílias em Portugal e na Europa. In *Portugal Social em Mudança: Portugal no Contexto Europeu em Anos de Crise*, ed. João Ferrão and Ana Delicado, 31–45. Lisbon: Instituto de Ciências Sociais.

Waldram, James. 2016. Narrative and the Construction of 'Truth' in a Prison-based Treatment Program for Sexual Offenders. *Ethnography* 8 (2): 145–169.

Worrall, Anne. 1990. *Offending Women: Female Lawbreakers and the Criminal Justice System*. New York: Routledge.

Zedner, Lucia. 2010. Security, the State, and the Citizen: The Changing Architecture of Crime Control. *New Criminal Law Review* 13 (2): 379–403.

———. 2013. Is the Criminal Law Only for Citizens? A Problem at the Borders of Punishment. In *The Borders of Punishment: Migration, Citizenship, and Social Exclusion*, ed. Katja Franko Aas and Mary Bosworth, 40–57. Oxford: Oxford University Press.

Index[1]

A

Agency, 9, 117, 123, 139, 154, 155
Anxiety, 6, 66, 94, 101, 109, 110, 123, 181, 203
Authority, 7, 55, 56, 123–144, 151, 153, 154, 158, 198, 211, 213

C

Children negligence/maltreatment, 63, 157, 161, 168
Confinement, pains/benefits, 99
Court/tribunal, 6, 10, 22, 33, 37, 51, 62, 81, 82, 88, 111, 114, 121, 129, 132, 148, 150, 151, 153–160, 162–164, 168, 173, 179, 181, 185, 186, 203, 204
Crime rates, 28

D

Deportation, 64, 145, 147, 148, 150, 151
Depression, 87, 91, 94, 117
Directorate-General of Prison Services, 2, 29, 52, 54, 79, 95n2, 129, 152, 208
Discipline, 54, 55, 123
Domestic violence, 9, 38, 63, 94, 157, 158, 167, 170, 171, 176, 183–186, 210
Drug-addiction/trafficking/smuggling, 9, 53, 54, 61, 63–65, 74, 79, 81, 84–88, 94, 106, 111, 119, 146, 148–152, 164, 169, 175, 193, 194, 198, 204, 210, 214
Drug laws, 36, 41, 42, 149

---

[1] Note: Page numbers followed by "n" refer to notes

E

Education, 8–10, 23n5, 32, 33, 45, 54, 77, 87, 94, 106, 107, 114, 117, 131, 135, 146, 155, 156, 160, 169, 170, 173, 179, 200, 211
Ethnicity, 15, 78, 88
Ethnography-methods/fieldwork, 3, 11
Everyday life, 3, 7, 11–21, 43, 55, 63, 67, 102, 114, 117, 139, 142, 146, 171, 197

F

Family, 8–10, 15, 21, 39, 41, 43, 45, 52, 54, 56, 64, 65, 67, 68n1, 73, 79, 81, 86, 87, 92, 93, 100, 101, 105–107, 111, 112, 117–119, 125, 132, 133, 141, 146–148, 150–152, 155, 156, 159–161, 164, 167–174, 177, 180, 181, 183, 186, 187, 194, 195, 197, 201, 204, 207, 211
Femininity, 82, 210
Friendship, 16, 54, 110, 112, 113, 183

G

Gender role, 10, 43
Gipsy community, 15, 43, 74, 78, 79, 83–90, 94, 113, 152, 178, 180, 192, 193, 209, 210

I

Identity, 7, 9, 10, 18, 19, 21, 39, 40, 68, 82, 86, 114, 153–156, 212, 213
Illiteracy, 8, 79, 180

J

Judicial rulings, 21, 157

M

Mental health, 94
Moral, 21, 32, 33, 66, 153, 154, 156, 158, 160
Motherhood, 8, 21, 41, 155, 156
Murder, 38, 105, 182, 184, 214

N

Narratives, 6, 9, 20, 43, 64, 68, 99, 107, 154, 157, 167, 168, 171, 179, 182, 211, 214

O

Overcrowding, 2–4, 17, 20, 29, 30, 35–37, 39, 44, 45, 55

P

Portugal, 1, 8, 10, 14, 16, 23n5, 27–47, 53, 64, 77, 78, 106, 129, 131, 133, 136, 146, 148, 151, 153, 193–196, 201, 214
Poverty, 8, 21, 64, 86, 87, 94, 100, 135, 167, 170, 177, 181, 204
Power, 16, 18, 32, 34, 39, 58, 66, 139
Prisoner rights, 45
Prison staff shortage, 4, 30, 45, 52, 129

R

Repentance, 149, 150, 164, 184

Robbery, 9, 64, 86, 108, 114–116, 119, 120, 169, 171, 173, 175, 178, 180

S

Secure training center, 161, 168, 171, 174, 176
Social welfare-benefits, 168
Solitude, 16, 105–118, 181
Stigma, 39, 41, 114, 183
Suicide, 91–93, 116

T

Tension, 4, 14, 59–61, 102, 123–144
Theft, 64, 81, 85, 86, 91, 108, 111, 114, 115, 161, 169, 172, 214

V

Victim Support Association, 170, 175, 183
Violence, 8, 9, 11, 21, 38, 39, 43, 63, 64, 67, 94, 100, 115, 157, 158, 167, 170, 171, 174, 176–178, 181–187, 210

W

Work, 1, 23n5, 28, 52, 58–62, 74, 100, 125, 146, 168, 179, 183, 191, 210

Y

Youth Protection Services, 9, 22, 160, 162, 175

CPI Antony Rowe
Eastbourne, UK
December 04, 2019